GLOBAL CONVERTIBLE INVESTING
The Gabelli Way

HART WOODSON

JOHN WILEY & SONS, INC.

Published by John Wiley & Sons, Inc., New York.
Published simultaneously in Canada.

Library of Congress Cataloging-in-Publication Data:

ISBN: 0-471-20982-1

Printed in the United States of America.

10 9 8 7 6 5 4 3 2 1

To Jenifer and Elizabeth

CONTENTS

LIST OF FIGURES

LIST OF TABLES

INTRODUCTION

We have had one goal since starting Gabelli Asset Management in 1977: to earn a superior risk-adjusted rate of return for our clients. Over the past 23 years, the value product at Gabelli has generated a compound annual rate of return of 21%, net of fees. This compares favorably with benchmarks such as the S&P 500 (16%), the Russell 2000 (14%), and inflation as measured by the consumer price index (CPI) plus 10% (15%). We started the firm as a private company with $100,000 under management. Today, Gabelli is a public company trading on the New York Stock Exchange under the symbol GBL, with $25 billion under management and an enterprise value of more than $1 billion.

Our approach is simple. We are focused, research-driven, long-term investors in the tradition of Graham and Dodd. We believe in value plus a catalyst. When investing in a stock, we are not just buying a piece of paper. We are buying a business. We become surrogate owners of the business for our clients. We like franchises that have pricing power. We like managements that understand how to create shareholder value. We like to invest with a margin of safety. And we like bargains. We like to buy straw hats in winter and assets for free. These are the tenets of value investing, which the late Professor Roger Murray impressed upon me so memorably during my days as a student at the Columbia University Graduate School of Business.

Fortunately, Mr. Market is constantly presenting us with attractive investment opportunities. There is only one problem: It often takes time for a catalyst to unlock this value. Enter the convertible security.

Convertibles offer a terrific overlay to our value style of investing because you "get paid to wait" for the catalyst to unfold. At Gabelli, we have been investing in convertible securities for more than 20 years and fondly refer to them as "stocks in drag." Convertible securities, because of their attractive risk-reward characteristics, help us to earn an attractive risk-adjusted rate of return for our clients. We use convertibles in dedicated portfolios, blended into straight equity portfolios, and as a component of our hedge arbitrage activities. When we decided to launch a series of global funds in 1993, it was only natural to include a global convertible fund as well. But who would manage it?

Marc Gabelli had worked on Lehman Brothers' convertible securities desk in London in 1992. So we asked, Who would be the best person to manage our new global convertible fund, a novelty in the domestic retail market? The word came back: Hart Woodson. One month later, Hart had left his perch in Amsterdam and was on board. Actually, unbeknownst to Hart, the real reason we hired him was that he was a graduate of the Thacher School in Ojai, California. Thacher is famous for its "extra-day" trips when freshmen are sent out on horseback for a week in the Sesbe National Forest. This wasn't quite like growing up on East Tremont Avenue in the Bronx, but by having survived the ordeal Hart had demonstrated sufficient character to join Gabelli. Besides, as a margin of safety, he had a master's degree in international affairs from Columbia University. Nine years later, Hart continues to manage our convertible product and has returned to Europe as our managing director in London. He has been an outstanding member of our management team. In his book, he has pulled together all that is essential in convertible securities investing for both the layperson and the professional. I hope you enjoy reading it as much as I have.

Congratulations, Hart!

MARIO J. GABELLI
Chairman and
Chief Executive Officer
Gabelli Asset Management, Inc.

Rye, New York
December 2001

PREFACE

In principle, convertible securities have been around for centuries. Yet few investors, even investment professionals, actually know what they are. Simply put, convertibles are hybrid securities that combine the attributes of both equities and bonds. They provide the income and relative safety of debt instruments with the upside potential of equities by virtue of an embedded call option. A call option gives the holder the right, but not the obligation, to purchase a security at a specified price for a predetermined period of time.

Debt instruments have been around since the Middle Ages, although a modern international bond market did not develop until the sixteenth century. One of the first accounts of an options contract is given in *Aristotle's Politics*, in which he recalls the story of Thales, a philosopher from Miletus in Greek Ionia. Cynical olive farmers had challenged Thales to prove the commercial relevance of philosophy. Thales, to set them straight, offered to pay cash today for the exclusive right to use their olive presses later in the autumn (i.e., an option premium). The harvest had been poor for the past several seasons and the farmers readily agreed. Sure enough, the new harvest yielded a bumper crop, and the farmers were beholden to Thales.

In modern times, convertible securities have been used to finance speculative, high technology businesses such as the railroads in the 1800s. In 1867, Jay Gould, the U.S. financier, went one step further when he used a convertible bond to dilute effectively Cornelius Vanderbilt's hostile takeover attack on the Erie Railroad. Today, little has changed. The market for global convertibles remains vibrant and dynamic. Young growth companies in telecommunications, technology, media, and health care continue to utilize the convertible market. This makes perfect sense because such companies enjoy a comparative advantage in the convertible market. Rather than being penalized for their weak and volatile capital structures, they are rewarded.

Instead of paying high interest rates to borrow funds in the high-yield market, they obtain low cost financing by offering investors a valuable call option on their stock. Conversely, many well-established companies utilize the convertible market as an avenue for inexpensive, tax-efficient financing.

My mentor, Mario Gabelli, amusingly refers to convertibles as "stocks in drag." I prefer to think of them as the Cadillac of all asset classes. After all, understanding convertible securities requires knowledge of stock selection, option pricing theory, credit analysis, and currency markets. The global convertible market is a large market totaling more than USD 400 billion. Although this represents less than 2% of the global equity market, it is nonetheless significant. My colleague Caesar Bryan, manager of the Gabelli Gold Fund, tells us the total equity market capitalization of the world's listed gold shares is only USD 40 billion. Yet every day you will find mention of the gold market in the *Wall Street Journal*. Although pricing and performance information on convertibles is available from publications such as *Barron's* and *Investors' Business Daily*, the product remains one of the capital market's best-kept secrets. Fortunately, the emergence of a number of excellent web sites, like www.convertbond.com, is adding visibility to the market.

The goal of this book is to bring convertibles into the open. The book is written for both the layperson and the professional. Consequently, it is divided into four sections as follows:

Part One, The Convertible Basics, is designed for the layperson. Chapters 1 through 6 describe what a convertible is, how they work, what to look for in a prospectus, how they have performed as an asset class, and conceptually how they are valued.

Part Two, Convertible Pricing and Valuation, offers an in-depth discussion of option pricing theory and convertible valuation techniques. Here, I have taken the academic literature and made it palatable for the mathematically impaired. Chapter 9 explains the language of options (i.e., delta, gamma, rho, theta, vega). The remainder of this section explores the various approaches to pricing convertibles including a bond plus a call warrant, a put plus yield-enhanced stock, and binomial trees. To provide consistency in proving each approach, a single example is used throughout.

Part Three, Convertible Hedging, explores hedging techniques. It is estimated that hedge arbitrageurs now control more than 60% of the global convertible market. Consequently, an understanding of this strategy is essential. Chapter 12 explains basic arbitrage strategies from the point of view of both an individual and institutional investor (leveraged and unleveraged). Chapter 13 considers the use of options as an alterative to common stock as a hedging instrument. Chapter 14 looks at the problem of hedging interest rate and default risk, including callable asset swaps and credit default swaps. Finally, Chapter 15 is devoted to the problem of hedging currency risk.

Part Four, Special Topics, focuses on a number of issues unique to the convertible market. Chapter 16 analyzes the phenomenon of Mandatory Convertible Securities (MCS). MCS are innovative structures that allow issuers to cross the insurmountable divide between debt and equity by combining the merits of both debt (i.e., tax deductibility) and equity (i.e., rating agency credit). Chapter 17 provides an overview of the busted convertible market, convertibles whose share prices have fallen significantly since issue. Chapter 18 lays out the basics of credit analysis by examining the attributes of both an old and new economy issuer. Finally, Chapter 19 is dedicated to the investment process. This chapter explains why a convertible portfolio is superior to a balanced portfolio of stocks and bonds, how to score and rank convertibles on their technical merits, and when to buy and sell. The chapter also includes a framework for valuing stocks, including a brief review of Mario Gabelli's Private Market Value (PMV) approach, Gabelli Growth Fund manager Howard Ward's Earning Valuation Model (EVM), and a simple discount cash flow model (DCF).

Convertibles have been a passion of mine for nearly 15 years. In this book, I have tried to provide the layperson with a simple understanding of the product, make option pricing theory fun, and break some new ground in the literature. In their book, *Security Analysis*, Graham and Dodd referred to convertibles as "the most attractive of all [securities] in point of form, since they permit the combination of maximum safety with the chance of unlimited appreciation in value." At Gabelli, we agree. Convertible investing is a win-win proposition.

ACKNOWLEDGMENTS

This book would not have been written without the help and encouragement of a number of individuals. First and foremost is Mario Gabelli. If Mario had not put me up to the task, there would be no book. At first I was daunted by the task, but soon realized that Mario had offered me a golden opportunity to give testimony to my 15 years as a convertible investor. Mario's longtime experience with convertibles, together with his boundless energy and intellect, inspired me. At Gabelli, we believe in content. Not only do we invest in content; we create it. This book marks the second in a series of Gabelli-inspired books on investing. The first, *Deals, Deals, and More Deals*, was written by my colleague Regina Pitaro and published by Gabelli University Press in 1999. Regina's success gave me the confidence that it could be done.

Although Mario presented me with the opportunity, the book would not have been completed without the support and encouragement of my wife Jenifer and daughter Elizabeth. The book took more than two years to write, which meant late nights, weekends, and holidays spent in solitude rather than with my family. Instead of complaints, they offered enthusiasm. The project began in the summer of 1998 and was completed in early 2001. I always enjoyed my eight-year-old daughter's musing that, "Daddy, when are you going to finish that book? You've been working on it for two centuries!" Millicent Dunham also provided loving editorial advice.

Several of my Gabelli colleagues provided invaluable assistance. Henry Van der Eb, president and portfolio manager of the Gabelli Mathers Fund, made a number of useful observations. Vincent Roche was instrumental in deriving the option pricing formulas concerning hedging cross-currency risk. Others either read the draft or contributed to its completion, including Bob Zuccaro and Jim McKee. A number of summer interns worked on the book, including Andrew Thomas, Marc

Picconi, Andrew Schenker, and Erin Fitzpatrick. The initial layout and production of the manuscript could not have been accomplished without the tireless devotion of Maureen Naccari, who, despite the rigors of her other responsibilities, was always of good humor. Mark Foundos did an excellent job formatting the graphs. I am grateful to the members of the board of directors of the Gabelli Global Convertible Securities Fund for their support and encouragement of this initiative: Anthony J. Colavita, John D. Gabelli, Karl Otto Pöhl, Werner J. Roeder, Anthonie C. van Ekris, and the late Felix J. Christiana.

I would like to thank my professional colleagues who took the time and effort to review various parts of the manuscript. These included Clive Gibbons in foreign exchange at MeritaNordbanken, Rich Lemanski in stock lending at Lehman Brothers, Kendrick Wakeman in mandatory convertibles at Wachovia Securities, and David Page in asset swaps at Merrill Lynch. Special appreciation goes to Lorraine Lodge at ING Barings, Rick Nelson at ABN AMRO, and Grant Mackie at Lehman Brothers for their prompt and through review of the entire text.

I am delighted to be a member of the global convertible community. I want to thank Menno de Jager, Marc Gabelli, and Richard Cunningham for making that possible as well as the many others who have made the experience both educational and rewarding.

Part One

THE
CONVERTIBLE BASICS

1

ANATOMY OF A CONVERTIBLE

WHAT IS A CONVERTIBLE?

Convertibles are a hybrid security. They combine the income of bonds with the capital appreciation of stocks. As with bonds, convertibles pay a fixed rate of interest that is generally higher than the dividend yield on the underlying common stock. However, because they are exchangeable into stock, convertibles also enjoy significant upside potential. At maturity, convertibles are worth either their cash redemption value or the market value of the shares into which they are convertible, whichever is greater.

WHY SHOULD AN INVESTOR CONSIDER CONVERTIBLES?

Historically, convertibles have generated equity-like returns with less risk (see Chapter 5). In bull markets, convertibles have trailed global equity markets by only a few percentage points, while in bear markets convertibles offer considerably more downside support. Ideally, convertible investors hope to earn two-thirds of the upside return with only one-third of the downside risk. Convertible securities are an appropriate investment vehicle for long-term investors seeking a high rate of total return but with less risk than common stocks.

WHY SHOULD A COMPANY ISSUE A CONVERTIBLE?

Convertibles are well suited for small, fast-growing companies. First, because these companies often lack a long-term track record and have volatile capital structures, if they issue debt they must offer a high coupon. However, in the convertible market this issuer can transform its high volatility into a benefit. It can achieve financing with a very low coupon in exchange for offering a call warrant on its stock. The more volatile the stock, the more valuable the warrant; thus the lower the coupon (see Chapter 7). Consequently, the issuer has a comparative advantage in the convertible market versus the fixed income markets.

Secondly, convertibles are appropriate for this type of issuer because as the firm grows (and its stock price rises), the company will likely call the bonds. When this happens, investors will exchange the convertible for common stock. This in turn will strengthen the company's equity base at the moment when it is most needed. If all goes well, the company will never have to repay the bonds at maturity— only about 25% of all convertibles issued are actually redeemed. In fact, even though the average maturity of a convertible bond is just over 12 years, the average life of a convertible is about 4.5 years. Assuming typical new issue terms, a stock's price needs only to rise by about 5% a year on average to insure conversion. This logic helps explain why over 50% of the U.S. convertible market is comprised of high-growth companies in the technology, telecommunications, media, and health care sectors.

However, large capitalization, mature companies also issue convertible securities. This has been especially true in Europe and Japan because of the nature of their capital markets (see Chapter 4). These issuers use convertibles to raise capital on extremely favorable terms. Exchangeable convertible securities are frequently used to monetize nonstrategic assets in a tax-efficient manner (see Chapter 2).

NOMENCLATURE

Understanding convertibles requires knowledge of their basic terms. To illustrate, we introduce the following hypothetical example. (See Table 1.1)

XYZ Corporation issued $150 million worth of convertible bonds due in five years. The bonds were priced at par, mature at par, and are noncallable. Each bond has a denomination of $1,000 and pays interest semiannually at a rate of 5% per annum. On the day of pricing the stock closed at $100. The stock pays no dividend. Because of these generous terms, the bond immediately traded up to its theoretical value of 118.54% (see Chapter 8).

At the time of issue, a conversion price was set at $125, or a 25% premium to the closing stock price. The conversion price is the price at which bondholders may exchange their bonds for stock in XYZ Corporation. But how many shares of stock will they receive? The conversion ratio is determined by dividing the bond's denomination by the conversion price.

Table 1.1 Convertible Bond Example: XYZ Corporation 5% due 25–Jan–05

Issuer	XYZ Corporation
Par value	$1,000
Size	$150 million
Term	Five years
Call protection	Five years
Coupon	5.00%
Payment frequency	Semiannually
Issue price	100%
Redemption price	100%
Denomination per bond	$1,000
Conversion price	$125
Stock price at issue	$100
Stock dividend	$0
Current stock price	$100
Current convertible price	118.54%

$$\text{Conversion ratio} = \frac{\text{Bond denomination}}{\text{Conversion price}}$$

$$= \frac{\$1,000}{\$125}$$

$$= 8$$

Each bond of $1,000 face amount is convertible into eight shares. This ratio is fixed at issue but is adjusted for stock splits (see Chapter 3).

Parity (or conversion value) represents the intrinsic value of a convertible bond. It is calculated by multiplying the current share price by the conversion ratio.

$$\text{Parity} = \text{Current share price} \cdot \text{Conversion ratio}$$

$$= \$100 \cdot 8$$

$$= \$800$$

With the stock price at $100, parity of the bond is $800. Parity establishes a minimum boundary condition for the price of the convertible. If the price falls below parity, an arbitrage opportunity exists. An arbitrageur can buy the convertible, sell eight shares of stock against it, convert the bonds, cover the short stock position, and make a risk-free profit (see Chapter 12).

The conversion premium describes the extra amount an investor is willing to pay to own a convertible security rather than a commensurate amount of common stock (eight shares). The premium is calculated as follows:

$$\text{Conversion premium} = \frac{\text{Convertible price} - \text{Parity}}{\text{Parity}}$$

$$= \frac{\$1,185 - \$800}{\$800}$$

$$= 48.13\%$$

With the bonds trading at 118.50% ($1,185 per bond), an investor is willing to pay 48.13% more to own the bonds rather than the eight shares of stock into which they are convertible ($800). Why should an investor pay this premium? First, compared to the stock, the convertible investor enjoys a yield advantage. The stock pays no dividend, while the bond pays a 5% coupon. Second, the convertible gives the investor downside protection should the stock price fall (see Chapter 8).

INVESTMENT VALUE

A convertible's investment value is its price as a regular straight bond. If the stock price falls such that the conversion privilege becomes worthless, the convertible will trade solely on its fixed income characteristics. This price, which is a function of the current level of interest rates and the company's credit spread, forms the second boundary condition for a convertible. If the convertible price falls below the investment value (i.e., the credit spread widens), then an arbitrage opportunity will exist. An arbitrageur can buy the convertible and sell an equivalent maturity Treasury security against it. The arbitrageur then sells the convertible to a fixed-income investor willing to pay the original investment value and makes a risk-free profit. Of course, this assumes that the original credit spread was correct for that quality issuer. If the credit deteriorates, the spread to Treasuries will widen and the investment value will fall.

The investment value is influenced by interest rates and credit spreads. It is impervious to movements in the share price until such time as a decline signals a credit problem. As the stock price approaches zero, the investment value curves downward reflecting the increased likelihood of bankruptcy. This principle is illustrated in Figure 1.1 where we have calculated the investment value for the XYZ convertible at a price of 84.78%, or $847.84 per bond (see Chapter 8). This price represents a yield to maturity of 8.83%, or 3.08% over the equivalent maturity Treasury yield of 5.75%.

The investment value premium is the difference between the market price of the convertible and its investment value, expressed as a percentage of the investment value.

$$\text{Investment value premium} = \frac{\text{Convertible price} - \text{Investment value}}{\text{Investment value}}$$

$$= \frac{\$1,185 - \$847}{\$847}$$

$$= 39.9\%$$

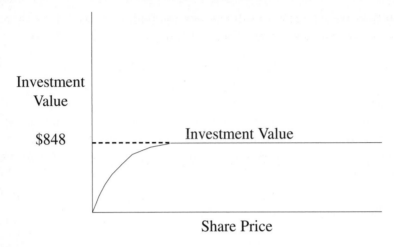

Figure 1.1   Investment Value for the XYZ Convertible

The investment value premium tells the investor how much more the investor must pay to own the convertible instead of an equivalent straight bond. The figure is useful as a measure of risk. A convertible with a low investment value premium will trade close to its investment value. Its price will be more influenced by interest rates than stock price movements. Alternatively, a high investment value premium indicates that the convertible is an equity surrogate with little downside protection.

A bond's current yield is calculated by dividing its annual coupon rate by its current market price. It gives an investor a static view of the return on investment. The current yield ignores any premium or discount that must be amortized over the life of the bond. This is captured by the yield to maturity, which measures the internal rate of return of the bond.

$$\text{Current yield} = \frac{\text{Annual coupon payment}}{\text{Convertible price}}$$

$$= \frac{\$50}{\$1,185}$$

$$= 4.22\%$$

If the current yield exceeds the stock's dividend yield, the convertible is said to enjoy a positive yield advantage.

$$\text{Yield advantage} = \text{Current yield} - \text{Dividend yield}$$
$$= 4.22\% - 0.00\%$$
$$= 4.22\%$$

CONVERTIBLE PERFORMANCE

After issue, the convertible price changes depending on where the stock price is relative to the conversion price. Figure 1.2 specifies the four main zones. The difference between the convertible price and the parity line is the conversion premium. On the downside, the conversion premium is influenced by the stability of the investment value. On the upside, it is influenced by the amount of call protection. Call protection insures that the issuer cannot call the bonds away from the investor. Under hard (absolute) call protection, the bonds cannot be called regardless of the stock price. With soft (provisional) call protection, the stock must trade above a certain hurdle price before the bonds can be called. Because an investor forfeits accrued interest

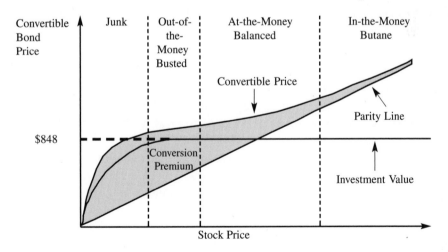

Figure 1.2 Secondary Market Performance

when forced to convert, a deep in-the-money convertible that is currently callable will lose its conversion premium faster than one that enjoys call protection.

Butane: In-the-Money (Stock Price > Conversion Price)

When the stock price exceeds the conversion price, the convertible is in-the-money. As the stock price rises, the convertible becomes more and more sensitive to changes in the stock price and less so to interest rates. As parity increases with the stock price, the conversion premium falls. The convertible may still retain a yield advantage, but the investment value premium will be high. The convertible trades in line with the common stock and offers little downside protection.

Balanced: At-the-Money (Stock Price = Conversion Price)

When the underlying stock price is close to the conversion price, the convertible is at-the-money. At this point, the convertible is balanced, meaning that it is influenced by both the stock price and interest rates. Here the convertible is in the sweet spot. Ideally, it will capture two-thirds of the stock's upside movement with only one-third of the downside.

Busted: Out-of-the-Money (Stock Price < Conversion Price)

When the stock price is less than the conversion price the convertible is out-of-the-money or busted (see Chapter 17). As the stock price declines, the convertible price declines, but at a reduced rate as the equity component diminishes and the conversion premium expands. At this point, the convertible price is dominated by interest rates and credit factors.

When the credit becomes distressed, the investment value breaks down and the convertible trades like junk. At this point, the convertible once again trades more like equity than debt (see Chapter 10).

2

CONVERTIBLE STRUCTURES
Let Me Count the Ways

In Chapter 1, we define the characteristics of a traditional convertible bond. However, convertible securities can be structured in a variety of forms. As noted in Figure 2.1, these structures cover a wide spectrum. The payoff profile ranges from being very bondlike to very equity sensitive. This flexibility explains the wide appeal of convertible securities for both issuers and investors. In this chapter, we explain these structures and highlight their most important characteristics.

ZERO-COUPON CONVERTIBLE BONDS (OID)

This type of convertible is the most bondlike of all convertibles. It has no current yield because it pays no coupon. However, because the bond is issued at a deep discount to par, it has a positive yield to maturity because it accretes to par over its life. Consequently, this structure is known as an original-issue discount (OID). To qualify as an OID structure, the bond's coupon must be below a certain limit specified by the tax code. The zero-coupon bond is the most

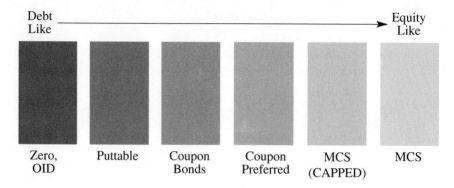

Figure 2.1 The Convertible Spectrum

extreme form of this structure. Similar structures may offer a merger coupon. From a tax perspective, the zero-coupon structure is very favorable to the issuer. The accreted value of the bond, which is treated as interest expense for tax purposes, can be deducted without actually having to pay the cash cost until final maturity. Maturities range from five to twenty years, by which time the bond is more likely to be converted than redeemed. Unfortunately, since the tax code is symmetrical, the investor (if taxable) must pay tax on the accreted value of the bond even though no cash interest is received. This is required even if the purchase price of the bond is above its accreted value. Similarly, if the bond is held to maturity, no capital gains tax is due.

Zero-coupon convertible bonds are usually issued with lower conversion premiums than traditional convertibles since the effective conversion price is always moving away from the investor. This is best illustrated with an example. Returning to our XYZ Corporation convertible (see Chapter 1), let us assume that the coupon is reduced from 5% to zero. In this case the issue price of the bond would fall from 100% to 78.21% to give a 5% yield to maturity. If at issue the initial conversion price is maintained at $125 (a 25% conversion premium), then the conversion ratio falls from 8 to 6.25 shares. The conversion ratio is determined by dividing the issue price ($781.20), and not the face value of the bond ($1,000), by the initial conversion price of $125. After this point, the conversion ratio remains fixed at

6.25 shares. With the conversion ratio fixed, as the bond accretes toward par, the conversion price rises. To see how this works, assume that one year passes and the bond has accreted in value by 5% to a price of 82.075% ($820.75). Now the conversion price has risen to $131.32 ($820.75/6.25). In other words, in order for it to be worthwhile for the investor to exchange the bond for equity, the stock price must rise at least as fast as the bond price accrues.

A variation of the OID structure is a convertible issued at par but with a redemption price at maturity above par. The premium redemption structure raises the security's investment value. For an issuer with a high dividend yield, the structure helps to overcome investors' disdain for a low yield advantage since current yield can be replaced by the yield to maturity. For the issuer, if the bond is redeemed, the premium paid at maturity is tax deductible.

PUTTABLE CONVERTIBLE BONDS

This structure allows the bondholder to put or return the bonds to the issuer at a predetermined price and time. Put dates range from one to several years, but always come due before the bond's final maturity. Put prices vary from the issue price to a premium over issue. The effect of the put is to shorten the maturity of the bond and effectively raise its investment value (see Chapter 1). This structure is commonly seen in zero-coupon bonds, which despite a twenty-year final maturity are usually puttable after three to five years. Put features are frequently offered by volatile emerging market issuers because investors demand better downside protection. Investors should make sure that such issuers make proper provisions to satisfy the put obligation.

COUPON PAYING CONVERTIBLE BONDS

The traditional convertible bond is issued at par and matures at par (par being defined as 100% of the bond's face value). It pays a fixed rate of interest (coupon). Typically, payment frequency is semiannually in the United States and Japan, and annually in Europe and non-

Japan Asia. The main difference from a normal, straight bond is that the coupon is generally lower and the convertible can be exchanged for stock at the bondholder's request.

CONVERTIBLE PREFERRED STOCK

Convertible preferred stock pays a fixed amount of interest (dividends) and is exchangeable into common stock at the holder's option. Generally, convertible preferred stock has no final maturity date, and this makes the investment value elusive. However, when issued from a trust, it may be redeemable at par within 10 to 30 years. Convertible preferred stock differs from a convertible bond in that dividend payments can be deferred for up to five years without triggering an event of default. Preferred shareholders take precedence over common shareholders for dividend payments. For the issuer, convertible preferred stock is treated like equity by the rating agencies and dividend payments are nontax deductible.

Exchangeable convertible preferred stock gives the issuer the option of exchanging its existing convertible preferred stock for a like convertible bond. The terms of the exchange are stated at issue. This gives the issuer more flexibility in its capital structure. It can exchange equity for debt on the balance sheet, and replace a nontax-deductible dividend payment with tax-deductible interest expense.

MANDATORY CONVERTIBLE SECURITIES (MCS)

Even more equitylike than convertible preferred stock are mandatory convertible securities (see Chapter 16). Because these securities are mandatorily convertible into common stock at maturity, they have no discernible investment value. Mandatory convertibles are effectively yield-enhanced common stock. They offer no downside protection to the investor apart from their higher yield. Yield is maximized when price appreciation is capped. From the issuers' perspective, these securities offer the best of both worlds because they enjoy both equity credit and tax deductibility.

OTHER FEATURES

Within the context of the structures described, convertible securities may contain additional features that enhance their defensiveness. Some of the most prominent are detailed next.

Resettable Convertibles

Reset features allow for the adjustment of the coupon, conversion ratio, conversion price, or maturity date of the security if certain stipulated events occur. For instance, if the stock price declines beyond a certain level, the reset feature enhances the bondholder's value. By increasing the conversion ratio or the coupon, the value of the bond is sustained. Speculative-grade issuers frequently offer these features.

Premium Protection (Make-Whole Provision)

Convertibles with little or no call protection sometimes offer investors premium protection. If a bond with soft-call protection is called early, premium protection allows the bondholder to convert the security and still receive a portion of the coupon payments remaining during the call-protection period. Premium protection preserves the value of the initial premium paid by the investor at issue.

OTHER CONVERTIBLE STRUCTURES

Convertible Stock Notes

Convertible stock notes pay either in common stock or cash at the issuer's option, instead of paying interest and principal in cash. These securities are often referred to as pay-in-kind (PIK), and are designed to give issuers flexibility in managing cash flow. Convertible stock notes are typically issued by companies in financial distress, making it difficult to compare their yields with those of other convertibles. These notes are issued most commonly through private placements.

Exchangeable Convertibles

These securities are issued by one company and exchangeable into the shares of a different company. This situation occurs if the issuer wants to monetize the value of a nonstrategic asset in a tax-efficient manner. By issuing an exchangeable convertible security, the issuer receives the proceeds of the sale immediately (and at a premium to the current share price), but does not have to pay capital gains tax until the bonds are actually converted several years in the future. Since the issuer wants to preserve this tax benefit for as long as possible, the bondholders' right to exchange the securities into common stock may be restricted. The structure is particularly popular in Europe, where it constitutes about 50% of the current market capitalization.

3

UNDERSTANDING THE PROSPECTUS
Caveat Emptor

The prospectus describes the terms and conditions of a convertible security. Legally, it is superseded only by the trust deed. The trust deed is a cumbersome document and so investors usually refer to the prospectus. Unfortunately, the language used in a prospectus is often legalistic and difficult to understand, and this can lead the investor to overlook important information. Under United States law, a company's obligation to its bondholders is a contractual rather than fiduciary responsibility. Although issuers do not purposely deceive investors: caveat emptor. Bondholders should feel free to contact the trustee directly with any questions concerning the prospectus. It is the trustee's responsibility to act in the bondholder's interest.

Table 3.1 outlines the main issues to consider when the investor is reviewing a convertible prospectus.

CALL PROTECTION

In the early 1970s and 1980s, convertibles often lacked call protection and were soon called away, stripping the holder of the premium.

17

Table 3.1   What to Look for in a Prospectus

Favorable	Unfavorable
• Long period of call protection	• Callability soon after launch
• Dilution protection	• Protection only against basic issues
• Compensation for extraordinary events such as special dividends	• No mention of bondholder compensation if equity bonus
• Ranking shares upon conversion	• Converted shares to not rank for the dividend for the first financial year
• Sleeping investor clauses	• Investor must remember to convert if in his or her interest
• Immediate and continuous convertibility	• Limited convertibility, or cash alternative
• Senior or unsubordinated	• Subordinated
• Protection in the event of change of control	• No reference to change of control
• Cross-covenants	• No reference to other debt
• Weak redemption structure	• Straightforward redemption
• Nonpayment of coupon/dividend would constitute a default	• Conditional income
• Adequate default protection	• Little default protection

Source: Merrill Lynch

Consequently, most convertibles now feature at least three years of hard-call protection. Recently, some issuers have offered only soft-call protection, albeit with high hurdles and make-whole provisions (see Chapter 2). Hard-call protection with the longest possible duration is most desirable for the investor.

DILUTION PROTECTION (EXTRAORDINARY DIVIDENDS)

Convertible investors are not compensated for normal dividend payments. However, if a company makes an extraordinary dividend payment, resembling a return of capital, convertible holders want to be compensated. Sometimes, to qualify as an extraordinary dividend, the dividend need only be labeled as extraordinary. In other cases, however, it must be specifically defined. For example, if the dividend payment in question yields more than a specified amount (e.g., 5%), any amount over the threshold will be compensated. An infamous case in which convertible investors were denied such compensation occurred in the spring of 1998 when Daimler–Benz, the German automaker, paid its shareholders a special stock dividend of DM 20 per share, representing about 12% of the then prevailing stock price.

RANKING SHARES

Typically, shares received from conversion rank for the dividend pertaining to the fiscal year in which the conversion took place. Unfortunately, in Euroland dividends declared for one fiscal year are usually not paid until the next fiscal year. This means that if an investor is forced to convert toward the end of the current fiscal year, he or she will not only lose the accrued interest but will have to wait until the following year to receive the dividend on the stock received. In convertible parlance this circumstance is fondly referred to as the double screw. In France, this can be particularly painful since French convertibles pay interest annually on January 1. Meanwhile, stock dividends are usually paid semiannually: a small interim dividend is paid in the first half of the year with the bulk paid at the end of the year. The investor must consider which payment is more meaningful: the accrued interest or the dividend payment. Conversions, which allow the investor to rank for the next payable dividend, are preferable. This seems fair given the loss of accrued interest.

SLEEPING INVESTOR CLAUSES

If at maturity parity is above the redemption price, a rational investor will exchange the convertible into stock. Investors should be notified, but they may fail to submit their conversion notice to the trustee. In that case, it is useful to have a sleeping investor provision in the prospectus. This clause permits the trustee to convert the securities on behalf of the investor if parity exceeds the redemption price by a specified margin, usually 5%.

CONVERTIBILITY

Immediate and continuous convertibility has obvious advantages over limited convertibility. Limited convertibility can hurt bondholders in cases of takeovers, mergers, or any other activity that may increase shareholder value. Exchangeable convertible securities often have limited convertibility to preserve the issuers' tax benefits (see Chapter 2).

RANKING: SENIOR OR SUBORDINATED

Convertible investors rank senior to common stockholders but may be junior or subordinated to other creditors. Investors should be wary as to where they rank in the company's capital structure and should favor securities with senior status. Whenever possible, convertible debt should share cross-covenants with the company's other debt obligations (i.e., cross default, negative pledge).

TAKEOVER PROTECTION

Takeover protection is found in the prospectus under the change of control provisions. Earlier convertible prospectuses did not contain these provisions. However, after a wave of merger and acquisition activity in the early 1980s, investors began to demand such protection. For the convertible investor, time is money. The investor has paid a premium to own the convertible and requires time to earn a yield advantage and to wait for the stock price to rise. A takeover or leveraged buyout accelerates investors' holding periods and robs them of this time value.

There are two methods of compensation. First, payment of the security may be accelerated. This is accomplished via a change of control put-at-par. This benefits the bondholder, provided the security is trading below par. If the security is trading above par, then the acceleration option is worthless. In fact, if the bid is in cash, the investor will lose the premium and the bonds may trade down in price (see Chapter 12). In the second method, the issuer can prevent the conversion premium from evaporating by increasing the conversion ratio to restore the premium to the average level seen before the takeover announcement. Unfortunately, such generosity is rare.

REDEMPTION TERMS (CASH OR STOCK)

Increasingly, issuers have been given the option of satisfying the redemption price in either cash or stock. If investors have not been previously converted, they should prefer to receive cash. Although technically the cash value of the shares must equal the cash redemption price, investors may suffer slippage in their redemption value as bondholders simultaneously sell shares to obtain cash.

CONDITIONAL INCOME

A convertible investor wants to be paid. Payment of dividends or coupons should not be conditional on the availability of funds. For a bond, failure to pay the coupon should trigger an event of default. For preferred stock, some dividend deferral is usually permitted, but payments should be cumulative and paid with interest as soon as funds become available.

CONCLUSION

The issues discussed here provide a checklist for the prudent convertible investor. Unfortunately, prospectuses lack consistency, and each one must be carefully reviewed. Until recently, convertible investors have not been organized as a group. In 1999, the Association of Convertible Bond Management (ACBM) was founded in Zurich, Switzerland. Its mission is to further the educational and networking needs of professionals in the convertible bond industry. Members of the Association include both investment banks and institutional portfolio managers. It is hoped that this organization will further the development of universal convertible standards that are fair to both issuers and investors alike.

4

GLOBAL
CONVERTIBLE MARKETS

SIZE

The capitalization of the global convertible market as of March 2001 is approximately USD 400 billion. To put this in perspective, it is larger than the gross domestic product (GDP) of Australia (USD 380 billion) but smaller than the market capitalization of General Electric (USD 415 billion). Last year, the United States overtook Japan as the world's largest convertible market. New issue activity in the United States has been running at a record pace, as many new economy companies have been drawn to the convertible market. In Japan, regulatory changes have stymied growth. Elsewhere in Asia (and in other emerging markets), new issue activity has been slow to recover since the currency devaluations in 1997. Companies in Europe have used convertibles to divest nonstrategic assets and to fund acquisitions. (See Figure 4.1.)

The overall size of the market has grown only marginally over the past several years. This is because convertible securities are generally callable after three years. Consequently, when equity markets perform well, net new issuance tends to be negative. Conversely, in

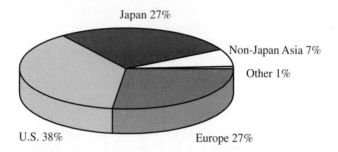

Figure 4.1   Global Convertible Market: Regional Breakdown
Source: Merrill Lynch, March 2001

Japan, following a 10-year bear market, nearly half of all outstanding convertibles are expected to mature without being converted by 2002.

CREDIT QUALITY

In the United States, many new economy companies have raised capital in the convertible market. These companies have a highly volatile capital structure and enjoy a comparative advantage in the convertible market relative to the straight fixed-income market. In the fixed-income market, these companies are forced to raise funds at very high yields. In the convertible market, on the other hand, they can achieve low yields by selling a call warrant on their equity. The more volatile the stock, the more valuable the warrant and the lower the coupon. This trend has led to a deterioration of the credit quality of the domestic U.S. market. Presently, about 46% of U.S. convertibles (ex-mandatories and preferreds) are rated as investment grade. By contrast, Europe enjoys the best credit ratings if we assume that unrated credits are assigned a rating. In Europe, almost 50% of the convertible market is unrated since many well-known issuers are unwilling to invest the time and money required to obtain a formal rating (i.e., Roche). However, after estimating an appropriate credit rating, about 90% of the European market is considered investment grade. Similarly, according to the local rating agencies, nearly 97% of the Japanese market is rated as investment grade. However, after applying more universally accepted standards, approximately 85% of the market is considered investment grade. In non-Japan Asia, (and other emerging markets), the majority of issuers are unrated and presumed to be subinvestment grade. (See Figures 4.2 and 4.3.)

SECTOR ALLOCATION

As of March 2001, about 35% of the U.S. market is made up of technology and telecommunications companies. By contrast, Japan retains a strong old economy bias since construction is tied with technology as the largest sector at 15%. In fact, the Japanese market is very broad, which allows for good diversification. Europe's convertible market differs from the underlying equity markets, but it is still more diverse than the U.S. market. For example, almost 75% of the Dow Jones Euro STOXX 50 Index can be replicated with convertibles. Non-Japan Asia is dominated by technology and telecommunications companies. (See Figure 4.4.)

CHARACTERISTICS

Table 4.1 reveals the basic characteristics of the global convertible market as a whole and by region (ex-mandatories and preferreds). As we would expect, conversion premiums in Japan and the rest of Asia are generally higher than the global average, reflecting the dominance of busted issues in that universe. Ironically, current yields there are low. This is because of the low coupons at issue. Yields to maturity or put are substantially higher. Investment value premiums are in line with the general level of conversion premiums and credit quality.

RECENT TRENDS

Europe

The fall of the Berlin Wall in November 1989 and the introduction of the euro in January 1999 have changed the face of Europe. Corporations have been forced to become more shareholder friendly and effi-

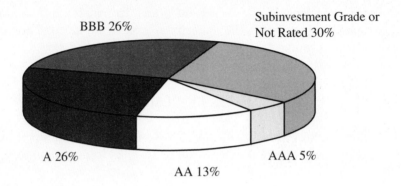

Figure 4.2 Global Convertible Market: Credit Breakdown
Source: Merrill Lynch, March 2001

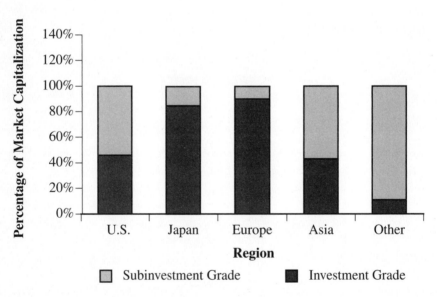

Figure 4.3 Global Credit Quality Comparison
Source: Merrill Lynch, March 2001

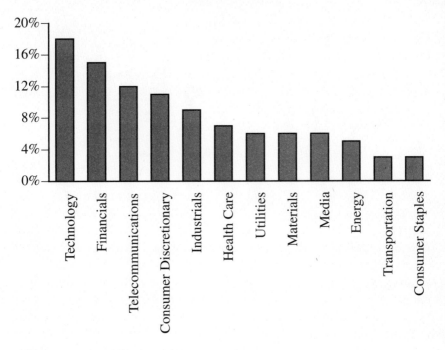

Figure 4.4 Global Convertible Market: Sector Breakdown
Source: Merrill Lynch, March 2001

Table 4.1 Global Convertible Characteristics

Region	Conversion Premium	Current Yield	Investment Value Premium
Global (G300)	45.0%	2.4%	18.9%
U.S.	74.2%	3.1%	27.5%
Europe	33.1%	2.4%	12.7%
Japan (domestic)	59.9%	1.1%	17.1%
Non-Japan Asia	108.6%	2.6%	0.8%

Source: Merrill Lynch, March 2001

cient. Convertibles have been used to fund acquisitions and to mone-tize nonstrategic assets in a tax-efficient manner. As Europe shifts from a bond-oriented culture to an equity culture, convertibles offer an attractive investment stepping stone. Demand for convertibles is expected to grow as an aging population increases their equity-related investments to fund retirement plans.

Japan

New issuance has been curtailed by both regulatory changes and a persistent bear market. To counter fears of a weak market, Japanese banks seeking to raise Tier 1 capital issued a host of resettable con-vertibles (also known as refixes) in the mid-1990s. The refix feature periodically resets the value of the convertible near par if the stock price declines, by increasing the conversion ratio. Unfortunately, the strategy backfired because the stock prices continued to drop, and hedge arbitrageurs increased their short positions and exaggerated the decline. Needless to say, these structures have fallen from popu-larity in recent years.

One unusual trait of the Japanese domestic market is that issuers typically do not call their bonds for fear of upsetting investors. Al-though this custom remains nearly intact (e.g., Tanabe Seiyaku), com-panies are beginning to price new issues with higher conversion premiums in keeping with international standards—for example, Nippon Electric Company (NEC). Traditionally, convertibles were seen as equity surrogates and were priced on premiums of only 2.5%.

United States

A recent trend in the U.S. convertible market is a growing prevalence of private placements under rule 144A. Under this rule, convertibles are not listed on an exchange or registered with the Securities and Exchange Commission. Consequently, only Qualified Institutional Buyers (QIB) can purchase these securities. A QIB is defined as an in-stitutional investor with a minimum of USD 100 million under man-agement. After a seasoning period, usually 180 days, these securities may be purchased by non-QIB investors. As of March 2001, 144A se-curities made up about 12% of the total U.S. market but they have been dominating recent new-issue activity. The ease with which rule

144A allows companies to issue convertibles means that this trend will continue. The implication for individual investors is that owning convertibles via mutual funds will become increasingly important.

Since their introduction in 1990, Mandatory Convertible Securities (MCS) have gained popularity (see Chapter 16). As of March 2001, they comprised about 14% of the market but accounted for about one-third of all new issuance in 1999. Issuers favor these securities because of their favorable tax treatment. In a bull market, these equity-like securities have been popular with investors. However, should the market turn down we would expect to see a relative decline in these issues relative to convertible bonds.

Finally, the latest innovation in the market has been zero-coupon convertible bonds with contingency features. These structures contain both contingent conversion and interest payment features. Issuers find these structures appealing because they provide favorable tax and accounting treatment. As of March 2001, zeros had grown to constitute about 30% of the U.S. convertible market in terms of market capitalization versus just 13% in December 1994.

Non-Japan Asia

Since the currency crisis in 1997, convertible issuance has been muted. In order to entice convertible investors to re-enter the market, more defensive structures have been introduced. Formerly, new issues were priced in ten-year maturities with low coupons, mid-teen conversion premiums, and five-year put options yielding U.S. Treasuries plus 200 basis points. New structures have sought to raise the investment value by introducing a rolling annual put at par.

5

BENCHMARKS
AND PERFORMANCE
Global and
Domestic Indices

BENCHMARKS

Benchmarks provide investors with a comparative view of the convertible universe and help them to monitor a manager's performance. Although investment managers are often evaluated against a benchmark, the benchmark may not accurately reflect the investor's objectives or may be impossible to replicate. When considering the appropriateness of a benchmark, investors should determine if the index is constructed in a manner that is consistent with their own investment guidelines and risk tolerance. Benchmarks should allow investors to relate performance to their investment goals and to assist them in making rational decisions.

CONVERTIBLE INDICES

In what follows we document the main characteristics of the major domestic and global convertible indices. We have limited our discussion to the broadest, most inclusive indices. Increasingly, the leading investment banks have further segmented the market into a whole host of sub-indices. These sub-indices slice the market by product type, credit quality, market capitalization, industry sector, and investment style. Sub-indices make it easier for investors to construct appropriate benchmarks. When considering an index, investors should be cognizant of how it is constructed. For example, what are the rules for inclusion and omission? How is the index calculated and how frequently? Surprisingly, the performances of apparently similar indices can be quite diverse. It is important to understand the reasons for this diversity when comparing results.

DOMESTIC CONVERTIBLE INDICES

Credit Suisse First Boston (CSFB)

The general convertible index of CSFB is a total return index comprised of convertible bonds and convertible preferred stock (mandatory and contingent convertibles are excluded). The index, which began in January 1982, is further segmented into two sub-indices: one for bonds and one for preferreds. The index is weighted by market capitalization, which means that the price of each issue is multiplied by the dollar value outstanding. There is no set number of issues in the index. As of March 2001, the index contained 319 issues with a total market value of USD 97 billion. The selection criteria for the securities in the index include:

I Minimum value of USD 50 million.
I If the issue is rated by S&P, the rating must be B– or better. If the issue is not rated, but has a value of at least USD 50 million, it will be included unless there are already some rated issues from the same company in the index.
I New issues are priced at the end of the month during which the security has been trading for the entire month.
I Issues are removed if they are valued at less than USD 50 million for more than six consecutive months.

Convertible bonds make up 77.8% of the index while convertible preferreds constitute 22.2%. CSFB also identifies the composition of issues in the index by credit rating. (See Table 5.1.)

Merrill Lynch All US Convertible Index (VXAO)

Merrill Lynch began tracking convertible performance in 1988 and extended its index in 1995 to create the new All US Convertible Index (VXAO) as a master index with many sub-indices. These sub-indices are divided into four subgroups: structure, credit quality, sector/industry, and style/size objective. The sub-indices satisfy the same selection criteria as the master index. The master index contains all types of convertible securities including mandatories and preferreds, and it also includes nonrated issues. The selection criteria are as follows:

- A minimum USD 50 million aggregate market value.
- The issue must be sold in U.S. dollars and must be publicly traded in the United States.
- The issuer's firm cannot currently be in bankruptcy.
- New issues are added at par value as of the issue date.
- An issue is removed at the end of the quarter if it is converted or if it depreciates below USD 40 million.
- If there is a forced conversion where the conversion parity exceeds the call proceeds, the redeemed issues are removed on the last conversion date. If there is a cash call where the call proceeds exceed conversion parity, then the issue is deleted at the redemption date.

Table 5.1 CSFB Domestic Convertible Index: Credit Quality

AAA	0.8%	BBB	29.7%	NA/NR	12.6%
AA	0.1%	BB	11.1%		
A	13.1%	B	32.6%		

Source: Credit Suisse First Boston, March 2001

The index is updated daily and is reevaluated quarterly to insure the liquidity and value of the convertibles in the index. As of March 2001, there were 507 issues in the index with a total market value of USD 159 billion. The average rating of convertibles in the index was BB+ and the conversion premium was 56.8%. The index also distinguishes issues by credit quality and company size. (See Table 5.2.)

Bear Stearns Convertible Securities Index

The Bear Stearns All Convertible Index is composed of all types of convertible securities including mandatories and preferreds. The index does not have a set number of issues and as of March 2001 it contained about 648 issues with a market capitalization of USD 177 billion. The selection criteria for the index include:

I The issue must have a minimum market value of USD 25 million.

I The company cannot currently be bankrupt.

I New issues are introduced into the index immediately at the issue price.

I Issues are removed if the underlying company is in danger of bankruptcy or if the issue becomes convertible into a fixed amount of cash.

The index is market capitalization-weighted and includes all types of credit ratings. The index is dissected into various subindices that provide more extensive information about historical returns.

Table 5.2 Merrill Lynch All US Convertible Index (VXAO): Credit Quality and Market Capitalization

Investment grade	48%	Large cap	64%
Speculative grade	40%	Mid cap	26%
Nonrated issues	12%	Small cap	10%

Source: Merrill Lynch, March 2001

Salomon Smith Barney Index

The Salomon Brothers indices divide into two categories: the Salomon Brothers Convertible Securities Index (SBCSI) and the Salomon Brothers Broad Convertibles Index (SBBCI). The SBCSI is composed of four distinct modules: cash-coupon convertible bonds, zero-coupon convertible bonds, convertible preferreds, and mandatories. Convertibles with limited upside potential, such as capped mandatory convertibles, are included in the SBBCI, together with all the different types of securities in the SBCSI.

Goldman Sachs Convertible 100 Index

The Goldman Sachs Convertible 100 was established in 1985. The index is rebalanced semi-annually to exclude issues with an equity market capitalization of less than USD 400 million, busted convertibles with a conversion premium of more than 100%, or deep in-the-money convertibles with parity more than 200% of par. The index includes the 100 largest convertible issues including bonds, preferreds, and mandatories. Fast add/delete rules accommodate large new issues or redemptions between rebalancings. Performance is calculated daily on both an equal-weighted basis and a market capitalization-weighted basis. This index seeks to capture the more balanced, liquid portion of the market.

GLOBAL CONVERTIBLE INDICES

Originally, global convertible indices were constructed by conglomerating existing regional indices. Recently, as interest in the global convertible market has grown (see Chapter 4), financial firms have come to recognize the utility of constructing global convertible indices.

Merrill Lynch Global Convertible Index (ML-G300)

Merrill Lynch's Global Convertible Indices track data commencing on January 1, 1995. The ML-G300 contains 300 issues and represents roughly one-third of the total global convertible market. (See Table 5.3.) The ML-G300 is reported daily and is weighted by market

Table 5.3   Regional Breakdown of the ML-G300 Index

Country/Region	ML-G300 Weighting (%)	Number of Constituents
Japan	27	72
United States	38	122
Europe	27	67
Asia	7	35
Other*	1	4
Total	100	300

*Other includes Latin America, South Africa, and Eastern Europe.
Source: Merrill Lynch, March 2001

capitalization. The selection process was originally based on size but has been revised to more accurately reflect the composition of the global market. The rules for selection in the index include:

I The convertible must have a minimum market value of USD 50 million.

I An issue will not be selected if the index already contains another issue that converts into the same underlying shares.

Issues are removed if

I The company defaults, goes bankrupt, or the underlying shares are de-listed.

I The issue matures, is called, or the conversion right expires.

I A takeover or merger results in the creation of two convertibles with the same underlying shares (one will be replaced).

I The market value of the issue remains below USD 40 million for two consecutive weeks.

Goldman Sachs/Bloomberg Global Convertible Indices

After developing the US Convertible 100 Index in 1985, Goldman Sachs introduced three additional indices to cover Japan, the rest of Asia, and Europe. In April 1998, Goldman Sachs joined forces with Bloomberg to produce a global index that combined all four of these regional indices. (See Table 5.4.) This global index is composed of the Goldman Sachs US Convertible 100 Index, the Goldman Sachs Liquid Fifty (GOLF) Index (Japan), the GSBB European 50 Convertible Index, and the GSBB Asian 25 Convertible Index.

The GSBB Global Convertible Index is reported daily on a market capitalization-weighted basis and an equal-weighted basis. A security is chosen to be included in the index if it meets certain requirements including:

❚ An equity market capitalization greater than USD 75 million.

❚ A convertible amount outstanding greater than USD 75 million.

❚ A parity value less than 200% of par.

❚ A conversion premium less than 100%.

Between the semi-annual rebalancing of the index, convertibles may be fast-added if there is a newly issued convertible, or fast-deleted if a convertible is called, matures, is put back to the company, or is repurchased.

UBSW Global Convertible Index

In June 1998, Union Bank of Switzerland (UBS) merged with Swiss Bank Corporation (SBC) to create UBS AG. The merged investment banks were unified as Warburg Dillon Read (WDR), and eventually became UBS Warburg in May 2000. The UBS Warburg Global Con-

Table 5.4 Regional Breakdown of the GSBB Global Convertible Index

Country/Region	GSBB Weighting (%)	Number of Constituents
United States	40	100
Japan	17	50
Europe	35	50
Asia	8	25
Total	100	225

Source: Goldman Sachs, March 2001

vertible Index (UBSW) followed the same guidelines as the original UBS Convertible Index that began in January 1994. UBSW is weighted on a market-capitalization basis and aims to reflect the liquid investable universe within the global convertibles market. (See Table 5.5.) The index does not have a set number of issues, unlike most of the other indices. If a convertible is large enough and liquid enough it is included in the index. When the liquidity of the total market declines, the index will have a smaller amount of constituents to portray the current market condition. Typically, the index contains 400–500 issues. The requirements for selection in the index include:

▌ A minimum market capitalization of USD 100 million at the time of review.

▌ Either a minimum of USD 100 million of exchange traded volume for the last quarter at the time of review, OR

▌ A minimum of USD 100 million of volume reported to Autex, the market tracking service, for the last quarter at the time of review, OR

▌ At least four market makers out of the top ten convertible underwriters quoting prices with a maximum 2-point bid/ask spread at the time of review.

The criteria for removal of an issue from the index are lower than for inclusion in order to avoid a large amount of turnover. Thus, an issue is removed if:

▌ The market capitalization of the issue is less than USD 75 million at the time of review.

Table 5.5 Regional Breakdown of the UBSW Global Convertible Index

Country/Region	UBSW Weighting (%)	Number of Constituents
Europe	40	168
United States	39	208
Japan	8	27
Other Asia	7	69
Other	6	16

Source: UBS Warburg, March 2001

I There is less than USD 75 million of average exchange traded volume for the last two quarters prior to review, AND

I There is less than USD 75 million of average volume reported to Autex for the last two quarters prior to review, AND

I There are less than three market makers out of the top ten convertible underwriters quoting prices with a maximum 2-point bid/ask spread at the time of review, OR

I The issue has been called, put, converted, or repurchased by the company, or has matured.

Jefferies Active Convertible Index (JACI) Global (USD)

Jefferies & Company was one of the first brokers to track the performance of the international convertible market. Although the JACI Global Index did not start until May 1998 with the inclusion of the JACI U.S. Domestic Index, the other component parts of the global index originated in January 1993. These included the JACI International Eurobond Index and the JACI Japan Domestic Index. Currently, the JACI Global Index consists of a blend of four regional indices: JACI Asia ex-Japan, JACI Japan, JACI Europe, and JACI U.S. (See Table 5.6.) The JACI Japan Index includes both domestic and euro-convertibles. Euro-convertibles are securities issued outside the issuer's home country. If a Japanese company issues a convertible that is listed outside Japan, the convertible is considered to be a euro issue. Originally, the term *euro* in this context stemmed

Table 5.6 Regional Breakdown of the Jefferies Active Convertible Index (Global)

Country/Region	JACI Weighting (%)	Number of Constituents
Asia-Pacific	12	14
Europe	50	69
United States	21	104
Japan	17	45

Source: Jefferies, March 2001

from the recycling of petrodollars during the 1970s oil crisis. It has nothing to do with currency denomination. The JACI U.S. Index excludes mandatory convertibles.

Price data is obtained in the open market from at least two market makers. Prices are calculated daily, and the index is reviewed monthly. Liquidity is a major determinant for inclusion in the index. The minimum issue size by market capitalization is USD 200 million. Issues that become illiquid after going too far in- or out-of-the-money are removed from the index. New issues are entered into the index on the corresponding payment date at the prevailing market price.

Table 5.7 summarizes the characteristics of the main global convertible indices.

CONVERTIBLES AS AN ASSET CLASS

In the 1990s, convertibles have emerged as a separate asset class. Growth in the size, depth, and transparency of the market has brought convertibles within the reach of all types of investors. At the same time, studies have illustrated the superior risk-adjusted performance of convertibles relative to bonds and equities.

An investor's choice of convertible strategy depends on his or her investment objectives and risk tolerance. Convertibles are versatile

Table 5.7   Global Convertible Indices Compared

	ML-G300	GSBB	UBSW	JACI
Beginning date	Jan-95	Jan-98	Jan-94	May-98
Total market value	$134 billion	$154 billion	$253 billion	$118 billion
Review	semiannually	semiannually	quarterly	monthly
Weighting	market	market	market	market
Method	capitalization	capitalization	capitalization	capitalization
No. of issues	300	225	488	232
Calculation frequency	daily	daily	daily	daily

Source: Merrill Lynch, Goldman Sachs, UBS Warburg Jefferies, March 2001

instruments, and portfolios using convertibles can be designed to accommodate both conservative and aggressive investors. Insurance companies view convertibles as part of their fixed-income allocation, while other investors see them as low-risk alternatives to equities.

Tables 5.8–5.18 illustrate the low-risk, high-return characteristics of the global convertible market in recent years. Table 5.8 shows that the historic risk and return of convertibles fall between those of bonds and equities.

The Sharpe ratio measures the return of a portfolio, over and above the risk-free rate of interest, relative to the amount of risk taken. Risk is defined as the volatility, or annualized standard deviation, of the portfolio returns (see Chapter 12). The ratio is calculated as follows:

$$\text{Sharpe ratio} = \frac{\text{Portfolio return} - \text{Risk - free rate}}{\text{Portfolio standard deviation}}$$

A higher Sharpe ratio indicates that the asset class produces a greater return given a certain level of risk. Table 5.9 presents

Table 5.8 Global Convertibles: Risk versus Return

	Bonds	Equities	Convertibles
Return	6.79%	13.95%	9.27%
Risk	5.07%	18.08%	7.48%

Bonds: JP Morgan Global Government Bond Index, USD, total return. Equities: Datastream Fairplay World, USD, total return. Convertibles: WDR Global Convertible Index, USD, total return. Return: Annualized returns over the period (CAGR). Risk: Volatility of daily USD returns over the period 31-Dec-93 to 5-Mar-99.
Source: UBS Warburg

Table 5.9 Global Convertibles: Historic Sharpe Ratios

	Bonds	Equities	Convertibles
Sharpe ratio	0.31	0.48	0.54

Risk-free rate over the period 31-Dec-93 to 5-Mar-99: 5.24% (yield on UST 8.875% 15-Feb-99.
Source: UBS Warburg

historic Sharpe ratios, illustrating the superior risk/return ratio for convertibles.

Table 5.10 shows performance statistics for the international convertible market (i.e., excluding the United States). Absent the strong U.S. equity market returns, international convertibles outperformed both stocks and bonds with moderate risk.

Table 5.11 illustrates the historic Sharpe ratios for international convertibles versus equities and bonds. During this period, the Sharpe ratios for convertibles were identical to that of bonds, which benefitted from the one-off convergence play associated with the introduction of the euro in January 1999.

The strong performance of international convertibles over both bonds and equities is partly explained by the poor performance of Asian equity markets. In Japan, while bonds performed best, convertibles managed to generate a positive return with much lower volatility than equities. (Table 5.12.)

The real test for convertibles comes during rising equity markets. In rising markets, convertibles should underperform equities. During the late 1990s, U.S. and European equity markets showed substantial gains that should have left convertibles trailing. However, when we

Table 5.10 International Convertible Markets: Risk versus Return

	Bonds	Equities	Convertibles
Return	7.18%	6.81%	7.38%
Risk	7.64%	12.77%	8.67%

Bonds: JP Morgan Global Government Bond Index ex U.S., USD, total return. Equities: MSCI World ex U.S., USD, total return. Convertibles: WDR Global ex U.S. Convertible subindex, USD, total return. Return: Annualized returns over the period (CAGR). Risk: Volatility of daily USD returns over the period 31-Dec-93 to 5-Mar-99.
Source: UBS Warburg

Table 5.11 International Markets: Historic Sharpe Ratios

	Bonds	Equities	Convertibles
Sharpe ratio	0.25	0.12	0.25

Over the period 31-Dec-93 to 5-Mar-99
Source: UBS Warburg

Table 5.12   Japanese Convertibles: Risk versus Reward

	Bonds	Equities	Convertibles
Return	5.53%	−3.52%	4.92%
Risk	4.43%	18.01%	6.13%

Bonds: JP Morgan Japan Government Bond Index in yen, total return. Equities: TOPIX, yen, total return. Convertibles: WDR Japanese Convertible Subindex, in yen, total return. Return: Annualized return over the period (CAGR). Risk: Volatility of daily yen returns over the period 31-Dec-93 to 5-Mar-99.
Source: UBS Warburg

look at the historic data for these markets, we find that convertibles produced only slightly lower returns with much lower volatility. (See Table 5.13.)

In Europe, the higher Sharpe ratio of convertibles further illustrates the attractiveness of these securities when compared to bonds or equities. (See Table 5.14.)

In the U.S. market, results are less conclusive because more small- to medium-sized companies issue convertibles than in foreign markets. This sets the U.S. convertible market apart from the rest of the world, where traditionally the large blue-chip companies have been the major issuers.

During the five-year period under review, large capitalization stocks in the S&P 500 outperformed all others. Table 5.15 illustrates this exceptional return, but also highlights the high return and low risk of convertibles.

In Table 5.16, the higher Sharpe ratio for equities results from the S&P 500's consistently strong performance. Nevertheless, convert-

Table 5.13   European Convertibles: Risk versus Reward

	Bonds	Equities	Convertibles
Return	9.23%	19.05%	16.34%
Risk	4.41%	15.15%	9.69%

Bonds: JP Morgan Global Europe Government Bond Index in euros, total return. Equities: Dow Jones STOXX, Euros, total return. Convertibles: WDR European Convertible Subindex, in Euros, total return. Return: Annualized return over the period (CAGR). Risk: Volatility of daily euro returns over the period 31-Dec-93 to 5-Mar-99.
Source: UBS Warburg

Table 5.14　European Markets: Historic Sharpe Ratios

	Bonds	Equities	Convertibles
Sharpe ratio	0.92	0.92	1.15

Risk-free rate over the period 31-Dec-93 to 5-Mar-99: 5.1541% (yield on German bond 7% 20-Apr-99)
Source: UBS Warburg

Table 5.15　U.S. Markets: Risk versus Reward (S&P 500)

	Bonds	Equities	Convertibles
Return	6.55%	24.08%	14.28%
Risk	4.29%	14.71%	8.62%

Bonds: U.S. Total All Lives Datastream Government Bond Index, in USD, total return. Equities: S&P 500, U.S., total return. Convertibles: WDR U.S. Convertible Subindex, USD, total return. Return: Annualized return over the period (CAGR). Risk: Volatility of daily USD returns over the period 31-Dec-93 to 5-Mar-99.
Source: UBS Warburg

Table 5.16　U.S. Markets: Historic Sharpe Ratios (S&P 500)

	Bonds	Equities	Convertibles
Sharpe ratio	0.30	1.28	1.05

Risk-free rate over the period 31-Dec-93 to 5-Mar-99: 5.24% (yield on UST 8.875% 15-Feb-99).
Source: UBS Warburg

ibles demonstrate a superior Sharpe ratio compared to bonds, and only a slightly lower ratio compared to equities.

Because U.S. convertibles are issued mostly by small- to medium-sized companies, the Russell 2000 index may be a fairer benchmark by which to judge performance. In this case, convertibles outperformed both the Russell 2000 index and the bond market. (See Table 5.17.)

The higher Sharpe ratio of convertibles again illustrates the attractiveness of these securities when compared to bonds or equities. In this case, the difference between the Sharpe ratio for convertibles and the ratio for both bonds and equities is substantial. (See Table 5.18.)

Table 5.17 U.S. Markets: Risk versus Reward (Russell 2000)

	Bonds	Equities	Convertibles
Return	6.55%	8.69%	14.28%
Risk	4.29%	13.25%	8.62%

Bonds: U.S. Total All Lives Datastream Government Bond Index, in USD, total return. Equities: Russell 2000, USD, total return. Convertibles: WDR U.S. Convertible Subindex, USD, total return. Return: Annualized return over the period (CAGR). Risk: Volatility of daily USD returns over the period 31-Dec-93 to 5-Mar-99.
Source: UBS Warburg

Table 5.18 U.S. Markets: Historic Sharpe Ratios (Russell 2000)

	Bonds	Equities	Convertibles
Sharpe ratio	0.30	0.26	1.05

Risk-free rate over the period 31-Dec-93 to 5-Mar-99: 5.24% (yield on UST 8.875% 15-Feb-99).
Source: UBS Warburg

This is interesting information, but how do convertibles perform over the long term?

The Ibbotson Study

In 1993, Scott L. Lummer and Mark W. Riepe of Ibbotson Associates, the investment-consulting firm, published their definitive article in the *Journal of Fixed Income*, "Convertible Bonds as an Asset Class." The study demonstrated that over the long-term (i.e., from December 1956 through December 1992), the domestic convertible market delivered returns that approached those of equities but with less risk. The major findings of the study, which is subsequently updated through 2000, are outlined in the following list.

I Over the period for which reliable long-run data is available, the total return performance of the domestic convertible market has approached that of the S&P 500, with significantly lower risk. Over the same period, convertibles have significantly outperformed long-term corporate bonds while demonstrating comparable risk.

I Convertibles have demonstrated a much higher correlation with the S&P 500 than with corporate bonds.

I Convertibles can help maximize performance in both equity and fixed-income portfolios.

There are three main reasons for the long-run outperformance of convertible instruments.

1. Inefficient company timing in calling convertible issues. If a deep in-the-money convertible enjoys a significant yield advantage over the common stock but is not called, it is likely to outperform the underlying stock. Companies may delay conversion for a number of reasons including balance sheet and rating agency considerations.

2. Attractive convertible pricing at issue. Typically, convertible securities are initially priced several percentage points cheap to their theoretical value in order to insure a successful launch. These securities often trade higher in the immediate aftermarket. Apparently, companies are prepared to offer attractive terms in order to assure entry to the capital markets and to enjoy the tax benefits offered by convertibles.

3. Exposure to a universe of significantly higher beta stocks (i.e., the New Economy sectors of telecommunications, technology, and health care) through a period of excess equity returns.

In the original study, it was shown that convertible returns from December 1956 to December 1992 stayed between that of the equity market (S&P 500) and the corporate bond market during the entire period. However, during the period from 1973 to 1992, convertibles produced a total return that actually exceeded that of the equity market, with significantly lower volatility. Table 5.19 provides the data for the returns and standard deviations for the period 1973 to 2000.

Table 5.19 shows that the 11.89% compound annual return for convertible bonds was only slightly lower than the 12.97% return of the S&P 500. However, convertible bonds produced a significantly

Table 5.19   U.S. Markets: Risk versus Reward (Ibbotson Study)

Asset Class	Compound Annual Return	Standard Deviation
Convertible bonds	11.89%	12.68%
S&P 500	12.97%	17.03%
Long-term corporate bonds	8.99%	11.90%

Period 1973–2000
Source: Ibbotson Associates, Goldman Sachs

lower standard deviation of 12.68%, compared to 17.03% for the S&P 500. During this period, convertible bonds outperformed long-term corporate bonds, with a similar level of risk.

During the period from 1973 to 2000, annual returns for the S&P 500 and convertibles demonstrated that convertibles and common stocks typically move together, but with yearly fluctuations tending to be lower for convertibles. The correlation between convertibles and the S&P 500's monthly returns over the January 1973 to December 2000 period is 0.82. Convertibles tend to be up (down) when stocks are up (down), but the extent of the monthly returns is smaller for convertibles. The Ibbotson Study found that while convertibles participated in 70% of upward equity market movements, they participated in only 52% of the downside. The correlation between convertibles and long-term corporate bonds over the comparable period is considerably lower at only 0.39.

The Efficient Frontier

Figure 5.1 illustrates the positive portfolio effects of including convertible securities, as managed by the Gabelli Asset Management Company (GAMCO), into a portfolio of stocks (e.g., S&P 500) and bonds (e.g., Lehman Brothers Intermediate Government/Corporate Bond Index). The curves represent risk/return values along the efficient frontier for each portfolio. The portfolio that includes convertibles results in a more efficient portfolio than the one consisting of just stocks and bonds. It generates higher returns with less risk. (See Additional Notes for an explanation of how to calculate the efficient frontier.)

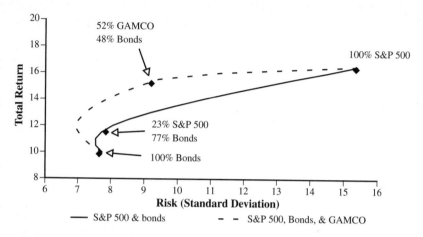

Figure 5.1 The Efficient Frontier with Convertibles (1980–2000)
Note: GAMCO = Gabelli Asset Management Company
Bonds = Lehman Brothers Intermediate Government/Corporate Bond Index
Source: Gabelli

ADDITIONAL NOTES

The following steps explain how the efficient frontier can be calculated for a portfolio (or group of portfolios).

1. Gather periodic total return data for the selected portfolios making sure that the data is from the same time intervals and periods for each portfolio. In our example, we use quarterly returns for the Gabelli Asset Management Company's convertible product, the S&P 500, and the Lehman Brothers Intermediate Government/Corporate Bond Index from 1980 through 2000. Our data series for the three portfolios is contained in columns B, C, and D, rows 5 through 88, respectively, of our Excel spreadsheet.

2. The average return and the standard deviation of each portfolio are then calculated. We have arranged this in Table 5.20.

3. The correlation of the indexes must also be calculated and these are shown in the second section on the spreadsheet.

4. The covariance of the portfolios is then calculated and arranged in a table. The covariance is calculated by multiplying the base portfolio's standard deviation (GAMCO) by the standard deviation of the given portfolio (S&P 500 or Lehman

Table 5.20 Efficient Frontier Calculations

	F	G	H	I
4		Standard Deviation	Average Return	
5	GAMCO	=STDEV(B5:B88)*(4^0.5)*100	=AVERAGE(B5:B88)*4*100	
6	S&P 500	=STDEV(C5:C88)*(4^0.5)*100	=AVERAGE(C5:C88)*4*100	
7	Lgov/Corp	=STDEV(D5:D88)*(4^0.5)*100	=AVERAGE(D5:D88)*4*100	
8				
9				
10	Correlation Matrix			
11		GAMCO	S&P500	Lgov/Corp
12	GAMCO	=CORREL(B5:B88,B5:B88)	=CORREL(B5:B88,C5:C88)	=CORREL(B5:B88,D5:D88)
13	S&P 500	=CORREL(B5:B88,C5:C88)	=CORREL(C5:C88,C5:C88)	=CORREL(C5:C88,D5:D88)
14	Lgov/Corp	=CORREL(B5:B88,D5:D88)	=CORREL(C5:C88,D5:D88)	=CORREL(D5:D88,D5:D88)
15				
16				
17	Covariance Matrix			
18				
19	GAMCO	=G5*G5*G12	=G5*G6*G13	=G5*G7*I12
20	S&P 500	=G5*G6*G13	=G6*G6*H13	=G6*G7*I13
21	Lgov/Corp	=G5*G7*G14	=G6*G7*H14	=G7*G7*I14
22				
23				
24	Efficient Frontier Portfolio for S&P and Bonds			
25		S&P 500	Bonds	
26	Weights	=F27	=F28	
27	1	=F27*G26*H20	=F27*H26*I20	

(Continued)

Table 5.20 (Continued)

	F	G	H	I
28	0	=F28*G26*H21	=F28*H26*I21	
29	=SUM(F27:F28)	=SUM(G27:G28)	=SUM(H27:H28)	
30				
31	Portfolio Variance:		=SUM(G29:H29)	
32	Portfolio Standard Dev:		=H31^0.5	
33	Portfolio Mean:		=F27*H6+F28*H7	
34				
35				
36				
37	Efficient Frontier Portfolio for S&P, Bonds, and GAMCO			
38		GAMCO	S&P 500	Bonds
39	Weights	=F40	=F41	=F42
40	0	=F40*G39*G19	=F40*H39*H19	=F40*I39*I19
41	1	=F41*G39*G20	=F41*H39*H20	=F41*I39*I20
42	0	=F42*G39*G21	=F42*H39*H21	=F42*I39*I21
43	=SUM(F40:F42)	=SUM(G40:G42)	=SUM(H40:H42)	=SUM(I40:I42)
44				
45	Portfolio Variance:	=SUM(G43:I43)		
46	Portfolio Standard Dev:	=H45^0.5		
47	Portfolio Mean:	=F40*H5+F41*H6+F42*H7		

Brothers Intermediate Government/Corporate) and finally by the correlation of the base and given portfolios.

5. Points on the efficient frontier are found by minimizing the standard deviation by changing the weights of the portfolios to arrive at a given return. We used Excel's Solver function (located in the Tools menu under Add-Ins) to make these calculations. We provided the Solver with a target (to minimize the standard deviation), and variables (the portfolio weights).

6. In addition to the target and variables, the Solver must also be given any constraints. For an unrestricted efficient frontier that allows short sales, but no leverage, one must restrict the sum of the portfolio weights to 100% and set the portfolio's expected return equal to a target return. If short selling is not allowed, as in our calculations, the portfolio weights must be restricted to positive numbers.

The Excel spreadsheet displays the steps described together with their formulas. The final weightings matrix is not shown because it contains only hard inputs and is easy to construct.

6

CONVERTIBLE VALUATION
A Cultural Overview

The process of convertible valuation may well be more of an art than a science. In fact, the very concept of value is often in the eyes of the beholder. Historically, the pricing and valuation of convertible securities have varied over time and among regions.

JAPAN: CONVERTIBLES AS AN EQUITY ALTERNATIVE

In Japan, convertibles have traditionally been viewed as an alternative to equities. Consequently, new issues are generally priced with only a 2.50% premium to the underlying equity. Traditionally, this contrasted with premiums in the mid-teens in Europe and the mid-twenties in the United States. From the issuers' points of view, Japanese convertibles were structured as equities in order to circumvent regulations that made issuing common stock difficult. The main buyers of Japanese convertible bonds were domestic tax-exempt institutions like public pension funds, which benefited from the so-called 5-3-3-2 rule. This rule required that these institutions hold no more than 30% of their portfolios in equities, with the balance being in bonds, foreign currency investments, and real estate. These institutions created a strong demand for low-premium convertible bonds, which gave them increased equity exposure but were classified as bonds. Subsequent to the deregulation of the Japanese economy, and the repeal of rule 5-3-3-2, the growth of the domestic convertible market has been stunted (see Chapter 4).

UNITED KINGDOM: THE DIVIDEND CROSS-OVER METHOD

In Europe, the convertible market was separated between the United Kingdom and the Continent. In the United Kingdom, domestic investors traditionally viewed convertibles as equities with an income advantage. Here the main emphasis was on the cash flow of the convertible versus the common stock. The appropriate premium to be paid was directly related to the income advantage. Once a company's dividend yield surpassed the current yield on the convertible, there would no longer be any reason to own the convertible. The investor should then switch into the stock. The point at which this switch should occur is known as the cross-over point. To predict this point, a dividend growth rate must be assumed. The dividend stream (and the coupons from the bond) are then discounted and compared to determine in which year the cross-over will occur. The discount rate is the risk-free rate plus a credit spread. The risk-free rate is the government bond yield with the same maturity and in the same currency as the convertible. This distinction is important for cross-currency bonds where the bond is issued in a different currency from the company's home currency. The credit spread is the difference between the risk-free rate and the market rate paid on the company's existing debt. Adjustments should be made to compensate for maturity differences and seniority status. If the company has no other debt outstanding, then the debt of similar companies in the same industry should be used as a proxy.

The concept of discounted yield advantage can be used to determine how much premium the investor should be willing to pay for a convertible. The first step is to determine the cash premium the investor is paying to own the stock via the convertible, as opposed to buying the stock outright. The cash premium is calculated as follows:

$$(\text{Conversion ratio} \cdot \text{Equity price})$$
$$- (\text{Convertible price} \% \cdot \text{Denomination})$$

The cash premium is then converted to a per-share basis by dividing it by the conversion ratio.

The next step is to determine the discounted yield advantage on a per-share basis and compare it to the cash premium above. If the yield advantage is greater than the cash premium, then it makes sense to own the convertible. In other words, the extra income you receive by owning the convertible more than makes up for the premium you are paying. The longer it takes for the dividend on the stock to catch up with the coupon on the bond, the more valuable the income advantage is to the investor. This technique is useful in that it helps the investor focus on the company's dividend policy. How large is the dividend? Is it secure? What is the dividend payout ratio? Once the investor forms a view of the dividend policy, it can then be determined whether or not the premium being paid for the convertible is fair or not. The faster the dividend grows, the less valuable the yield advantage, and the lower the premium. Conversely, if a company reduces or eliminates its dividend, the more valuable the yield advantage becomes and the higher the premium. Thus, the company's dividend policy is important in determining a convertible's value.

Equity investors have always appreciated this fact since over the past 60 years more than one-third of their returns have come from dividends. Today, share buy-backs may represent a more tax-efficient way to return surplus cash flow to investors. Nevertheless, dividends still matter. In fact, by comparison to U.S. investors, European investors have traditionally been more income oriented. Perhaps this is why they have given so much attention to the relative yield advantage of the bond over the stock when they are determining the value of a convertible.

An example of this valuation method is given in Table 6.1. The theoretical price of the convertible is the sum of parity plus the discounted income advantage. Parity is easily calculated, being the sum of the conversion ratio (33.33) times the stock price ($25.00) or $833.33. The discounted yield advantage calculation requires two assumptions: the dividend growth rate and the discount rate. The other two variables, the coupon and the initial cash dividend, are known. In this case, we assume that the 2.4% dividend yield grows at a rate

Table 6.1 Income Valuation Model

Issue Details	Bond	Stock
Issuer	XYZ Corp.	XYZ Corp.
Denomination	$1,000	
Convertible price	92.000%	
Coupon	5.000%	Price	$25.000
Stock price	$25.000	Dividend	$0.600
Conversion premium	20.000%	Yield	2.400%
Conversion price	$30.000	Growth	15.000%
Conversion ratio	33.333	Discount rate	9.000%
Discount rate	9.000%		
Cash premium (1)	−$86.67	Parity	$833.33
Income differential (2)	$99.94	Inc. adv.	$99.94
Total (1 + 2)	$13.27	Theo. value	$933.27
Per share adv/disadvantage		Price	93.327%
of buying shares through the convertible	−$2.60		
Income advantage	$99.94		
Advantage per share	$3.00		

Year	Bond Cash Flow	PV Bond Cash Flow		Stock Dividends	PV Stock Cash Flow	
1	$50.00	$ 45.87	$ 45.87	$20.00	$ 18.35	$ 18.35
2	$50.00	$ 42.08	$ 42.08	$23.00	$ 19.36	$ 19.36
3	$50.00	$ 38.61	$ 38.61	$26.45	$ 20.42	$ 20.42
4	$50.00	$ 35.42	$ 35.42	$30.42	$ 21.55	$ 21.55
5	$50.00	$ 32.50	$ 32.50	$34.98	$ 22.73	$ 22.73
6	$50.00	$ 29.81	$ 29.81	$40.23	$ 23.99	$ 23.99
7	$50.00	$ 27.35	$ 27.35	$46.26	$ 25.31	$ 25.31
8	$50.00	$ 25.09	$ 0.00	$53.20	$ 26.70	$ 0.00
9	$50.00	$ 23.02	$ 0.00	$61.18	$ 28.17	$ 0.00
10	$50.00	$ 21.12	$ 0.00	$70.36	$ 29.72	$ 0.00
Total		$320.88	$251.65		$236.30	$151.71

of 15% per annum and that all cash flows are discounted at 9%. Beginning in the eighth year, we see that the present value of the dividend payment on the stock has overtaken the present value of the coupon payment on the bond. This tells us that the optimal time to sell the convertible and switch into the stock will be the year before this occurs, in year seven. This is the cross-over date. After this date, we prefer to benefit from the higher income paid by the stock's growing dividend.

Since we will be selling the convertible bond after the cross-over date, we cease to include any cash flows after this date in our calculation of the discounted income advantage. The discounted income advantage is the difference between the sum of the bond's discounted cash flows and the stock's discounted dividend payments through the cross-over period. In our example, this equals $99.94. Thus, the theoretical price of the bond is $933.27, being parity ($833.33) plus the income advantage ($99.94). Expressed as a percentage of its $1,000 face amount, this is a value of 93.327%. Since the convertible bond is being offered at 92%, it is reasonably priced relative to its income advantage.

Of course this method has numerous drawbacks. It does not take into consideration the most important element of a convertible bond: its optionality. As we shall see, more sophisticated approaches seek to value the embedded call warrant, which is a function of the stock price volatility. The more volatile the stock price, the greater the likelihood that it will go into the money and benefit the convertible holder. Moreover, the method does not consider that the bond may be called away from the investor before its final maturity. This would reduce the potential yield advantage of the bond over the stock, and tend to overstate its theoretical price. The benefit of the method is that it focuses the investor's attention on the yield advantage and seeks to quantify it. A company's dividend policy is relevant even for those employing option-pricing models to value convertibles. In fact, sensitivity to cultural biases across markets can identify attractive buying opportunities. For example, because the discounted yield advantage method does not consider the value of the convertible's embedded warrant, a domestic U.K. investor using this method might be a willing seller to a U.S. investor who values the warrant more highly.

The analytical power of the discounted yield advantage model becomes clear once we sensitize the dividend assumption. In our example, we assumed a dividend growth rate of 15%, which produced a theoretical value of 93.327%. If the company increases its dividend rate by only 5%, the theoretical value rises to 99.83%. Conversely, should the company accelerate its dividend growth rate to 20%, the theoretical value will fall to 91.57%.

NETHERLANDS: THE TOTAL PREMIUM METHOD

Everyone knows that the Dutch are excellent businesspeople after having purchased Manhattan Island for $24 in 1626. For a country of 16 million people, twice the size of New Jersey, the Dutch are among the largest investors in the United States. Their success is testimony to the wonders of compound interest. Of course the Dutch are also known for their frugality. The history and culture of the Dutch have affected their view of pricing convertible bonds. In Holland, when one speaks of a convertible's premium, one refers to the concept of total premium. This is not solely the conversion premium, as is the case elsewhere. The total premium also includes a component to account for the opportunity cost of owning a lower-yielding convertible versus a normal straight bond. The consensus view is that total premiums should lie in the range between 35% and 45%. Once again, this method fails to take into consideration the bond's optionality or call features. Nevertheless, the method is useful in that it forces the investor to focus on the relative value of the convertible's income advantage versus straight debt. This concept spawned a simple trading rule in other markets such as the United States. If the current yield spread between the convertible and an equivalent straight bond is greater than 2%, the convertible is expensive.

Table 6.2 shows how the total premium method is calculated. The total premium is the sum of the conversion premium and the present value of the forgone interest, expressed on a per-share basis. The irony of this method is that the total premium can be manipulated by changing the maturity of the bond. The longer the maturity, the larger the forgone interest income, and the higher the total premium. Under this method, the interest component domi-

Table 6.2 Total Premium Model

Issuer	XYZ Corp.
Issue price	100.00%
Issue size	€250,000,000
Notional amount	€1,000
Coupon	5.0%
Term (years)	10
Stock price	€200.000
Conversion premium (1)	12.00%
Conversion price	€224.000
Conversion ratio	4.464
Parity	89.29%
Dividend yield	3.00%
Yield advantage	2.00%
Payback (years)	6.00
Government bond yield	6.00%
Credit spread	2.50%
Straight bond yield	8.50%
Yield give up	3.50%
Interest loss	€350.00
Interest loss (present value)	€229.65
Discount rate	8.50%
Interest loss per share (present value)	€51.44
Percent loss per share (2)	25.72%
Total premium (1 + 2)	37.72%

nates the total premium. Consequently, the conversion premium tends to be relatively low. Once again, understanding cultural biases toward convertible pricing can provide interesting opportunities for the global investor.

OPTION PRICING MODELS

Although the above pricing methods provide interesting insights into some of the factors affecting convertibles, they are flawed because they ignore the convertible's option component. The world of pricing financial assets and liabilities changed forever in 1972 when Fisher Black and Myron Scholes published their now-famous paper in the *Journal of Finance*, "The Valuation of Option Contracts and a Test of Market Efficiency." As global financial markets have become more integrated, the use of option theory to price convertible securities has become more widely accepted. Today, pricing anomalies among markets is more a function of the inputs to the model than mere tradition.

Part Two

CONVERTIBLE PRICING AND VALUATION

7

OPTION PRICING THEORY

INTRODUCTION

There are two types of options: calls and puts. A call option gives the holder the right to purchase an underlying asset by a certain date, at a specified price. A put option gives the holder the right to sell an underlying asset by a certain date, at a specified price. The date at which the option expires is known as maturity, the exercise date, or the expiration date. The purchase or selling price specified in the option is called the strike price or exercise price.

Options come in two varieties, European and American, although these names have nothing to do with the markets in which the options are sold. A European option can be exercised only on its date of maturity. An American option, on the other hand, can be exercised at any time before maturity, thus giving the holder much greater flexibility. Unlike forward contracts, options give the holder the opportunity to take a course of action rather than an obligation to do so. At maturity, the holder of an option can choose not to exercise the option, at which time its price becomes zero.

ESTABLISHING THE BOUNDARY CONDITIONS OF A CALL OPTION

A valuation method similar to that used for forward contracts (see Chapter 15) can be used to calculate a theoretical floor for call options and, more importantly, to show that it is never optimal to exercise a nondividend-paying American call option prior to its maturity. Consequently, American and European call options on nondividend-paying stocks are equivalently priced. To see this, consider the following two portfolios:

> Portfolio 1: one call option plus a discount bond worth K at time T
>
> Portfolio 2: one share of the underlying nondividend-paying stock

If the call option is exercised at any time, t, its value is the underlying stock price minus the strike price, $S - K$. Likewise, the value of the discount bond at any time, t, is $Ke^{-r(T-t)}$. Portfolio 1 is thus worth

$$S - K + Ke^{-r(T-t)}$$

where S = the current stock price
$\quad\quad K$ = the strike price of the option
$\quad\quad t$ = the current time
$\quad\quad T$ = the maturity date of the option

when the call is exercised prior to maturity. Since portfolio 2 is always worth S, it can easily be seen that portfolio 1 is worth less than portfolio 2 at any time prior to maturity. At maturity, however, portfolio 1 is worth

$$\text{Max}(0, S_T - K) + K = \text{Max}(K, S_T)$$

which is always worth at least as much as portfolio 2, whose value is S_T at time T.

Because portfolio 1 is worth at least as much as portfolio 2 at maturity, portfolio 1 must sell at a higher price than portfolio 2 in order to prevent arbitrage. If this were not the case, an investor could short portfolio 2 and purchase portfolio 1 with the proceeds. At maturity, the investor could then use portfolio 1 to close out his or her short position and thus obtain a risk-free profit from the initial price differential. A lower limit is thus established for the call price,

$$C + Ke^{-r(T-t)} > S$$

or, put more concisely,[1]

$$C > S - Ke^{-r(T-t)}$$

or, more conservatively,

$$C > S - K \qquad\qquad (7.1)$$

where C = the price of the American call option

Because portfolio 1 is more expensive, it is not optimal to exercise the call prior to maturity since this will result in a lower profit than portfolio 2 (i.e., a person exercising the call early would be better off holding the second portfolio). This means that an investor owning an American call will not exercise it prior to maturity and thus there is no price difference between American and European calls on nondividend-paying securities. Intuitively, a call option provides insurance to the holder by limiting the downside potential of a security while maintaining the upside. Since the security pays no dividends and, since the call can be converted into the security at any time, holding the call is equivalent to holding the underlying security, with the added bonus of a protective price floor set at the exercise price. By exercising an American call early, the holder unnecessarily surrenders the price premium paid for the protective insurance. If an investor believes the stock price will fall in the future, he or she would be better off selling the call option and being compensated for the insurance premium rather than exercising the option and selling the stock.

The above relationships can be used to graphically illustrate the basic value structure of a call as it varies with the stock price.

---

[1]This relationship is the weaker form of the previous equation and is based on the fact that $K > Ke^{-r(T-t)}$ for all positive values of r. This therefore implies that $C > S - Ke^{-r(T-t)} > S - K$ and thus, by transitivity, $C > S - K$. This is used as a time invariant lower bound for the call value.

Figure 7.1 illustrates several aspects of a call's valuation. The price of the underlying stock provides an upper bound for the value of a call as evidenced by the top diagonal line in the figure. This is because, at exercise, an in-the-money call is worth the stock price minus the strike price, while an out-of-the money call is worth zero even though the underlying stock maintains a positive value. The lower bound in Figure 7.1 corresponds to Equation 7.1 and represents the payoff if the call was exercised immediately. As demonstrated earlier, the insurance provided by the call provides a premium to the call valuation above the exercise payoff. It is this premium that is surrendered when a call is exercised prior to maturity.

Consider the call valuation at the three points denoted A, B, and C in Figure 7.1.

Point A: At point A the stock's value is zero and therefore the call has no chance of ever being in-the-money. If the stock had any possibility of upward movement it would have a positive value. The call will expire out-of-the-money and worthless. This unique point is the only time at which the stock price and the call price will be equally valued.

Point B: At point B the stock's value is equal to the strike price. Exercising the option at this point would result in a zero net gain. All of the call's value at this point is due to its insurance premium. The call has the potential for upside gains with no downside risk. If the stock rises, the exercise value becomes positive. If the stock falls, the worst possible payoff remains zero.

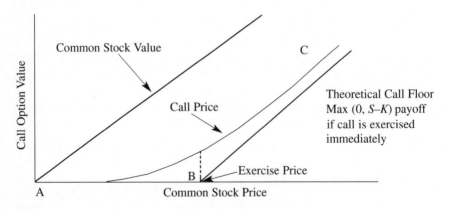

Figure 7.1   Call Valuation as a Function of Stock Price

Point C: At point C, the call is deep in-the-money and the likelihood of the stock falling below the strike price is minimal. When a call is deep in-the-money, its conversion into stock is a near certainty. On a nondividend-paying stock this is essentially equivalent to owning the stock. If exercise were an absolute certainty, buying a call could be viewed as buying the underlying stock, but financing part of the purchase by borrowing. The amount borrowed is implicitly the present value of the exercise price. Looked at from another perspective, one is paying the stock price S in two installments, an amount C today, and an amount K in the future. The value of the call would therefore be:

$$C = S - Ke^{-r(T-t)}$$

which is the theoretical floor we calculated earlier.

HOW TO PRICE A CALL OPTION: A LEVERAGED POSITION IN THE STOCK

In the previous section, we defined the boundary conditions for a European call option at expiration on a nondividend-paying stock. Now we want to calculate the current price of the option.

A call option is like owning a leveraged position in the stock. This is logical because with an investment of less than the price of the stock (i.e., the call price), the option holder can benefit from the complete movement in the stock price. Therefore, one way to price a call option is to replicate the payoff of the call by creating an equivalent portfolio consisting of a partial investment in the stock plus a loan. If we can create a portfolio with the same payoff as the option at expiration, the two portfolios must have the same price today. If not, it would be possible to make a risk-free profit by selling the expensive portfolio and buying the inexpensive portfolio. To illustrate this concept, consider the following example:

Stock price	$100
Exercise price	$100
Term	1 year
Risk-free interest rate	5%

Assume that after one year the stock price can move either up or down by 25% to $125 or $75, respectively. Since we know the final price of the stock, we can calculate the price of the option at expiration. If the stock price is below the exercise price of $100, the option will expire worthless. If the stock price is above the exercise price, the option will be worth the stock price at expiration (S^T) minus the exercise price (K) or in this case $25 (i.e., $125 minus $100 equals $25). These outcomes are illustrated below.

Beginning stock price	$100.00	
Ending stock price	$75.00	$125.00
Option value at expiration	$0.00	$25.00

Step 1: How Much Stock to Purchase?

The first step in establishing the replication portfolio is to determine how much stock to purchase. To do this we want to know how sensitive the option price is to a change in the stock price. This sensitivity is measured by the option's delta or hedge ratio. The hedge ratio can be calculated as follows:

$$\text{Hedge ratio} = \frac{\text{Variation of the option price}}{\text{Variation of the stock price}} = \frac{\Delta C}{\Delta S}$$

In our example, the hedge ratio is 50% as illustrated below.

$$\text{Hedge ratio} = \frac{\$25 - \$0}{\$125 - \$75} = \frac{\$25}{\$50} = 50\%$$

Thus, to create the replication portfolio, we need to purchase half a share of stock worth $50 (i.e., $100 · 50% equals $50). (Note: Of course in reality it is not possible to purchase just half a share of stock. Exchange-traded options control 100 shares of stock. In our example, we would have purchased 50 shares of stock to replicate 1 call option). We calculated the hedge ratio using unrealistically simple assumptions. We assumed that the stock price moved only once over the term of the option and that we knew in advance what the future stock prices would be. We have used these simple assumptions to illustrate the principle of option pricing by building an equivalent portfolio of stock and debt. Later in this chapter we will modify these assumptions to accommodate more realistic assumptions. The Black–Scholes option pricing formula provides for a continually moving stock price rather than a one-step process. In addition, the formula, by incorporating a stock's expected return and volatility, creates a range of possible future stock prices.

Step 2: How Much Should We Borrow?

The next step is to decide how much to borrow to complete the replication portfolio. The amount of money we want to borrow is the present value of the difference between the payoffs from the option and the delta neutral amount of stock we purchased. The delta neutral amount of stock is the amount of stock needed to replicate the option position. As illustrated next, the difference between the payoffs is $37.50, regardless of whether the stock goes up or down. The present value of $37.50 for one year discounted at the risk-free rate of 5% is $35.71 (i.e., $37.50/1.05 equals $35.71).

Beginning stock price	$100.00	
Ending stock price	$75.00	$125.00
Hedge ratio	50%	50%
(1) Stock payout	$37.50	$62.50
(2) Option value at expiration	$0.00	$25.00
Difference between (1) and (2)	$37.50	$37.50

Thus, the replication portfolio consists of half a share of stock worth $50 minus the liability of a one-year loan of $35.71 compounding interest at 5% per annum. Let us test this hypothesis and see if it gives the same payoff as the call option at expiration.

Beginning stock price		$100.00

	$75.00	$125.00
Ending stock price	$75.00	$125.00
Hedge ratio	50%	50%
(1) Stock payout	$37.50	$62.50
(2) Repay loan plus interest	−$37.50	−$37.50
Total payoff (1) plus (2)	$0.00	$25.00
Call option value at expiration	$0.00	$25.00

Since the replication portfolio and the call option have the same payoff at maturity, they must be equivalently priced today. If not, it would be possible to arbitrage one against the other. Therefore, the value of the call option is:

$$
\begin{aligned}
\text{Value of call option} &= (\text{Option delta} \cdot \text{stock price}) - \text{Loan} \\
&= (50\% \cdot \$100) - \$35.71 \\
&= \$50.00 - \$35.71 \\
&= \$14.29
\end{aligned}
$$

NO ARBITRAGE OPPORTUNITY

If the call option were overpriced and selling at $20, we could make a risk-free profit of $5.71 by selling (writing) one expensive call for $20

Beginning stock price		$100.00

	$75.00	$125.00
Ending stock price	$75.00	$125.00
Hedge ratio	50%	50%
Cash flow payoff at expiration		
Write one call for $20	$20.00	−$5.00
(− $25 + $20 = −$5)		
Buy half a share for $50	−$12.50	+$12.50
Borrow $30 (pay interest @ 5% p.a.)	−$1.50	−$1.50
Total payoff	+$6.00	+$6.00

and then locking in our profit by buying half a share of stock for $50 and borrowing $30 to fund the balance of the long stock position. The cash flows from this arbitrage are shown on the opposite page. As noted, regardless of whether the stock price goes up or down we lock in a $6 profit at expiration, which on a present value basis discounted at 5% per annum is worth $5.71 today.

Similarly, if the call option was selling cheaply at $10, we could make a risk-free profit of $4.29 by buying the call for $10 and then locking in our profit by selling half a share of stock for $50. We use $10 of our $50 proceeds to buy the call option and lend the remaining $40 for one year at 5% interest. No matter what happens to the stock price, we are assured of a $4.50 profit at expiration, which has a present value of $4.29 today.

Beginning stock price	$100.00	
Ending stock price	$75.00	$125.00
Hedge ratio	50%	50%
Cash flow payoff at expiration (+$25 − $10 = $15)		
Buy one call for $10	−$10.00	$15.00
Sell half a share for $50	+$12.50	−$12.50
Lend $40 (earn interest @5% p.a.)	+$2.00	+$2.00
Total payoff	+$4.50	+$4.50

Using a replication portfolio to value a call option illustrates the importance of interest rates to option pricing. Buying a call option is like borrowing money. When we buy a call option, the interest on the loan is implicitly included in the price of the option. The higher the interest rate and the longer the term, the more valuable the loan, and the greater the option price. We also saw that there can be only one correct price for the option; otherwise arbitrage would occur. The inability to arbitrage is a function of the borrowing (or lending) rate of interest. In our example, we assumed that these rates were equivalent and equal to the risk-free rate of interest. In other words, the option price does not depend on the investor's view toward risk. If an arbitrage profit exists, it will be exploited until equilibrium returns.

This suggests an alternative method for pricing a call option, described next.

HOW TO PRICE A CALL OPTION: DISCOUNTED EXPECTED RETURN

In a risk-free world, the expected rate of return on a stock is equal to the risk-free rate of interest. In a risk-free world, investors need no additional incentive to invest in stocks. This means that the expected rate of return on a stock must be equal to the risk-free rate of interest, or 5% in our example. We already know that the stock price can go either up by 25% to $125 or down by 25% to $75 over the next year. We can calculate the probability of the stock price going up or down. Once we know these probabilities, we can apply them to the possible option payoffs and determine the expected option value.

Step 1: Determining the Probability of a Stock Price Rise

Using the preceding information, we can calculate the probability of the stock price rising (p) to be 60%.

$$\text{Expected return} = 25\% \cdot p - 25\% \cdot (1 - p)$$
$$\text{Risk-free rate} = 5\%$$
$$\text{Expected return} = \text{Risk-free rate}$$
$$25\% \cdot p - 25\% \cdot (1 - p) = 5\%$$
$$p = \frac{30\%}{50\%} = 60\%$$

We can re-write this equation to solve for the probability of a stock price rise (p) as follows:

$$p = \frac{(1 + r) - (1 + d)}{(1 + u) - (1 + d)}$$

where r = the risk-free interest rate
d = the ratio of a downward move in the stock price
u = the ratio of an upward move in the stock price

The probability of the stock price falling is 1 minus the probability of its rising, or 40%. The expected price of the call option is then $15.00.

Beginning stock price	$100.00	
Ending stock price	$75.00	$125.00
Option value at expiration	$0.00	$25.00
Probability	40%	60%
Expected value	$0.00	$15.00

Step 2: Discounting the Expected Return

We know that the fair value of the option is $15 at maturity. However, we must pay for the option today. The cost of financing the position must be deducted from the expected return to obtain the current fair value of the option. Discounting the expected return of $15 at 5% gives a fair value of $14.28 as follows:

$$\text{Call option fair value} = \frac{\$15}{1.05} = \$14.28$$

This produces the same result as the stock plus loan methodology described above under method 1.

DERIVING A GENERAL FORMULA TO PRICE A CALL OPTION

Previously, we knew with certainty the future price of the stock. The stock price could only go up or down in a binomial process. We can write a general equation to price a call with only one period to expiration as follows.

The One-Step Binomial Option Pricing Formula

$$C = \frac{p \cdot C(Su) + (1-p) \cdot C(Sd)}{1+r}$$

where C = the price of the call option

            p = the probability of a stock price rise

   $C(Su)$ = the value of the call at expiration if the stock price rises

   $C(Sd)$ = the value of the call at expiration if the stock price falls

            r = the risk-free rate of interest over the term of the option

The Two-Step Binomial Option Pricing Formula

We can take our analysis one step further by allowing the stock to move twice during the term of the option. In this case, we have the following possible outcomes for the stock price:

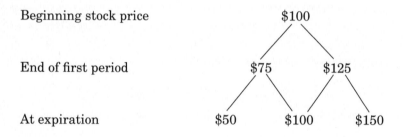

We can describe this process in more general terms where S equals the current stock price, Sd is the price of the stock at the end of the first period if the stock goes down and Su is the price if it goes up, and so on.

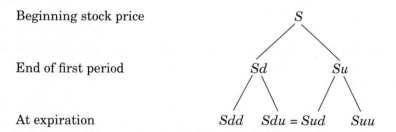

Similarly, we can describe the price of the call option at each of these steps in the binomial tree as follows:

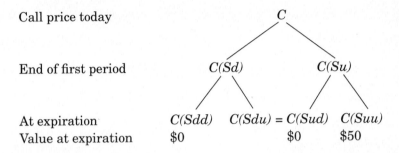

Call price today

End of first period

At expiration
Value at expiration

If the price of the call option is C with two periods remaining to expiration, its value will be $C(Su)$ or $C(Sd)$, depending on whether the stock price goes up or down in the next period. At expiration, its price will be $C(Sdd)$, $C(Sdu) = C(Sud)$, or $C(Suu)$ depending upon the path of the stock price. Upon expiration, the value of the call at each of these four nodes will be Max(0, Sdd–K), Max(0, Sdu–K), Max(0, Sud–K), or Max(0, Suu–K), respectively.

It is apparent that if the stock price is Su with one period remaining, the option price (Cu) will be:

$$C(Su) = \frac{p \cdot C(Suu) + (1-p) \cdot C(Sud)}{1+r}$$

$$= \frac{60\% \cdot \$50 + 40\% \cdot \$0}{1.05}$$

$$= \frac{\$30}{1.05} \qquad (7.2)$$

$$= \$28.57$$

And if the stock price is Sd, the option (Cd) will have a value of:

$$C(Sd) = \frac{p \cdot C(Sud) + (1-p) \cdot C(Sdd)}{1+r}$$

$$= \frac{60\% \cdot \$0 + 40\% \cdot \$0}{1.05} \qquad (7.3)$$

$$= \$0$$

Recalling that the value of a call option with only one period remaining to expiration is given by the following formula, we can solve for the value of a two-step call option accordingly:

$$C = \frac{p \cdot C(Su) + (1-p) \cdot C(Sd)}{1+r}$$
$$= \frac{60\% \cdot \$28.57 + 40\% \cdot \$0}{1.05} \qquad (7.4)$$
$$= \$16.32$$

If we substitute equations 7.2 and 7.3 into equation 7.4, we can derive the formula for a call option with two periods remaining to expiration.

$$C = \frac{p^2 \cdot C(Suu) + 2p \cdot (1-p) \cdot C(Sud) + (1-p)^2 \cdot C(Sdd)}{(1+r)^2}$$
$$= \frac{60\%^2 \cdot \$50 + 2 \cdot 60\% \cdot (1-60\%) \cdot \$0 + (1-60\%)^2 \cdot \$0}{1.05^2}$$
$$= \$16.32$$

THE BLACK–SCHOLES OPTION PRICING FORMULA

We have shown how a call option can be priced with one and two steps remaining to maturity. We can extrapolate this process to include many steps to maturity. Finally, we will arrive at a state where the steps become infinitesimally small and the stock price will be seen to be moving continuously. In 1972, Fischer Black and Myron Scholes introduced the first really practical model for pricing a European call option on a nondividend-paying stock. The model is practical because it requires only five inputs (S, K, r, T, and σ) and does not depend on the investor's view of future stock prices or risk. The model is based on the key principles we have established previously. First, determine all the possible stock prices and relevant probabilities at expiration. Second, calculate the expected return of the option. Third, discount the option's expected return by the risk-free rate of interest. We can still price the option through a leveraged investment in the stock, but we need to adjust the amount of stock and debt continuously as the stock price moves and time passes. The Black–Scholes formula is given next and is broken down into its stock and loan components as follows:

Value of a call option = (Option delta · stock price) – (loan   )
$$= (N(d_1) \qquad \cdot \qquad S) - (N(d_2) \cdot Ke^{-rT})$$

$$d_1 = \frac{\ln\dfrac{S}{K}\left(r + \dfrac{\sigma^2}{2}\right) \cdot T}{\sigma\sqrt{T}}$$

$$d_2 = d_1 - \sigma\sqrt{T}$$

where $N(d)$ = cumulative normal probability density function
       K = exercise price of the option
       r = the risk-free rate of interest
       T = time to the exercise date in years
       S = the stock price today
       σ = the volatility of the stock price

In our previous examples, we knew with certainty what the future stock prices would be. In other words, the variance of the stock price, σ^2, was zero. When the variance is zero, both d_1 and d_2 become very large and the value of the normal distribution functions, $N(d_1)$ and $N(d_2)$ will equal one. In this case, the Black–Scholes model reduces to the value of a European call option as derived earlier in this chapter.

$$C = S - Ke^{-rT}$$

When the future stock price is uncertain, the variance, σ^2 is greater than zero. When the variance is greater than zero, the normal distribution functions, $N(d_1)$ and $N(d_2)$, will range between zero and one. This means that the relative weighing of stock and debt in the Black–Scholes formula will range between zero and one. As we demonstrated earlier, the relative weightings will be such that no arbitrage profit will be possible.

ADJUSTING FOR STOCKS PAYING A KNOWN DIVIDEND YIELD

In our example, XYZ Corporation paid no dividend. We can make two simple adjustments to the Black–Scholes model to accommodate stocks that pay a known dividend yield. Later, using the binomial model, we will illustrate how discrete dividend payments can be incorporated.

The payment of a dividend causes the stock price to drop by the amount of the dividend. Therefore, the payment of a continuous dividend yield causes the stock price to grow at a slower rate. In a risk-free world, the total return of the stock is equal to the risk-free rate of interest, r. The continuous dividend yield provides a return of q. The expected growth rate in the stock price is then $r - q$. We make this adjustment in the calculation of d_1 as follows:

$$d_1 = \frac{\ln\frac{S}{K} + \left(r - q + \frac{\sigma^2}{2}\right) \cdot T}{\sigma\sqrt{T}}$$

The second adjustment is to alter the current stock price to a price that reflects the payment of a continuous dividend. The stock price, S, is then reduced to Se^{-qT} so that the terminal stock price is the same in both cases. The formula for a European style call option on a stock paying a continuous dividend yield is then:

$$C = S \cdot e^{-qT}N(d_1) - Ke^{-rT}N(d_2)$$

8

USING THE BLACK–SCHOLES MODEL TO PRICE A CONVERTIBLE BOND

BOND PLUS A CALL WARRANT

One method of valuing a convertible bond is to combine a straight bond plus a call option on the stock. However, there are two important distinctions between a traditional call option and the option embedded in a convertible bond. First, the embedded call option is actually a warrant and therefore creates dilution. Second, conversion is made by exchanging the convertible for stock and not by paying cash. This means that the strike price of the call warrant is variable.

WARRANT VERSUS OPTION: DILUTION

The difference between a call option and a call warrant is that upon exercise a call option does not increase the number of shares outstanding, whereas a warrant creates dilution. The dilution effect causes the warrant to sell for less than the option, all else being equal. How much less is a function of the number of warrants outstanding relative to the number of shares outstanding. In pricing a convertible bond, we can adjust the Black–Scholes derivation of the call option to obtain the value of the embedded call warrant as follows:

$$\text{Value of a warrant} = \frac{1}{1+\lambda} \cdot \text{call option}$$

where λ = the ratio of outstanding warrants to the number of outstanding shares, assuming each warrant is exercisable into one share

This methodology may be most relevant when pricing a new issue. At the time of issue, or even before, the stock price is likely to discount the probability of conversion. Once this information is in the market it may no longer be necessary to adjust the price of the warrant for dilution since it is already reflected in the stock price. This could explain why the stock price does not necessarily fall when conversion is actually made. Moreover, if it appears that no conversion will be made as expiration approaches, adjusting for dilution would be incorrect.

CASH PAY VERSUS EXCHANGE

At expiration, call options and warrants require the cash payment of an exercise price in exchange for stock. With a convertible bond, a cash payment is not made. Instead, the convertible bond is exchanged with the issuer for stock according to the conversion ratio. Consequently, the exercise value is equal to the future coupon and principal payments which are forgone when they are exchanged for stock. This value is equal to the investment value of the convertible, which changes with time, interest rates, and credit spreads. The exercise price is determined by dividing the convertible's investment value by its conversion ratio. In other words, a convertible bond is like a straight bond plus a call warrant on the stock, with a changing exercise price equal to its investment value.

Consider a newly issued convertible bond with the following characteristics. We can determine its fair value by breaking it down into its two component parts: an ordinary straight bond, and a five-year warrant struck at the investment value. (See Table 8.1.)

Table 8.1 Convertible Bond Example:
XYZ Corporation 5% Due 25–Jan–05

Issuer	XYZ Corp.
Par value	$1,000
Size	$150 million
Term	Five years
Call protection	Five years
Coupon	5.00%
Payment frequency	Semiannually
Issue price	100.00%
Redemption price	100.00%
Stock price at issue	$100
Conversion price	$125
Conversion premium at launch	25.00%
Denomination per bond	$1,000
Conversion ratio	8.00
Credit rating	BB
Risk-free five-year interest rate	5.75%
Credit spread	3.08%
Existing shares outstanding	15 million
Shares created by the convertible	1.2 million
Dilution caused by the convertible	8.00%
Dividend	0.00%
Stock price volatility	40.00%

THE INVESTMENT VALUE

The investment value is equal to the sum of the present values of the expected future cash flows. (See Table 8.2.) In our example, a five-year bond with a 5% coupon paying interest semi-annually and yielding 8.83% to maturity is worth 84.78% today. The yield to maturity is determined by adding the five-year, risk-free rate of interest (5.75%) to the assumed credit spread for a BB credit of 3.08%.

$$\text{Investment value} = \sum_{t=1}^{n} \frac{CPN}{(1+YTM)^t} + \frac{PAR}{(1+YTM)^n}$$

where CPN = coupon rate
   PAR = par value (face value of the bond)
   YTM = discount rate (yield to maturity)
   n = number of payment periods to maturity

ADJUSTMENTS TO INVESTMENT VALUE: MATURITY DATE AND ACCRUED INTEREST

In our simple example, we use a convertible bond with five years to maturity and five years of call protection. There is no possibility of early conversion. However, if the bond had only three years of call protection, we would have to estimate when the convertible might be called. This will affect both the maturity of the bond and the term of the warrant.

Table 8.2 Investment Value Calculation

Par value	$1,000
Coupon	5.000%
Payment frequency	Semi-annually
Term (years)	5
Discount rate p.a.	8.830%
Discount rate s.a.	4.415%

Period (t)	Cash Flow	Present Value Cash Flow
0.5	$25.00	$23.94[a]
1.0	$25.00	$22.93
1.5	$25.00	$21.96
2.0	$25.00	$21.03
2.5	$25.00	$20.14
3.0	$25.00	$19.29
3.5	$25.00	$18.48
4.0	$25.00	$17.69
4.5	$25.00	$16.95
5.0	$1,025.00	$665.42
Total		$847.84[b]

[a]$25/(1.04415)^{(t/0.5)}$
[b]Total of all the discounted cash flows

If the convertible is called before maturity, the issuer generally is required to give the investor 30 days' notice. Usually, the issuer will call the convertible early only if it is in-the-money and trading above its call price. In this case, the investor will be better off converting the bond rather than being called away. This is known as a forced conversion. In a forced conversion, the investor exchanges the convertible for stock but loses any accrued interest. Under these circumstances, the maturity of the convertible will be 30 days and the price will have to be adjusted for the loss of accrued interest.

THE WARRANT VALUE

We can calculate the warrant value of the convertible by plugging in the relevant inputs into the Black–Scholes model. As noted earlier, we will adjust the exercise price (i.e., the conversion price) from the stated amount of $125 to $105.98 to reflect the exchangeable characteristic of the convertible.

$$\text{Adjusted exercise price} = \frac{\text{Investment value}}{\text{Conversion ratio}}$$
$$= \frac{\$847.84}{8}$$
$$= \$105.98$$

Therefore, the price of one embedded call warrant is calculated as follows:

$$\begin{aligned}
\text{Value of a call warrant} &= (\text{Warrant delta} \cdot \text{stock price}) - (\text{loan} \quad) \\
&= (N(d_1) \quad \cdot \quad S) - (N(d_2) \cdot Ke^{-rT}) \\
&= (0.7593 \cdot \$100) - (0.4243 \cdot \$105.98 \cdot e^{-0.0575 \cdot 5}) \\
&= \$42.20
\end{aligned}$$

$$d_1 = \frac{\ln\dfrac{S}{K} + \left(r - q + \dfrac{\sigma^2}{2}\right) \cdot T}{\sigma\sqrt{T}}$$
$$d_2 = d_1 - \sigma\sqrt{T}$$

where $N(d)$ = cumulative normal probability density function
q = annualized continuous dividend yield
K = exercise price of the option
r = risk-free rate of interest
T = time to the exercise date in years
S = stock price today
σ = volatility of the stock price

Since each convertible bond of $1,000 par value gives us the right to convert it into eight shares of common stock, we must multiply the price of the call warrant by the conversion ratio to derive the value of the call component embedded in each bond. This gives a value of $337.60 per bond. Adjusting for dilution, the value of the warrant is $312.93.

The theoretical value of the XYZ convertible bond is 118.54%, or $1,185.44 per bond. This represents the sum of the straight investment value (i.e., 84.78%) plus the warrant value (i.e., 33.76%). On a fully-diluted basis, the value of the bond falls to 116.08%, or $1,106.77 per bond.

9

SENSITIVITY ANALYSIS
The Greeks

In order to appreciate the price behavior of convertible securities, we need to understand how the various inputs to the Black–Scholes model affect valuation. A summary of these inputs and their impact is given in Table 9.1.

Using XYZ Corporation's five year, noncallable, 5% convertible bond (see Chapter 1) as an example, we consider the pricing effects of each of these inputs next.

CHANGING SHARE PRICE: DELTA

Figure 9.1 illustrates that the price of a convertible bond increases when the price of the stock rises. When the stock price is high above the exercise price, the convertible is deep in-the-money and trades one-for-one with the stock. When the stock price is far below the exercise price, it is deep out-of-the-money and the convertible will have a low sensitivity to any change in the stock price.

A change in the price of a convertible bond due to a change in the stock price is measured by its delta or hedge ratio. The delta is the

Table 9.1 Sensitivity of a Call Warrant

If . . .	The call price will . . .	Measurement
The stock price rises	rise	$\text{Delta} = \dfrac{\delta C}{\delta S}$
The stock price falls	fall	
Volatility rises	rise	$\text{Vega} = \dfrac{\delta C}{\delta \sigma}$
Volatility falls	fall	
Interest rates rise	rise	$\text{Rho} = \dfrac{\delta C}{\delta r}$
Interest rates fall	fall	
Time increases	rise	$\text{Theta} = \dfrac{\delta C}{\delta T}$
Time decreases	fall	

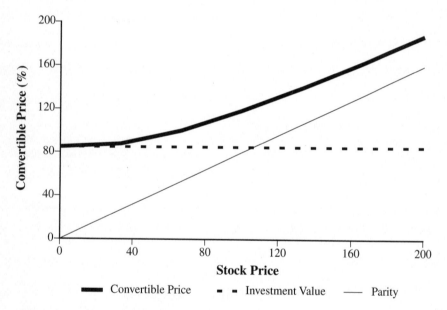

Figure 9.1 Convertible Price Behavior

first derivative of the convertible's price with respect to its underlying share price. In our convertible bond pricing model, we separated the convertible into two parts: the bond and the warrant. Under normal circumstances, the warrant is the only part of the convertible that is affected by a change in the stock price. Later, we will see how a deteriorating stock price leads to an increase in credit risk, thus affecting the convertible's investment value as well. At this juncture, we can measure the convertible's delta by measuring the warrant's delta. In the previous chapter, we define the delta of a call option in a risk-free world as the change in the option price divided by the change in the stock price. In an uncertain world, we introduce the Black–Scholes model as a way of generating a range of expected stock prices based on the expected return and volatility of the stock price. Using this formula, it can be shown that for small changes in the stock price the option, or warrant, delta can be given as:

$$\text{Call warrant delta} = \frac{\delta C}{\delta S}$$

$$= \frac{\delta\left(S \cdot e^{-qT} N(d_1) - Ke^{-rT} N(d_2)\right)}{\delta S}$$

$$= e^{-qT} N(d_1)$$

$$d_1 = \frac{\ln\dfrac{S}{K} + \left(r - q + \dfrac{\sigma^2}{2}\right) \cdot T}{\sigma\sqrt{T}}$$

$$d_2 = d_1 - \sigma\sqrt{T}$$

where $N(d)$ = cumulative normal probability density function
q = the annualized continuous dividend yield
K = exercise price of the option
r = the risk-free rate of interest
T = time to the exercise date in years
S = the stock price today
σ = the volatility of the stock price

Thus, in our example, the delta of the convertible bond at issue is 75.92%. This means that if the stock price moves up (or down) by $1, we would expect the convertible bond price to move up (or down) by $7.59 or 0.0759% of its $1,000 face value.

Figure 9.2 illustrates the delta of our convertible bond for a wide range of stock prices.

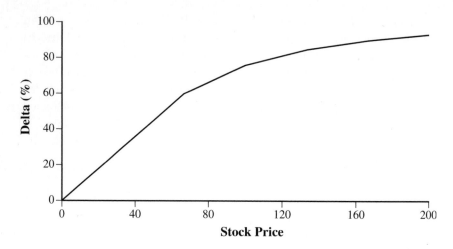

Figure 9.2 Convertible's Delta versus Stock Price

RATE OF CHANGE OF DELTA: GAMMA

Notice that the delta does not change at a constant rate. The delta's
rate of change due to a change in the underlying share price is known
as its gamma. Gamma is the second derivative of the warrant's price
with respect to the share price.

$$\text{Gamma} = \frac{\text{Change in warrant delta}}{\text{Change in share price}}$$

$$= \frac{\delta \Delta}{\delta S} = \frac{\delta^2 C}{\delta S^2}$$

Using the terms of the Black–Scholes formula, we can translate
this equation as follows:

$$\text{Option gamma} = \frac{N'(d_1) \cdot e^{-qT}}{S\sigma\sqrt{T}}$$

$$d_1 = \frac{\ln\dfrac{S}{K} + \left(r - q + \dfrac{\sigma^2}{2}\right) \cdot T}{\sigma\sqrt{T}}$$

$$d_2 = d_1 - \sigma\sqrt{T}$$

where $N(d)$ = cumulative normal probability density function
q = the annualized continuous dividend yield
K = exercise price of the option
r = the risk-free rate of interest
T = time to the exercise date in years
S = the stock price today
σ = the volatility of the stock price

Figure 9.3 illustrates the gamma of our convertible bond example for a wide range of stock prices. At issue, the gamma of the convertible was 0.0035. This means that for a $1 change in the stock price, the convertible's delta will change by 0.35 of 1%. A $10 increase in the stock will increase the delta by 3.50%, and vice versa.

When the stock price is either very low or very high, the gamma approaches zero. This makes sense because if the stock price is low, the warrant will be out-of-the money and a small change in the stock price will not improve the chances that the warrant will be exercised. Consequently, the warrant price and its delta will not change. In terms of the convertible, the warrant will be virtually worthless and the convertible will trade solely on its fixed-income characteristics. Any small change in the share price will not affect the convertible price. Similarly, if the share price is high and the warrant is deep in-the-money, the warrant will trade one-for-one with the stock. In this case, a small change in

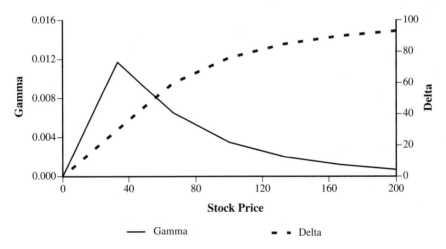

Figure 9.3 Convertible's Gamma and Delta versus Stock Price (5-Year Term)

the stock price will not alter this relationship. The delta of the warrant, and thus the convertible, will remain close to 100.

WHERE IS GAMMA MAXIMIZED?

Gamma is maximized at the stock price given by the following formula:

$$S_{gm} = Kr^{-T}(e^{-3/2\sigma^2 T})$$

where S_{gm} = the stock price where gamma is maximized
K = the exercise price of the option
r = the risk-free rate of interest
T = time in years to the exercise date
σ = the volatility of the stock price

If the term of the warrant is long, gamma is maximized when the stock price is far out-of-the-money. In the equation a five-year warrant struck at \$105.98 maximizes its gamma when the stock price is \$24.14. When the term of the warrant is short, gamma is maximized at- or slightly out-of-the-money. In Figure 9.4, shortening the term of the warrant to six months maximizes the gamma at \$91.44. Understanding the delta and gamma of convertible securities is important to all convertible investors. For outright investors, these measurements quantify the risk-

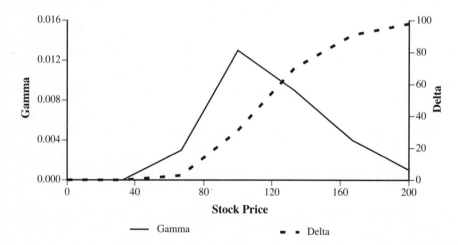

Figure 9.4 Convertible's Gamma and Delta versus Stock Price (6-Month Term)

reward profile. For hedge arbitrageurs, maintaining a delta-neutral position is essential for monetizing market inefficiencies.

CHANGES IN VOLATILITY: VEGA

Warrants, and convertible bonds, are positively correlated to changes in volatility. The more volatile the stock price, the greater the chance it will rise above the exercise price by expiration. The more volatile the stock, the more valuable the warrant and thus the convertible. The rate of change of the value of the warrant with respect to the volatility of the stock price is known as the warrant's vega. From the Black–Scholes model we can define vega as:

$$\text{Vega} = \frac{\delta C}{\delta \sigma}$$

$$= \frac{\delta \left(S \cdot e^{-qT} N(d_1) - K e^{-rT} N(d_2) \right)}{\delta \sigma}$$

$$= S\sqrt{T} \cdot e^{-qT} N'(d_1)$$

$$d_1 = \frac{\ln \dfrac{S}{K} + \left(r - q + \dfrac{\sigma^2}{2} \right) \cdot T}{\sigma \sqrt{T}}$$

$$d_2 = d_1 - \sigma \sqrt{T}$$

where $N(d)$ = cumulative normal probability density function
q = the annualized continuous dividend yield
K = the exercise price of the option
r = the risk-free rate of interest
T = time to the exercise date in years
S = the stock price today
σ = the volatility of the stock price

In our convertible example, the vega is 0.6968. This means that for a 1% change in the stock's volatility, the convertible price will change by $6.96 per bond of $1,000. Figure 9.5 shows how a 10% increase or decrease in volatility will affect the price behavior of our sample convertible.

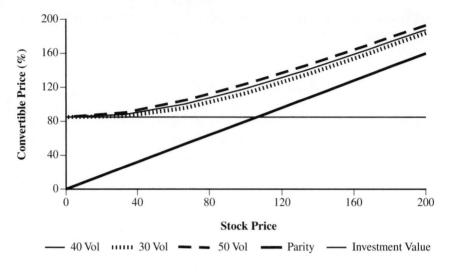

Figure 9.5 Impact of Volatility on Convertible Price

WHAT IS VOLATILITY?

All the inputs to the Black–Scholes model can be readily observed except for one: the stock price volatility. There are three types of volatility: historic, implied, and future. We want to know the future volatility of the stock price because it determines the stock's potential return. How do we determine the stock's future volatility? Calculating the stock's historic and implied volatility can be a helpful predictor.

Historic volatility is calculated by measuring a stock's returns over a certain time period (see Chapter 12). Assuming no major changes in the company's business, this can be a good indicator of how the stock will move in the future. An important question to ask when the investor is calculating historic volatility is what time period should be used. For instance, suppose a stock's historic volatilities are as follows:

30-day volatility: 20%

90-day volatility: 40%

180-day volatility: 30%

What period is best to use? Is the lower 30-day volatility an indicator of more solid company fundamentals, or simply a temporary lull? Likewise, is the high volatility experienced in the past 90 days a result of some traumatic event in the industry a few months back, or is it a good indication of how choppy the returns in the industry can be? Perhaps the 180-day volatility is providing the best overall summation of the company's movement, or maybe the older data no longer accurately reflects the company's current position. There are no easy answers to those questions. Estimating future volatility is both a science and an art. An investor must consider which period most accurately describes the company's position and use these numbers. In general, studies show that using 90 to 180 trading days of data tends to be a good compromise. One can also perform a weighted average of the various periods to derive a number for future volatility. For instance, an investor may predict

$$\text{Volatility} = (.45) \cdot 20\% + (.30) \cdot 40\% + (.25) \cdot 30\% = 28.5\%$$

This process weights the recent historic volatilities more heavily than the older ones in an effort to reflect their relative importance.

The second method of predicting volatility is to look at the price of an option, and back out the only variable that is not known with certainty, the volatility. The volatility calculated in this manner is known as the implied volatility and represents the market's current perception of the stock's volatility. This number is extremely important because it not only gives the consensus opinion on the stock's volatility, but also represents the volatility that is being priced in the market. For convertible arbitrageurs, implied volatility is the key metric in determining the merits of a hedge trade (see Chapter 12).

CHANGES IN INTEREST RATES: RHO AND DURATION

Figure 9.6 shows how a 1% change in interest rates affects our sample convertible bond. The figure makes it clear that a change in interest rates has its largest effect when the convertible is out-of-the-money. It is at this juncture that the convertible's investment value has the greatest influence on the convertible's price. However, in order to fully appreciate the effect of interest rate changes on the price of a convertible bond, we must dissect the convertible into its component parts: the bond and the warrant.

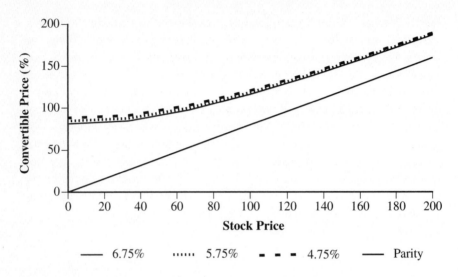

Figure 9.6   Impact of Interest Rates on Convertible Price

THE BOND EFFECT: DURATION

Bond prices are inversely correlated to interest rates. When interest rates fall, bond prices rise and vice versa. We can calculate the price sensitivity of a bond to a change in interest rates by first determining the weighted average duration of its respective cash flows and then measuring the sensitivity of these cash flows to a change in interest rates. The weighted average duration of the cash flows is known as Macaulay's duration, which was formulated in 1938. It is given by the following formula:

$$\text{Macaulay's duration} = \sum_{t=1}^{n}\left[\frac{PV(CFt)}{TPV}\cdot t\right]$$

where $PV(CFt)$ = the present value of the nominal cash flows received in year t

TPV = the total present value of all of the bond's future cash flows

t = time remaining until the receipt of cash flow CFt

n = number of payment periods to maturity

In our example, the duration of a five-year bond paying 5% semi-annually and yielding 8.83% to maturity (i.e., price of 84.78%) is 4.43 years. Each cash flow payment is discounted to its present value using the bond's yield to maturity and then weighted as a percentage of total payments. These percentages are then time-weighted to arrive at Macaulay's duration. (See Table 9.2.)

Once we know the duration of the cash flows, we can calculate the sensitivity of these cash flows for a given change in interest rates. This calculation is known as the modified duration and is given in the next formula.

Table 9.2 Calculation of Macaulay's Duration

Par value	$1,000
Coupon	5.000%
Payment frequency	Semi-annually
Term (years)	5
Discount rate p.a.	8.830%
Discount rate s.a.	4.415%

Period (t)	Cash Flow	Present Value Cash Flow	Price Weights	Price Weighted Maturities (years)
0.5	$25.00	$23.94[a]	0.028[c]	0.014[d]
1.0	$25.00	$22.93	0.027	0.027
1.5	$25.00	$21.96	0.026	0.039
2.0	$25.00	$21.03	0.025	0.050
2.5	$25.00	$20.14	0.024	0.059
3.0	$25.00	$19.29	0.023	0.068
3.5	$25.00	$18.48	0.022	0.076
4.0	$25.00	$17.69	0.021	0.083
4.5	$25.00	$16.95	0.020	0.090
5.0	$1,025.00	$665.42	0.785	3.924
Total		$847.84[b]	1.000	4.431[e]

[a]$25/(1.04415)^{(t/.5)}$
[b]Total of all the discounted cash flows
[c]$23.94/$847.84
[d]0.028 · 0.5 years
[e]Duration is the total of all price weighted maturities

$$\text{Modified duration} = \frac{\text{Macaulay's duration}}{1+YTM}$$

where YTM = the yield to maturity of the bond

In our example, the modified duration is 4.07 years. This means that for a 1% change in interest rates, the investment value of the convertible will change by approximately 4.07%, or $34.50 ($847.84 · 0.0407 = $34.50).

THE WARRANT EFFECT: RHO

The price of a call warrant is directly correlated to interest rates. As explained earlier, a call warrant is like owning a leveraged position in the stock. The higher the interest rate, the more valuable the loan, and the higher the option price. A change in the warrant price due to a change in interest rates is known as the warrant's rho, and is defined as follows.

$$\text{Rho} = KTe^{-rT}N(d_2)$$
$$= \frac{105.98 \cdot 5.00 \cdot 2.71828^{-0.0575 \cdot 5.00} \cdot 0.4243635}{100}$$
$$= 1.687$$

$$d_1 = \frac{\ln\dfrac{S}{K} + \left(r - q + \dfrac{\sigma^2}{2}\right) \cdot T}{\sigma\sqrt{T}}$$
$$d_2 = d_1 - \sigma\sqrt{T}$$

where $N(d)$ = the cumulative normal probability density function
q = the annualized continuous dividend yield
K = the exercise price of the option
r = the risk-free rate of interest
T = time to the exercise date in years
S = the stock price today
σ = the volatility of the stock price

This means that for a 1% increase (decrease) in interest rates, the price of a warrant will increase (decrease) by $1.6881. Since there are eight embedded warrants in each convertible bond, the warrant component of the convertible will change by $13.50.

In the case of a convertible bond, the exercise price (i.e., K) is a function of the investment value. An increase in interest rates will lower the investment value and reduce the exercise price of the embedded call warrant. A lower exercise price will, in turn, increase the value of the warrant. The combined effect of a 1% change in interest rates for our convertible example is calculated in Table 9.3.

The interest rate sensitivity of the convertible is about 1% for a 1% change in interest rates. The four-year duration of the convertible's investment value is largely neutralized by the warrant effect. To hedge the interest rate risk, we would short a fixed-income security with a duration of approximately one year (see Chapter 14).

THE PASSAGE OF TIME: THETA

The price of a convertible is also affected by the passage of time. For the warrant, the shorter the time to expiration, the smaller the possibility that the warrant will expire above its exercise price. The shorter the warrant's term, the lower its value. A warrant's time decay, or theta, is measured as follows.

$$\text{Theta} = \frac{SN(d_1) \cdot \sigma^{-qT}}{2\sqrt{T}} + qS \cdot N(d_1) \cdot e^{-qT} - rKe^{-rT} \cdot N(d_2)$$

Table 9.3 Interest Rate Sensitivity

	Base Case	Interest Rates +1%	Change	Interest Rates −1%	Change
Investment value (1)	$ 847.84	$ 812.75	−$35.09	$ 884.74	+$36.90
Warrant value (2)	$ 337.66	$ 362.58	+$24.92	$ 312.72	−$24.94
Exercise price	$ 105.98	$ 101.59	−$4.39	$ 110.59	+$4.61
Exercise price impact			+$11.41		−$11.49
Interest rate impact			+$13.51		−$13.49
Total (1 + 2)	$1,185.50	$1,175.33	−$10.17	$1,197.47	+$11.92
Percent change			−1.02		+1.19

$$d_1 = \frac{\ln \frac{S}{K} + \left(r - q + \frac{\sigma^2}{2}\right) \cdot T}{\sigma \sqrt{T}}$$

$$d_2 = d_1 - \sigma \sqrt{T}$$

where $N(d)$ = the cumulative normal probability density
function
q = the annualized continuous dividend yield
K = exercise price of the option
r = the risk-free rate of interest
T = time to the exercise date in years
S = the stock price today
σ = the volatility of the stock price

In our example, the warrant's theta is 0.007625, so the convertible's theta is eight times this, or 0.061. This means that, all else being equal, the convertible's price will fall by 6 cents a day, or $22.26 (2.22%) over one year.

HOW MUCH TIME DO I HAVE LEFT?

In our simple example, we assumed that the convertible was not callable. Consequently, we knew with certainty that the term of both the bond and the warrant would be five years. What if the bond had only three years of call protection? When would the issuer likely call the bond?

One way to answer this question is to ask how long it will take for the stock price to reach the conversion price. In our example, we know the current stock price is $100 and the conversion price is $125. Since the call price is typically par (i.e., 100%) or higher, the issuer is not likely to call the bond until the stock price is at least as high as the conversion price. At that point, the intrinsic value of the bond (i.e., parity) will be 100%, since $125 times the conversion ratio of eight shares per bond equals $1,000. Since the issuer wants to be assured of a forced conversion and does not want to pay cash to the convertible holders, the issuer will probably wait until its stock price has risen comfortably above the conversion price before calling the bonds. Studies have indicated that convertible issuers on average wait until their stock price is between 15% to 20% above the conversion price before calling their bonds. For our purposes, assume that the issuer will call its bonds once the stock price reaches $140 or 12% above the conversion price.

From our discussion on volatility to come (see Chapter 12), we know that the price of a $100 stock (i.e., the mean) with a 40% annual volatility is likely to be between $60 and $140, 68.26% of the time during a one-year time period. This means that 31.74% of the time the stock price will be either below $60 or over $140. We are interested only in the probability of the stock price being greater than $140, which is only 15.87% of the time. This is a rather low probability. Assume that we want to be at least 50% certain that the stock price will be $140 or greater. We can solve for the time (in years) required to reach this target as follows.

$$\text{Time (in years) to reach price target } = \frac{\log(1 - Po)}{\log(Pno)}$$

where Po = the desired probability of the event occurring
Pno = the probability of the event not occurring

$$\text{Time (in years) to reach price target } = \frac{\log(1 - 0.5)}{\log(0.84134)}$$
$$= 4.012 \text{ years}$$

In our example, there is a 50% chance that the stock price will be equal to or greater than $140 in 4.012 years. Shortening the term of our original convertible bond to four years implies a price of 116%, or 2% lower than the original noncallable bond. This methodology provides the investor with a flexible yet quantifiable approach to determining the term of a callable convertible bond.

The only difficulty in using this methodology is in determining the probability that the desired event will not happen. In other words, what is the area of the normal distribution curve to the left of our desired price target? For any given stock price, target price, and

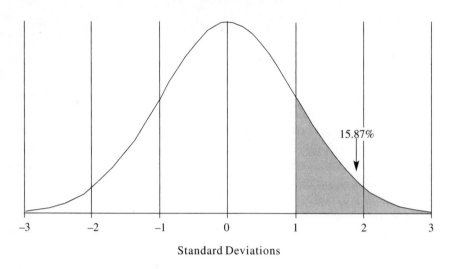

Figure 9.7   Normal Distribution Function

volatility this can be obtained by referring to statistical tables or by using the function NORMDIST in Microsoft Excel. (See Figure 9.7.)

Suppose that we were wrong about the stock price volatility and it was actually 50% and not 40%. Intuitively, we would assume that our price target should be met more quickly. Solving the normal distribution function, we observe that the probability of the event not occurring has fallen to 0.78814 and thus the likely time to call is reduced to 2.91 years.

10

CONVERTIBLE BOND PRICING
Binomial Trees

INTRODUCTION

In the previous chapter, we show how the Black–Scholes model can be used to price a convertible bond. However, we found that there are two main weaknesses to this approach. The first problem is how to adjust the price of the call warrant for stock dividends. Although we were able to make an adjustment for a continuously compounding dividend, the Black–Scholes model could not accommodate discrete dividend payments. The second problem was that we could not value other complications like the issuer's right to call the bonds. We attempted to solve this problem by introducing a methodology to estimate the likely time to call. In this chapter we seek a more elegant solution to these problems.

Recalling our discussion of how a call option is priced, (see Chapter 7), we started with a simple one-step model. We then extended this approach to a multi-step model and finally to the continuous-time Black–Scholes formula. Returning to the multi-step binomial tree, we can see how the payment of a dividend or the test of a call can be incorporated into the tree at the appropriate moment. Using this approach gives us the flexibility to incorporate any number of changes to the convertible's structure. By including a sufficient number of steps in the tree, we can reasonably estimate the convertible's fair value.

Previously, we used the binomial process to price a call option. In our simple example, the stock went either above or below the exercise price. In the up-state, the option was worth the stock price less the exercise price. In the down-state, the option expired worthless. When adapting the tree to model a convertible bond, in the up-state the bond will be worth parity (i.e., conversion ratio times the stock price) and in the down-state it will be worth its par value, not zero. In this case, we assume the issuer will not default.

In order to determine which value to place in the tree at any given node, we must construct a separate tree for both the stock price and the bond price and then select the correct value. To illustrate, consider our previous example of the XYZ Corporation's 5% convertible bonds due 25-Jan-05 (see Chapter 1). In constructing our tree, we will break the bond's five-year term into ten equal periods of half a year each.

BUILDING THE STOCK TREE

In our earlier example of pricing a call option, we knew with certainty how the stock price would move. Now we want to devise a more general explanation of how the stock price behaves. Stock prices appear to follow what is known as a stochastic Markov process. This means that a stock's change in price is uncertain (stochastic) and that its history cannot predict its future performance (Markov process). Stock prices follow a particular type of Markov process known as a Wiener process or geometric Brownian motion. In physics, this is used to describe the motion of a particle that is subject to a large number of molecular shocks (see Chapter 12). For our purposes, let it suffice to say that stock prices follow a random walk in which they fluctuate with equal probability around their average return. This process is affected by the volatility of the stock and the passage of time. In our example, we know that the stock price is $100 and has an annual volatility of

40%. We can calculate the up-move (u) in our stock price over one six-month period as follows:

$$u = e^{\sigma\sqrt{\Delta t}}$$

$$= 2.71828^{0.40 \cdot 0.7071}$$

$$= 1.3269$$

where e = a random sample from a standard normal distribution (i.e., a normal distribution with a mean of zero and a standard deviation of 1.0)

σ = the annual volatility of the stock price

t = time period of one step expressed in years

A down move (d) over the same period is defined as follows:

$$d = \frac{1}{u}$$

$$= 0.7536$$

Now that we know the degree by which the stock price will move up or down at each step, we can build out the tree of expected future stock prices as shown in Table 10.1.

Since we know the future stock prices, we can easily calculate the parity of the convertible bond at each node by multiplying the share price by the conversion ratio of 8 shares per bond. This produces the values shown in Table 10.2.

BUILDING THE BOND TREE

In building the bond tree, we use a process known as backward induction. Here we start at the final maturity date of the bond in period 10. Assuming no default risk, we know that at maturity we will receive the bond's par value ($1,000) plus a final semi-annual coupon of $25. To calculate the value of the bond one period earlier, we need to determine the present value of the period 10 payment. What discount rate should we use? In our example, the risk-free rate of interest is 5.75% and the additional credit spread required for a BB rated issuer is

Table 10.1 Stock Price Tree

Period 0	1	2	3	4	5	6	7	8	9	10
$100.00	$132.69	$176.07	$233.62	$309.99	$411.33	$545.79	$724.20	$960.94	$1,275.07	$1,691.88
	$ 75.36	$100.00	$132.69	$176.07	$233.62	$309.99	$411.33	$545.79	$ 724.20	$ 960.94
		$ 56.80	$ 75.36	$100.00	$132.69	$176.07	$233.62	$309.99	$ 411.33	$ 545.79
			$ 42.80	$ 56.80	$ 75.36	$100.00	$132.69	$176.07	$ 233.62	$ 309.99
				$ 32.26	$ 42.80	$ 56.80	$ 75.36	$100.00	$ 132.69	$ 176.07
					$ 24.31	$ 32.26	$ 42.80	$ 56.80	$ 75.36	$ 100.00
						$ 18.32	$ 24.31	$ 32.26	$ 42.80	$ 56.80
							$ 13.81	$ 18.32	$ 24.31	$ 32.26
								$ 10.41	$ 13.81	$ 18.32
									$ 7.84	$ 10.41
										$ 5.91

Table 10.2 Parity Tree

Period 0	1	2	3	4	5	6	7	8	9	10
$800.0	$1,061.5	$1,408.5	$1,869.0	$2,479.9	$3,290.6	$4,366.3	$5,793.6	$7,687.5	$10,200.5	$13,535.1
	$602.9	$800.0	$1,061.5	$1,408.5	$1,869.0	$2,479.9	$3,290.6	$4,366.3	$5,793.6	$7,687.5
		$454.4	$602.9	$800.0	$1,061.5	$1,408.5	$1,869.0	$2,479.9	$3,290.6	$4,366.3
			$342.4	$454.4	$602.9	$800.0	$1,061.5	$1,408.5	$1,869.0	$2,479.9
				$258.1	$342.4	$454.4	$602.9	$800.0	$1,061.5	$1,408.5
					$194.5	$258.1	$342.4	$454.4	$602.9	$800.0
						$146.6	$194.5	$258.1	$342.4	$454.4
							$110.5	$146.6	$194.5	$258.1
								$83.3	$110.5	$146.6
									$62.7	$83.3
										$47.3

3.08%. Therefore, we discount the period 10 payment by the risk-adjusted semi-annual rate of 4.415%. To this sum we add the current coupon payment received in period 9 of $25. This gives a value for the bond of $1,006.66 in period 9 as follows.

$$\text{Value of the bond in period } 9 = \frac{\$1,025}{1+0.04415} + \$25$$
$$= \$981.65 + \$25$$
$$= \$1,006.66$$

If we repeat this process back to the current time period, we arrive at a present value for the bond of $847.84 today. (See Table 10.3).

COMBINING THE TREES TO PRICE THE CONVERTIBLE BOND

The convertible bond tree will also be built by backward induction. To do this, we need to determine the value of the convertible at maturity. As we noted earlier, the convertible will be worth the greater of parity or its redemption value plus the final coupon payment. To see how this works, we take a point in the middle of the ninth period when the stock price is $132.69. In the next period, we know that the stock price can move only up to $176.07 (parity of $1,408.52) or down to $100.00 (parity of $800.00). In the up-state, $1,408.52 is greater than the bond's final value of $1,025 and so at this node we will use parity. In the down-state, parity of $800 is lower than the bond's final value, so we will use the investment value of $1,025 at this node. Continuing this process, we fill out each node in the final period of the tree. Now, by discounting back we can obtain the fair value of the convertible.

WHICH DISCOUNT RATE TO USE?

Unfortunately, one problem remains. Which is the appropriate discount rate? When the stock price falls and the final value of the convertible is its straight investment value, the risk-adjusted periodic rate is correct. On the other hand, if the stock rises and the final value

Table 10.3 Bond Price Tree

Period 0	1	2	3	4	5	6	7	8	9	10
$847.84	$885.27	$898.25	$911.80	$925.96	$940.73	$956.16	$972.27	$989.09	$1,006.66	$1,025.00
	$885.27	$898.25	$911.80	$925.96	$940.73	$956.16	$972.27	$989.09	$1,006.66	$1,025.00
		$898.25	$911.80	$925.96	$940.73	$956.16	$972.27	$989.09	$1,006.66	$1,025.00
			$911.80	$925.96	$940.73	$956.16	$972.27	$989.09	$1,006.66	$1,025.00
				$925.96	$940.73	$956.16	$972.27	$989.09	$1,006.66	$1,025.00
					$940.73	$956.16	$972.27	$989.09	$1,006.66	$1,025.00
						$956.16	$972.27	$989.09	$1,006.66	$1,025.00
							$972.27	$989.09	$1,006.66	$1,025.00
								$989.09	$1,006.66	$1,025.00
									$1,006.66	$1,025.00
										$1,025.00

of the convertible is parity, then the risk-free rate is correct. What do we do for points in between when the convertible has characteristics of both stock and bond?

The way to overcome this dilemma is to calculate the convertible's delta at each node. This will tell us the portion of the convertible's value that is equity sensitive. The appropriate discount rate is then a combination of the risk-free rate applied to the equity portion of the convertible and the risk-adjusted rate for the balance.

$$\text{Discount rate} = \text{Delta} \cdot \text{Risk-free rate}$$
$$+ (1\text{--Delta}) \cdot \text{Risk-adjusted rate}$$

This approach is consistent with the risk-neutral framework we established earlier when valuing a call option. For example, if the convertible is deep in-the-money, it can be equated to a stock that is paying its dividend in the form of a coupon. If the delta is 100%, then an investor could fully hedge all the equity-related risk of the convertible by selling short eight shares of stock. If the issuer went bankrupt, the investor would be fully hedged and thus the risk-free rate is the correct discount rate. The tree in Table 10.4 is built out in this manner and arrives at a fair value of the convertible of 119.73%. This value is very close to the 118.54% result we derived in Chapter 8. Absent the interest rate adjustment, if we increased the number of nodes in our tree, the two values would converge.

MODIFICATIONS TO THE BINOMIAL TREE

In this section, we demonstrate how the binomial tree can be modified to accommodate stock dividends, other embedded options like calls and puts, and credit risk.

DIVIDENDS

The binomial tree gives us the flexibility to adjust our model for the payment of dividends. When the stock goes ex-dividend, the share price will fall by the amount of the dividend payment. We can accommodate various ways of incorporating the dividend. We can make the

Table 10.4 Convertible Valuation with Blended Discount Rate

Period										
0	1	2	3	4	5	6	7	8	9	10
$1,197.3	$1,412.4	$1,688.7	$2,084.8	$2,643.0	$3,414.4	$4,462.2	$5,866.5	$7,736.8	$10,225.5	$13,535.1
	$1,074.2	$1,193.7	$1,372.8	$1,639.5	$2,029.7	$2,587.6	$3,363.5	$4,415.6	$5,818.6	$7,687.5
		$986.3	$1,055.5	$1,161.7	$1,326.7	$1,581.3	$1,966.5	$2,529.2	$3,315.6	$4,366.3
			$943.8	$980.8	$1,036.6	$1,125.2	$1,270.3	$1,509.1	$1,894.0	$2,479.9
				$932.9	$953.4	$980.0	$1,018.7	$1,081.5	$1,193.8	$1,408.5
					$940.7	$956.2	$972.3	$989.1	$1,006.7	$1,025.0
						$956.2	$972.3	$989.1	$1,006.7	$1,025.0
							$972.3	$989.1	$1,006.7	$1,025.0
								$989.1	$1,006.7	$1,025.0
									$1,006.7	$1,025.0
										$1,025.0

adjustment at a continuous rate as with the Black–Scholes model, or we can allow for discrete dividend payments at any given node. Table 10.5 shows how the nodes in the stock tree would change because of a $1 dividend paid semi-annually and growing at a 5% annual rate.

The bond tree remains unchanged. Combining the new parity tree with the old bond tree reduces the value of the convertible by 2.00%, from 119.73% to 117.33% (see Table 10.6).

ADJUSTING FOR CALL OPTIONS

Most convertible bonds are callable by the issuer. After a designated time period, the issuer enjoys the right to take the bond back from the investor at a specific price. This option is valuable because it preserves the issuer's flexibility to change its capital structure or refinance if interest rates fall. The issuer's gain is the investor's loss. Thus, a callable bond should be worth less than a noncallable bond, but by how much?

The binomial model gives us the flexibility to answer this question. In Chapter 3, we explain the different types of calls used by issuers. In the example following, we assume that the base case XYZ Corporation convertible is now callable at a price of 102% beginning in the fourth year, declining to 101% during the fifth year. We assume that the issuer will act in its own best interest. Therefore, it will not call the bond if the call price is higher than the convertible price. Likewise, the issuer will call the bond only if the convertible price is higher than the call price. If the issuer calls the convertible, it is obliged to pay the accrued interest. However, this is irrelevant because the issuer is likely to call the convertible only when it is in the investor's best interest to convert. In a forced conversion, the investor loses the accrued interest. This means that once the bond becomes callable and is above the call price in our tree, the maximum value at that node will be parity. If the value in the tree is less than the call price, the value at that node will remain unchanged.

To see how this works, consider the uppermost value at period 6 when the call price is $1,020 and the convertible is worth $4,366.3 (see Table 10.7). This value corresponds to parity when the stock price is at $545.79 (i.e., $545.79 · 8 equals $4,366.32) (see Tables 10.1 and 10.2). This is the correct value for this node when the call is in effect, since it is lower than our original value of $4,462.2 when the convertible was

Table 10.5 Stock Tree Adjusted for Dividends

Period	0	1	2	3	4	5	6	7	8	9	10
Div.		$1.00	$1.02	$1.05	$1.08	$1.10	$1.13	$1.16	$1.19	$1.22	$1.25
	$100.00	$131.69	$173.71	$229.45	$303.38	$401.45	$531.56	$704.16	$933.16	$1,237.00	$1,640.12
		$74.36	$98.22	$129.87	$171.85	$227.54	$301.42	$399.44	$529.50	$702.05	$931.00
			$55.02	$72.97	$96.80	$128.41	$170.35	$226.00	$299.85	$397.83	$527.85
				$40.41	$53.92	$71.85	$95.64	$127.23	$169.14	$224.76	$298.58
					$29.38	$39.53	$53.02	$70.92	$94.70	$126.25	$168.14
						$21.04	$28.66	$38.80	$52.26	$70.15	$93.90
							$14.73	$20.44	$28.05	$38.17	$51.62
								$9.94	$14.22	$19.93	$27.52
									$6.31	$9.50	$13.77
										$3.54	$5.92
											$1.42

Table 10.6 Convertible Valuation with Blended Discount Rate and Dividends

Period	0	1	2	3	4	5	6	7	8	9	10
Div.		$1.00	$1.02	$1.05	$1.08	$1.10	$1.13	$1.16	$1.19	$1.22	$1.25
	$1,173.3	$1,378.6	$1,641.8	$2,021.1	$2,558.1	$3,303.8	$4,319.4	$5,682.3	$7,497.1	$9,911.3	$13,121.0
		$1,059.2	$1,171.3	$1,340.0	$1,592.6	$1,964.9	$2,500.9	$3,251.4	$4,272.7	$5,634.5	$7,448.0
			$978.1	$1,042.3	$1,140.9	$1,294.5	$1,533.5	$1,898.8	$2,439.2	$3,202.7	$4,222.8
				$940.3	$974.6	$1,025.7	$1,106.4	$1,238.7	$1,458.6	$1,819.7	$2,388.6
					$932.0	$951.6	$976.4	$1,011.4	$1,066.6	$1,163.1	$1,345.2
						$940.7	$956.2	$972.3	$989.1	$1,006.7	$1,025.0
							$956.2	$972.3	$989.1	$1,006.7	$1,025.0
								$972.3	$989.1	$1,006.7	$1,025.0
									$989.1	$1,006.7	$1,025.0
										$1,006.7	$1,025.0
											$1,025.0

Table 10.7 Callable Convertible Valuation with Blended Discount Rate

Period 0	1	2	3	4	5	6	7	8	9	10
Div.	$0.0	$0.0	$0.0	$0.0	$0.0	$0.0	$0.0	$0.0	$0.0	$0.0
$1,116.4	$1,313.1	$1,574.4	$1,964.4	$2,529.2	$3,315.6	$4,366.3	$5,793.6	$7,687.5	$10,200.5	$13,535.1
	$1,007.6	$1,103.7	$1,257.8	$1,504.9	$1,894.0	$2,479.9	$3,290.6	$4,366.3	$5,793.6	$7,687.5
		$940.4	$986.0	$1,059.5	$1,185.0	$1,408.5	$1,869.0	$2,479.9	$3,290.6	$4,366.3
			$921.2	$942.1	$969.0	$1,006.3	$1,061.5	$1,408.5	$1,869.0	$2,479.9
				$928.0	$944.4	$963.1	$985.8	$1,016.1	$1,061.5	$1,408.5
					$940.7	$956.2	$972.3	$989.1	$1,006.7	$1,025.0
						$956.2	$972.3	$989.1	$1,006.7	$1,025.0
							$972.3	$989.1	$1,006.7	$1,025.0
								$989.1	$1,006.7	$1,025.0
									$1,006.7	$1,025.0
										$1,025.0
Call Price	—	—	—	—	—	$1,020.0	$1,020.0	$1,010.0	$1,010.0	

113

noncallable (see Table 10.4). This is because the investor gives up any accrued interest if he or she converts. Now consider the case when the stock price is at the lowermost node in period 6, of $18.32 (see Table 10.1). At this point, parity is $146.56 and the straight investment value is $956.16 (see Tables 10.2 and 10.3). At this node, $956.16 is the correct value in the convertible tree, since it is the minimum value of the convertible and the issuer will not call the security at $1,020. The effect of adding the call reduces the value of the convertible by 6.76%, from 119.73% to 111.64% (see Table 10.7).

The model can be easily adjusted to accommodate other refinements to the call. For example, many convertible bonds include soft-call (or provisional) protection, whereby the stock price must rise above the conversion price by a set percentage (e.g., 130%) for 30 consecutive days before the call becomes effective. Many issuers wait until their stock prices rise above the call price before issuing a call. This is done to insure that a forced conversion takes place and guards against the stock price falling below the call price once the call has been announced. In that case, the issuer would have to deliver cash to pay the call price because the investor would no longer exchange the bond into stock at a parity below the call price. Studies have indicated that this hurdle may be as high as 40% above the original conversion price.

ADJUSTING FOR PUT OPTIONS

Occasionally, the issuer will offer the investor a put option. This is common with zero-coupon convertible bonds and from emerging market issuers. The put option gives the investor the right to return the convertible to the issuer at a specific time and price. The put may be payable in cash (i.e., hard) or in stock (i.e., soft). The put increases the value of the convertible by raising its effective investment value.

In Table 10.8, we add a discrete put at 110% to our callable convertible bond at the end of year 3. If we look again at period 6 when the stock price was at $100 (see Table 10.1), we can see that the value of the original convertible was $1,125.2 (see Table 10.4) when the bond was neither callable nor puttable. With the bond callable at 102% or $1,020 at the beginning of year 4, we saw that the value of the convertible fell to $1,006.3 at this node (see Table 10.7). However, when we add the put of 110% at this juncture, the investor will elect to put the bond. The put

Table 10.8 Callable/Puttable Convertible Valuation with Blended Discount Rate

Period	0	1	2	3	4	5	6	7	8	9	10
Div.	$0.0	$0.0	$0.0	$0.0	$0.0	$0.0	$0.0	$0.0	$0.0	$0.0	$0.0
	$1,186.7	$1,366.5	$1,607.3	$1,977.2	$2,529.2	$3,315.6	$4,366.3	$5,793.6	$7,687.5	$10,200.5	$13,535.1
		$1,101.3	$1,182.3	$1,313.6	$1,531.7	$1,894.0	$2,479.9	$3,290.6	$4,366.3	$5,793.6	$7,687.5
			$1,058.3	$1,094.9	$1,149.6	$1,241.1	$1,408.5	$1,869.0	$2,479.9	$3,290.6	$4,366.3
				$1,060.1	$1,080.8	$1,102.4	$1,125.0	$1,061.5	$1,408.5	$1,869.0	$2,479.9
					$1,080.8	$1,102.4	$1,125.0	$985.8	$1,016.1	$1,061.5	$1,408.5
						$1,102.4	$1,125.0	$972.3	$989.1	$1,006.7	$1,025.0
							$1,125.0	$972.3	$989.1	$1,006.7	$1,025.0
								$972.3	$989.1	$1,006.7	$1,025.0
									$989.1	$1,006.7	$1,025.0
										$1,006.7	$1,025.0
											$1,025.0
Call Price	—	—	—	—	—	—	—	$1,020.00	$1,010.00	$1,010.00	—
Put Price	—	—	—	—	—	—	$1,100.00	$1,020.00	—	—	—

115

price plus accrued interest then fills the node at this point (i.e., $1,125). The effect of adding the put increases the price of the convertible bond by 6.30% from 111.64% to 118.67% (see Table 10.8).

ADJUSTING THE MODEL FOR CREDIT RISK

As discussed previously, one of the problems of the binomial model is deciding what discount rate to use at each node. We used a blended rate of the risk-free and risk-adjusted rates to reflect the composition of the convertible at each node. For the warrant portion that can be hedged, we used the risk-free rate. For the portion representing the bond, we used the risk-adjusted rate. Now we want to go one step further and change the risk-adjusted rate to reflect deteriorating credit quality. Experience tells us that as the stock price (i.e., parity) falls, the credit risk increases. In practice, this is painfully apparent when the convertible's investment value fails to hold when the stock price declines.

In our hypothetical XYZ example, the bond is rated BB and the credit spread is 308 basis points (i.e., 3.08%). In Figure 10.1, we can see that once parity falls below 60%, the credit spread begins to widen.

We can quantify the relationship between parity and credit

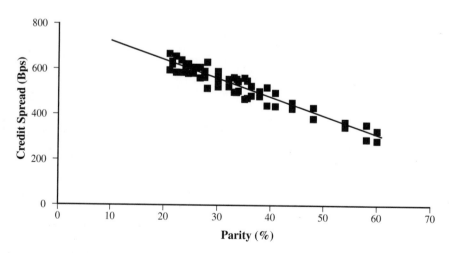

Figure 10.1 Credit Spread Estimates for BB Credits

spread using a linear regression technique. Once the points are plotted, a best-fit line can be drawn through the points. (See Figure 10.2.) This line has a slope (b) and an intercept on the y-axis (a). The equation for the best-fit line is $y = bx + a$. Thus, for any point on the x-axis (i.e., parity), we can calculate the credit spread (y). In this case the slope of the line is –8.3 and the y intercept is 806 basis points. The closer the points are to the regression line, the better the fit and the more confident we can be about our projections. The regression line has a fit (i.e., R-squared) of 94%, which means that 94% of the time a change in credit spread is directly related to a change in parity.

To adjust the binomial model, we use an "if statement." If parity is greater than 60%, we use the initial credit spread to calculate the risk-adjusted rate of interest. If parity is less than 60%, we use the maximum of the initial spread, or parity times the slope of the regression line plus the credit spread at the y intercept. Table 10.9 illustrates this adjustment to the nodes in the tree as the convertible price falls by 0.79% from 119.7% to 118.7%. Notice that in contrast to Table 10.4, the nodes at the bottom of the tree are discounted at higher rates as parity declines. The more busted the convertible becomes, the greater the impact of the credit spread adjustment.

This adjustment is useful in modeling the delta of busted convertibles (see Chapter 17). Without the adjustment, the delta of the convertible declines as the stock price falls. With the adjustment, the

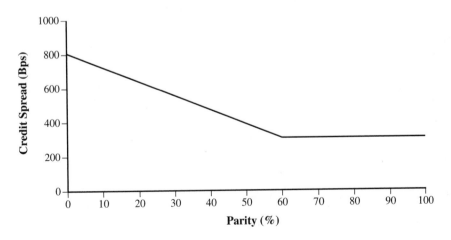

Figure 10.2   Credit Spread Profile for BB Credits

Table 10.9 Convertible with Blended and Credit Adjusted Discount Rate

Period 0	1	2	3	4	5	6	7	8	9	10
Div.	$0.0	$0.0	$0.0	$0.0	$0.0	$0.0	$0.0	$0.0	$0.0	$0.0
$1,187.9	$1,408.4	$1,687.4	$2,084.6	$2,643.0	$3,414.4	$4,462.2	$5,866.5	$7,736.8	$10,225.5	$13,535.1
	$1,058.4	$1,186.5	$1,370.4	$1,639.0	$2,029.7	$2,587.6	$3,363.5	$4,415.6	$5,818.6	$7,687.5
		$959.6	$1,042.7	$1,157.1	$1,325.7	$1,581.3	$1,966.5	$2,529.2	$3,315.6	$4,366.3
			$904.6	$958.2	$1,027.7	$1,123.1	$1,270.3	$1,509.1	$1,894.0	$2,479.9
				$882.7	$920.0	$962.9	$1,014.2	$1,081.5	$1,193.8	$1,408.5
					$884.5	$915.9	$948.1	$979.4	$1,006.7	$1,025.0
						$901.1	$932.6	$965.0	$996.7	$1,025.0
							$924.0	$957.0	$991.1	$1,025.0
								$952.5	$987.9	$1,025.0
									$986.1	$1,025.0
										$1,025.0

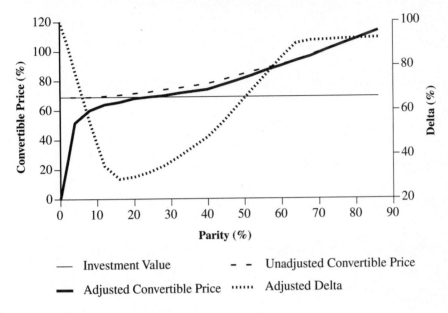

Figure 10.3   Credit Spread Adjusted Fair Value

delta increases at low levels of parity. This model more accurately re-flects the actual performance of convertibles as the investment value holds, deteriorates, and then disappears. In the junk stage with no in-vestment value, the convertible price becomes very volatile and trades again like equity. In Figure 10.3, we assume that the XYZ convertible has deteriorated to a CCC credit with an 800 basis point initial credit spread, a best-fit regression line with a slope of –30, and a y intercept of 2,500 basis points (i.e., 25%).

11

CONVERTIBLE BOND PRICING
Put plus Stock plus Yield Advantage

An alternative way to value a convertible bond is to treat it as yield-enhanced stock plus a put option. In this case, the put option represents the investment value. In effect, we are long a put option struck at the investment value, and long yield-enhanced common stock.

Returning to the XYZ Corporation example (see Chapter 1), we can break the convertible down into its component parts as follows.

THE EQUITY PORTION

This is an easy calculation. For each bond of $1,000 face amount, we are long eight shares of stock (i.e., the conversion ratio) times the current stock price of $100, for a value of $800.

THE PUT OPTION

A put option has the opposite payoff from a call option. The holder of a put option has the right to sell the underlying asset at a designated price over the term of the option. The holder benefits if the price of the asset falls. A European-style put can be exercised only at maturity. The price of a European-style put is easily determined by virtue of a relationship known as put-call parity. This is explained as follows.

Consider the following two portfolios.

Portfolio 1: A share of stock, a European put on the stock with strike price K, and borrowing the present value of the strike price, $Ke^{-r(T-t)}$.

Portfolio 2: A European call option with strike price K.

The payoff of these two portfolios is the same at expiration, namely:

Portfolio 1: $S - \text{Max}[0, K - S] - K = \text{Max}[S - K, 0]$

Portfolio 2: $\text{Max}[S-K, 0]$

Using an arbitrage argument, it is clear that both portfolios must be equally priced at any time, t, prior to the expiration date. If not, a savvy trader would short the more costly portfolio and purchase the cheap portfolio, locking in a risk-free profit. This equality gives a pricing relation between a European put and call option as follows:

$$c = S \cdot e^{-qT} + p - K \cdot e^{-rT}$$

or by rearranging:

$$p = -S \cdot e^{-qT} + c + K \cdot e^{-rT}$$
$$p = K \cdot e^{-rT} \cdot N(-d_2) - S \cdot e^{-qT} \cdot N(d_1)$$
$$= \frac{B}{CR} \cdot e^{-rT} \cdot N(-d_2) - S \cdot e^{-qT} \cdot N(-d_1)$$
$$= 105.98 \cdot e^{-t.75\% \cdot 5} N(0.1909) - 100 \cdot N(-0.7041)$$
$$= 79.50 \cdot 0.5757 - 100 \cdot 0.2407$$
$$= 45.77 - 24.07$$
$$= 21.70$$

where c = price of a European call option
         p = price of a European put option

S = the stock price today
q = annualized continuous dividend yield
T = time to the exercise date in years
K = exercise price of the option
B = investment value
CR = conversion ratio
$N(d)$ = cumulative normal probability density function

$$d_1 = \frac{\ln\frac{S}{K} + \left(r - q + \frac{\sigma^2}{2}\right) \cdot T}{\sigma\sqrt{T}}$$

$$d_2 = d_1 - \sigma\sqrt{T}$$

THE YIELD ADVANTAGE

Previously, we estimated the value of a convertible bond (CB) as the sum of its investment value (B) plus a call warrant (C):

$$CB = B + CR \cdot C$$

Using the put-call parity relationship, the price of the convertible is expressed as follows:

$$CB = B + CR \cdot S \cdot e^{-qT} + CR \cdot p - CR \cdot \frac{B}{CR} e^{-rT}$$

$$= CR \cdot p + B \cdot \left(1 - e^{-rT}\right) + CR \cdot S \cdot e^{-qT}$$

We introduce parity into the equation by adding and subtracting $CR \cdot S$:

$$CB = CR \cdot p + B \cdot (1 - e^{-rT}) + CR \cdot S \cdot e^{-qT} + CR \cdot S - CR \cdot S$$

By rearranging:

$$CB = CR \cdot S + CR \cdot p + B \cdot (1 - e^{-rT}) - CR \cdot S \cdot (1 - e^{-qT})$$

Now we have expressed the convertible bond as the sum of parity, plus a put, plus the yield advantage. In our XYZ convertible bond example, the stock pays no dividend. Consequently, we can calculate the yield advantage as follows:

$$
\begin{aligned}
B \cdot (1 - e^{-rT} - CR \cdot \text{S} \cdot (1 - e^{-qT}) &= 848 \cdot (1 - e^{-5.75\%.5}) - 800 \cdot (1 - e^{-0}) \\
&= 848 \cdot (1 - 0.7501) - 800(1 - 1) \\
&= 211.88
\end{aligned}
$$

Therefore, by combining the three component parts we arrive at the following valuation:

$$
CB = \$800 + 8 \cdot \$21.70 + \$211.8 = \$1{,}185.4
$$

This result is consistent with our previous Black–Scholes valuation where we described the convertible as the sum of a straight bond plus a call warrant (see Chapter 8).

Part Three

CONVERTIBLE HEDGING

12

CONVERTIBLE ARBITRAGE

IS A PURE ARBITRAGE POSSIBLE?

Arbitrage, strictly defined, is the process of making a risk-free profit by buying and selling the same asset in two different markets simultaneously. Convertible securities are derivative products. We expect them to trade in line with the underlying stock into which they are convertible. Convertibles trade within certain boundary conditions. If these boundaries are violated, an arbitrage profit is possible. If the convertible trades below parity, it can be purchased while simultaneously shorting an amount of stock equal to the conversion ratio. Upon conversion, the stock received can be used to cover the outstanding short position, locking in a profit. Of course, pure arbitrage opportunities are rare in efficient markets. Convertible securities sell at a discount to parity only in markets where it is difficult (or impossible) to short the stock. This often occurs in developing countries and offers long-term investors attractive opportunities.

WHY HEDGE?

If a convertible is trading at a discount to its fair value, we can extract this value by buying the convertible and selling the stock short. A convertible's fair value is a function of its key inputs volatility, credit spread, dividends, and so on. If we sell short an amount of stock equal to the delta of the convertible, we can establish a market-neutral position. If we maintain a delta-neutral position, no matter which way the stock price moves, the net change of our position will be zero (excluding carry considerations). Once the convertible returns to fair value, we can unwind the position and lock in a profit.

Waiting for the convertible to return to fair value is not the only way to profit from convertible arbitrage. The convertible is cheap because its implied volatility is lower than the historic volatility of the stock. This presents an opportunity. The convertible is a cheaper way to own the stock. We can extract this cheapness by setting up a delta-neutral hedge and then waiting for the stock price to move. As soon as the stock price moves, we are no longer delta neutral. If the stock price rises, the delta of the convertible increases, making us long to the position. At that moment, we are underhedged. We need to sell more stock in order to return to a delta-neutral position. If the stock price falls, so too does the delta of the convertible. Now we are overhedged or short the position. To return to a neutral position, we need to buy back stock. Each time we readjust our hedge back to delta neutral, we lock in a small profit. The more volatile the stock, the more opportunities we have to make a profit. The trick is to determine when to return to a delta-neutral position. On the one hand, we want to lock in our gain quickly so as not to miss the opportunity. On the other hand, we want to avoid losing all our profits on transaction costs.

By hedging the equity component of the convertible, we are limiting our risk and isolating the cheap component: the volatility. This is known as trading the convertible's vega. Vega is the change in the convertible price given a change in the volatility of the stock price. Convertible hedge arbitrage seeks to monetize this cheapness. This is achieved in incremental stages as the hedge is continually readjusted back to a delta-neutral position.

WHAT TO HEDGE?

Although we may have correctly identified a cheap convertible, there are a number of other risks that influence its price. These include the following.

Interest-Rate Risk

As explained in Chapter 14, changes in interest rates have a dual and inverse effect on convertible securities. Rising interest rates are negative for the convertible's investment value, but positive for its warrant value, and vice versa. The sensitivity of a convertible's price with respect to a change in interest rates is given by its rho and duration (see Chapter 9). This risk can be hedged by taking a short position in another fixed-income security or interest-rate-derivative product.

Default Risk

The price of a convertible is a function of its investment value and its warrant value. The general level of interest rates and the creditworthiness of the issuer directly affect the investment value. Default risk can be hedged through an asset or default swap (see Chapter 14).

Currency Risk

The convertible market is global. Hedge arbitrageurs are presented with many interesting opportunities outside of their home markets. Convertible securities denominated in foreign currencies present the arbitrageur with currency risk. Exchangeable convertibles may be subject to currency risk even if denominated in the arbitrageur's home currency. This is because the underlying stock is denominated in a foreign currency. The parity of the bond is affected by exchange rates regardless of stock price movements. These risks can be hedged with spot- or forward-currency agreements (see Chapter 15).

WHO HEDGES?

Hedge arbitrageurs include hedge funds and market makers. In the United States, it is estimated that this strategy accounts for more than 60% of the total convertible market. Consequently, it is important to understand the dynamics of hedge arbitrage in order to appreciate how convertibles are priced and traded.

THE IDEAL HEDGE CANDIDATE

There are two types of hedge arbitrage positions: the carry trade and the volatility trade. The carry trade seeks to achieve an attractive return on invested capital from the income generated by the position. This can be achieved in two ways. First, a busted convertible with a high current yield can be lightly hedged according to its delta. Assuming the investment value holds, this will generate high income with little downside risk. Second, a deep in-the-money convertible can be fully hedged. This transaction requires very little capital and so can be highly leveraged. If the position enjoys even a modest yield advantage it can generate an attractive return on capital (see Additional Notes at the end of this chapter). The second type of arbitrage trade is a volatility trade. This position may have a negative carry. To be profitable, the position must be traded. This requires a volatile stock and a convertible with a large positive gamma (see Chapter 9). Positive gamma means that the convertible will move sharply in the same direction as the stock. The important considerations for a hedge trade are as follows.

Conversion Premium

On a carry trade, the premium can be either high or low to be effective. An out-of-the-money convertible with a high premium and a low delta can be lightly hedged to generate good current income with low risk to the stock price. The main concern here is that the investment value will hold. If the convertible is deep in-the-money with a low premium, the carry trade can be achieved with high leverage. The hedge eliminates credit risk, but the return will be sensitive to the investor's cost of funds and stock loan fees.

On a volatility trade, gamma should be maximized. For short-dated options, gamma is greatest when the stock price is close to the warrant's exercise price. For the convertible, this translates into a low premium of between 10% and 20%. If the premium is too low, the convertible will trade just like the stock. The delta will be 100% and the gamma will be zero. There will be no opportunity to adjust the delta and capture a profit. If the convertible is deep out-of-the-money, it will have very little equity sensitivity. Its delta and gamma will be zero and there will be little opportunity to trade the position.

Investment Value

The arbitrageur, like all other convertible investors, prizes a strong, predictable investment value. The closer the convertible is to its investment value, the sooner it will find support should the stock price fall. However, if the credit deteriorates to junk status, the investment value will not hold and the convertible will trade down in lock step with the common stock (see Chapter 10). This is disastrous for the arbitrageur who is assuming a low delta at this juncture and will thus be woefully underhedged.

Call Protection

The hedge arbitrageur does not want to be exposed to the risk of forced conversion. If the convertible is unexpectedly called, the arbitrageur will lose both the premium and the accrued interest. If the convertible already reflects the call risk by trading at parity less accrued interest, a hedge position may still be attractive.

Yield Advantage

The arbitrageur earns the accrued income on the convertible but must pay away any dividend on the short-stock position. Thus, the greater the yield advantage of the convertible over the common stock, the better the carry on the arbitrage position.

Borrowability

Hedge arbitrage requires that the stock be easy and cheap to borrow. In many developing markets, lending and shorting stock is not allowed. In other markets, borrowing stock may be difficult. This is true in Japan during the months of March and September. In Japan, shareholders must be holders of record to be eligible for the dividend payments. If the stock is called in by the lender, the arbitrageur might be forced to sell the position at an inopportune moment. Lending rates are typically low at less than 50 basis points per annum. However, if the stock is in high demand, lending rates can soar to greater than 10%.

Liquidity

The arbitrageur appreciates good liquidity in both the stock and the convertible. This makes it possible to initiate, trade, and exit a position.

Cheapness

The arbitrageur seeks to identify, lock in, and monetize theoretical cheapness in convertible securities. This cheapness may be relative either to the stock's own historic volatility or to the prior trading history of the convertible.

Volatility

The arbitrageur is concerned about two types of volatility. First, he or she wants to purchase a cheap convertible where the implied volatility of the embedded warrant is lower than the historic volatility of the stock. Second, the arbitrageur wants the volatility of the underlying stock to be high so that the opportunity to monetize this cheapness will be maximized. Because volatility is intangible, it is a difficult concept to understand. However, since it is perhaps the most important element in determining the success of a hedge trade (except for carry trades), we devote the next section to explaining volatility and how to calculate it.

VOLATILITY UNMASKED

One of the critical factors affecting the price of a convertible is the volatility of the underlying stock. Volatility is a method of describing the magnitude of price swings a stock undergoes around its average return. It describes the price range of the stock and explains the likelihood of seeing the price within that range over a given time period.

Stock prices are said to follow a stochastic Markov process. This means that a stock's price change is uncertain over time (i.e., stochastic), and that its past history is irrelevant in determining its future performance. The Markov process implies that the current stock price incorporates all the market's known information. Moreover, stock prices follow a particular type of Markov process known as a Wiener process. This model views stock returns as undergoing a random walk in which they fluctuate with equal probability around their average return.

To gain a better understanding of the fluctuation in returns, consider the following example. Envision a game in which Ping-Pong balls are dropped through a 15-stage pyramid of wooden pegs and into numbered bins as in Figure 12.1. At each stage, a ball hits the peg below and is equally likely to bounce left or right. The ball is, in essence, undergoing a random walk down the pyramid. If enough balls are dropped, the resulting shape, or distribution, of the balls will resemble a bell, as shown in Figure 12.2. This shape is known as a normal distribution and demonstrates how a random process, repeated often enough, generates a predictable distribution.

The mean and the standard deviation are two statistics used to describe a given distribution. The mean is the average outcome and locates the peak of the bell curve. In Figure 12.2 the mean is 7.5 and can be thought of as the divider between bins 7 and 8. A ball that is dropped would therefore most likely fall into bin 7.5. Since there is no such bin, for a given ball there is an equal likelihood that it will fall into bin 7 or bin 8.

The standard deviation describes the dispersion of the balls around the mean value. A small standard deviation would indicate that a vast majority of the balls fell into the bins around 7 and 8, with few balls located in the tail end bins (i.e., those around 0 or 15). A large standard deviation would imply a much more even dispersion of balls. The majority would still be concentrated around 7 and 8, but a much higher percentage would be located in the outlying bins. In a normal distribution, a certain percentage of the data (or balls) will be located within each standard deviation from the mean. The percentages are:

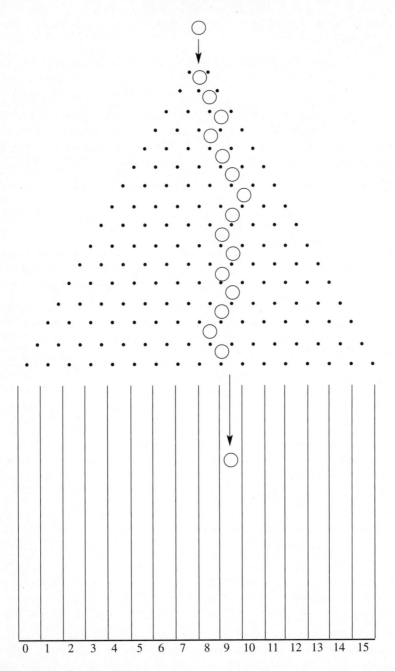

Figure 12.1 Random Walk
Source: Natenberg

Figure 12.2 Normal Distribution
Source: Natenberg

± 1 Standard Deviation	68.3%
± 2 Standard Deviations	95.4%
± 3 Standard Deviations	99.7%

In the Ping-Pong ball example, the standard deviation is approximately 2. This means that 68% of the balls dropped will fall between 7.5 ± 2, or into bins 6 to 9. Likewise, 95% of the balls dropped will fall within 7.5 ± 4, or into bins 4 to 11. Almost all the balls, 99.7%, should fall into bins 2 to 13. Very few balls will fall into the extremes. The mean and the standard deviation are descriptive statistics because they show both where data is centered and how it is distributed.

Assume that the Ping-Pong balls represent a stock's annual return, currently at 7.5%, and that each of the 15 levels represents the change in the stock's annual return in a given day. Suppose your boss comes in and asks what you expect the return of the stock to be when the quarter closes in 15 days. From the above analysis, you can predict a 7.5% return, the stock's mean. Furthermore, you can sleep fairly well at night since you know that there is a 68% chance you will not be off by more than 2%.

Consider a second example. Suppose another stock's return varies twice as much each day. This could be modeled by expanding our triangle and placing wooden shelves between pairs of pegs, as in Figure 12.3. The Ping-Pong balls will now fall from above, hit a shelf, and roll one way or another before falling again. This means that the stock price (or bin number) will change by 1% each day rather than .5% each day, as in the previous example. What will the new distribution look like? Calculating the mean and standard deviation, we get 7.5 and 4, respectively. The distribution maintains the bell shape of a normal distribution, but is now more spread out. Of the returns 68% now fall into a much larger region, 7.5 ± 4, or into bins 4 to 11. There is even a 2.5% probability that we will experience a negative return. If your boss now asks for your prediction, you will once again tell him or her that you predict a 7.5% return. However, you may toss and turn at night due to the stock's (and perhaps your job's) increased volatility.

The terms volatility, standard deviation, and variance are all used to describe the magnitude of a stock's fluctuations. These terms are all mathematically related and, when specificity is not required, can be used interchangeably. We will show the mathematical relationship

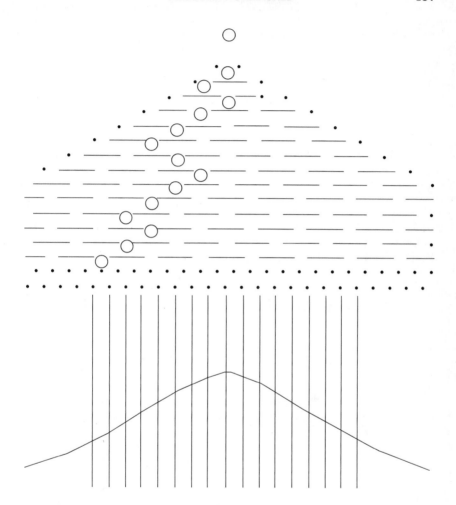

Figure 12.3 High Volatility Distribution
Source: Natenberg

between these three terms in the next section. Most practitioners use volatility to describe a stock's riskiness. Since a low volatility stock, as we demonstrated, yields a fairly stable and predictable return, it entails less risk than a high volatility stock. For this reason, investors will normally require a greater expected return (i.e., mean) from a higher volatility stock than from a low volatility stock in order to compensate for the increased risk they must bear.

The normal distribution of returns that is assumed in option analysis results in what is known as a lognormal distribution in a stock's price. Figure 12.4 shows the lognormal distribution in relation to a normal distribution. This upwardly skewed distribution results from the fact that a return on a low priced stock will cause a smaller price increase than the same return on a high priced stock. Consider a stock that is trading at $100. If it experiences a 10% increase, it will trade at $110. If it experiences a 10% decrease, it will trade at $90. Now suppose that in the next period the $110 stock increases 10% again. It will now be up $11 at $121. Likewise, if the low priced stock decreases by 10% again, it now trades down $9 to $81. Because its price is lower, the same percentage change causes a lower decrease in price. The same magnitude of return has thus resulted in an upward movement of $21 but a downward movement of only $19. The lognormal distribution reflects this asymmetry in stock prices.

CALCULATING HISTORIC VOLATILITY

Historic volatility is defined as the annualized standard deviation of a given set of returns. Standard deviation is the square root of variance.

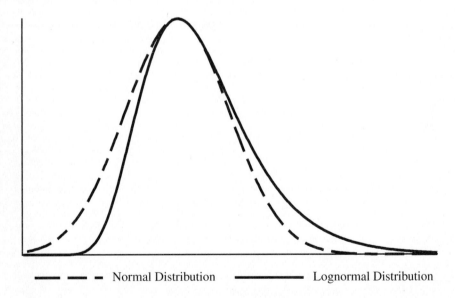

Figure 12.4 Lognormal versus Normal Distribution

Variance is the variability of a distribution around its mean. Given a set of historic stock price returns, the example below illustrates how to calculate historic volatility.

Step One: Calculate the Mean of the Lognormal Returns

In Table 12.1, we lay out the closing price of XYZ Corporation's stock price at the end of each week for 10 weeks (column 1). Next, we calculate the 10 weekly returns of the stock. We calculate this on a price-relative basis by taking the current week's stock price and dividing it by last week's price. Thus, in the first case 102% equals 1.020000 (column 2). If we wanted to calculate volatility assuming prices change at fixed intervals, we would convert 1.020000 to a percentage by subtracting one (1.02 − 1.00 = .02 or 2%). However, because the Black–Scholes model assumes continuously changing prices, we take the natural logarithm of

Table 12.1 Calculating Historic Volatility

Week	Stock Price (1)	$R_t = P_t/P_t - 1$ (2)	$\log(R_t)$ (3)	$\log(R_t) - u$ (4)	$(\log(R_t) - u)^2$ (5)
0	100				
1	102	1.020000	0.019803	0.014924	0.000223
2	103	1.009804	0.009756	0.004877	0.000024
3	98	0.951456	−0.049762	−0.054641	0.002986
4	102	1.040816	0.040005	0.035126	0.001234
5	105	1.029412	0.028988	0.024109	0.000581
6	107	1.019048	0.018868	0.013989	0.000196
7	103	0.962617	−0.038100	−0.042979	0.001847
8	97	0.941748	−0.060018	−0.064897	0.004212
9	103	1.061856	0.060018	0.055139	0.003040
10	105	1.019417	0.019231	0.014352	0.000206
Total			0.048790		0.014548
Mean			0.004879		
Variance					0.001616
Annualized variance					0.084055
Annual volatility					28.9922%

the price-relative returns, as in column 3 (0.019803). To calculate the mean (u) of these returns, we total them and divide by the number of observations ($n = 10$) to get 0.004879.

Step Two: Calculate the Variance of the Returns

Now that we know the mean of the returns, we can easily calculate how much each weekly return differs from the mean. In the first case, subtracting the return from the mean equals 0.014924 (column 4). To calculate the variance, we square the individual fluctuations from the mean, total them, and divide by the number of observations adjusted for $n - 1$ degrees of freedom (0.001616). We square the fluctuations from the mean so that negative and positive divergences do not cancel each other out. Direction plays no role in calculating volatility.

$$\text{Variance of returns} = \frac{1}{n-1} \sum_{i=1}^{n} (R_i - \overline{R})^2$$

where n = number of observations
R_i = return of ith occurrence
$\overline{R}$ = mean return

Step Three: Annualize the Weekly Variance

Since volatility is expressed annually, we need to convert the weekly variance to an annual figure. We do this by multiplying the weekly figure by the number of weeks in a year, or 52 (0.084055). If our observations had been monthly, or daily, we would multiply by 12 or 250, respectively. There are 250 trading days in a year.

Step Four: Convert the Annualized Variance to an Annualized Standard Deviation

In the final step, we take the square root of the variance to arrive at the standard deviation or volatility of 28.99% per annum (0.289922). In the variance equation, units are measured in percentages squared. This is a difficult concept to visualize. By taking the square root of the variance, we return the measurement to a percentage. Standard deviation, or volatility, is a more natural way of expressing variance because its units are the same as the object being measured.

To better visualize the data in Table 12.1, we graph the weekly stock price movements (See Figure 12.5.)

If, as hedge arbitrageurs, we seek to trade volatility, it may be helpful to graph the logged returns shown in column 3 of Table 12.1. In Figure 12.6, we can see the percentage change in the stock price. The taller the bars, the more volatile the stock.

Finally, if we plot the relative frequency distribution of the logged returns, we can see how often the stock price moves. The wider the distribution, the more volatile the stock. (See Figure 12.7.)

CONVERTIBLE HEDGING STRATEGIES

Returns from a convertible hedge position are influenced by the size of the hedge and the amount of the leverage employed. The size of the hedge determines the payoff profile. An investor who seeks solely to monetize the theoretical cheapness of the security or to trade its

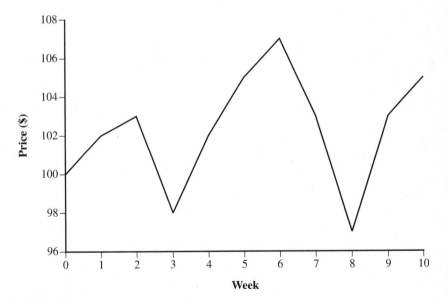

Figure 12.5 Weekly Stock Price Movements

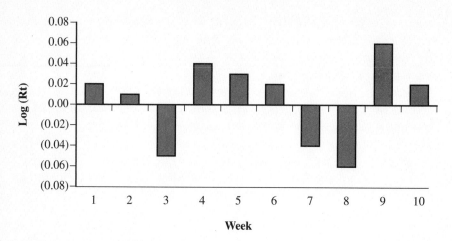

Figure 12.6   Log Returns

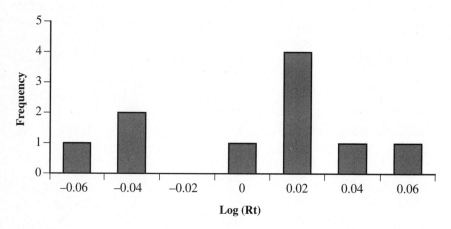

Figure 12.7   Relative Frequency Distribution

volatility will establish a market-neutral position. This strategy will be equally profitable in both up and down markets. However, an investor who has a view on the stock price can bias the hedge. The hedge can be designed so that if the investor is wrong about the direction of the stock price, the loss will be minimal. However, if the investor is correct, the gain will be amplified. The return from any of these payoffs can be magnified by the use of leverage. We will explain how both an individual and an institutional investor can use leverage.

CREATING THE SHORT POSITION

A necessary component of a hedge trade is creating an offsetting short-stock position against the convertible. A short-stock position can be created in several ways. Here, we consider selling the underlying stock short. Later, we will investigate other techniques like buying put options, selling call options, or combining strategies.

THE INDIVIDUAL INVESTOR

To short a stock, an investor must first borrow it from a broker. The broker in turn borrows the stock from an owner. The broker pays the owner a fee. This fee may vary from as little as 0.25% to more than 10.00% per annum depending on the demand for the stock. The fee is calculated on the current market value of the stock and its availability in the market. A short sale can be done only in a margin account. For a U.S.-based investor, regulation T of the Federal Reserve Board governs margin accounts. A margin account is composed of two subaccounts: a general account and a short account. Proceeds from the short sale are deposited into the short account. There must always be sufficient cash in the short account to cover the current value of the short position. As the stock price falls, money can be released from the short account and transferred to the general account. If the stock price rises, additional funds must be added to the short account. The general account earns interest on credit balances and pays interest on debit balances.

The two subaccounts of the margin account must be segregated. Proceeds in the short account cannot be used to offset a debit in the general account. The investor earns no interest on the proceeds in the short account. The broker is entitled to this interest income. Consequently, the broker pays the stock-lending fee. Of course, the broker is not obliged to lend stock that costs more to borrow than the interest earned on the short account. When the arbitrageur is setting up a hedge trade, the long convertible position is held in the general account. If the stock price rises, the investor does not have to top up the funds in the short account. The broker will lend these funds out of the general account being content to hold the convertible as collateral. If the stock price falls, proceeds are moved to the general account where they earn interest. Credit balances earn interest at the Broker Loan Bid Rate less a spread. Debit balances pay interest at the Broker Loan Offer Rate plus a spread depending upon the customer's creditworthiness. Under regulation T, shorting stock against a long convertible position is considered a covered short sale. No additional margin is required to support the short sale. The maximum leverage allowed is 50% of the original long position. As the stock price falls, gains on the short position may be moved to the general account and can be used to reduce the investor's loan or debit balance. If the stock price rises, the broker will lend the investor additional funds to top up the short account. This will increase the investor's loan amount. Thus, the cost of financing a leveraged position under regulation T will fall as the stock price falls and rise as the stock price rises.

THE INSTITUTIONAL INVESTOR

For an institutional investor, the mechanics change. The difference is that proceeds from the short sale earn interest at the Broker Loan Bid rate less a stock loan fee and a credit spread. Resident institutions remain governed by regulation T, which allows only 50% leverage. The exception is brokerage firms that are allowed up to 10 times leverage.

THE NONRESIDENT INVESTOR

Nonresident investors, like hedge funds located offshore, are not subject to regulation T. They enjoy the same arrangements as U.S. institutional investors except that they are allowed greater leverage. Each broker will have its own margin requirements. Typically, the margin requirement is 30% of the unhedged portion of the position plus the lesser of the conversion premium or 10% of the unhedged portion. Convertibles issued as private placements under rule 144A cannot be leveraged because the stock underlying them is not registered and so cannot be held by the broker as collateral against the short sale.

EXECUTING A SHORT SALE

A U.S. resident investor is subject to certain rules governing short sales laid out by the Securities and Exchange Commission. The principle behind these rules is that a stock cannot be shorted in a falling market. The plus tick rule states that an investor may sell short when the last stock price is higher than the preceding price. The zero plus tick rule allows the investor to sell short if the last sales price is unchanged but higher than the preceding different sale price. The only exception to these rules is if a short sale is made with the intention of covering it with stock from the conversion of a convertible security. This short exempt rule allows the investor to immediately lock in the value of the convertible without waiting for the time delay associated with conversion.

THE NEUTRAL HEDGE: NO LEVERAGE

In this strategy, the investor does not have a view on the stock price. The goal is to establish a market-neutral position by shorting the appropriate number of shares against the long convertible position. The arbitrageur will profit if the convertible, being theoretically cheap, returns to fair value. The trade can then be unwound, locking in a profit. The arbitrageur will also profit from the stock's volatility. If the stock moves up, the once-neutral position will become a long position as the delta of the convertible increases. Conversely, as the stock price falls, the position will become overhedged as the convertible's delta declines and the investor profits by being net short the stock. If the stock price stands still, the investor will have locked in the yield advantage (or disadvantage) of the convertible.

Returning to our XYZ Corporation convertible bond example (see Chapter 1), we illustrate the payoff from an unlevered neutral hedge position. In each of our illustrations, we assume a 50% up or down move in the stock price over a one-year time horizon. This is a reasonable price range since the stock price is $100 and has a historic volatility of 40%. Statistically, we expect the stock price to move up or down by 40% (or $40) two-thirds of the time (one standard deviation) over one year. Referring to Chapter 9, we can tailor the price movement of our payoff scenario to match the specific volatility of the stock and the expected holding period of the trade. We can also determine the probability of achieving a targeted return from our hedge position. This methodology is helpful in determining a realistic payoff for the trade and for ranking the attractiveness of trades. For example, if XYZ's stock price had only a 20% volatility, we would use a plus or minus $20 price range to forecast the success of our hedge trade.

In Table 12.2, we purchased 1,000 bonds at a price of 118.576%. Each bond has a denomination of $1,000 for a total investment of $1,185,760. The bonds were purchased on 25 January 2000, so there is no accrued interest. Each bond is convertible into eight shares of XYZ Corporation's common stock. The total number of shares underlying the position is 8,000. To set up the neutral hedge, we sold short 6,000 shares. This represents a hedge ratio of 75% (6,000/8,000). If

Table 12.2 XYZ Corporation Convertible Bond
Neutral Hedge: 75%
No Leverage

Strategy: Buy 1,000 bonds at 118.57% and short 6,000 shares at $100							
Stock price % change	−50%	−33%	−16%	0	+16%	+33%	+50%
Assumed stock price	50.0	66.7	83.3	100.0	116.7	133.3	150.0
Estimated cvt. price (%)	93.1	100.2	108.9	118.6	129.1	140.1	151.6
Current yield (%)	5.4	5.0	4.6	4.2	3.9	3.6	3.3
Conversion premium (%)	132.6	87.9	63.3	48.2	38.2	31.3	26.3
Parity (%)	40.0	53.3	66.7	80.0	93.3	106.7	120.0
Delta (%)	47.2	59.9	69.1	75.9	80.9	84.7	87.6
P/l convertible ('000)	−255	−183	−96	0	+105	+215	330
P/l stock ('000)	+300	+200	+100	0	−100	−200	−300
Bond interest ('000)	+50	+50	+50	+50	+50	+50	+50
Stock dividend ('000)	0	0	0	0	0	0	0
Total p/l ('000)	+95	+67	+53	+50	+55	+65	+80
Amount invested ('000)	1,185	1,185	1,185	1,185	1,185	1,185	1,185
Leverage	0	0	0	0	0	0	0
ROI (%)	8.0	5.6	4.5	4.2	4.6	5.5	6.7
Convertible unhedged							
Convertible p/l ('000)	−205	−133	−47	+50	+155	+265	+380
ROI (%)	−17.3	−11.2	−3.9	+4.2	+13.0	+22.3	+32.1

the stock price is unchanged, we will earn accrued interest on the long bond position of $50,000 ($1,000,000 times 5.00% for one year). This is a return on our original investment of 4.2%. We have locked in the convertible's yield advantage. The yield advantage is the current yield on the bond (4.2%) less the dividend yield on the stock (0.0%). If the stock price rises 50% to $150, the position will earn $80,302 or a return on investment of 6.77%. This profit consists of $50,000 in accrued interest plus a $330,302 gain on the convertible and a $300,000 loss on the short stock position. If the stock price falls by $50, we will earn $94,887, for a return on investment of 8.00%. The returns are very symmetrical for moves up and down in the stock price of up to 33%. At the 50% level, we make a better return on the downside because the investment value holds steady throughout. In practice, we would expect the issuer's credit quality to decline as the stock price falls, which would lower the investment value and reduce our return (see Chapter 10).

Considering that the risk-free rate of interest is 5.75%, these returns are hardly awe inspiring. This is not surprising. We purchased the convertible at its fair value so there was no opportunity to profit from a rerating. By adopting a market-neutral hedge, we basically created a risk-free asset which should earn the risk-free rate. Finally, we have used no leverage and have received no interest on our short-stock position. (See Figure 12.8.)

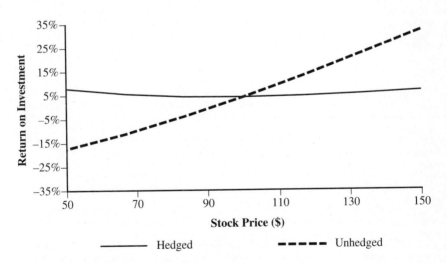

Figure 12.8 Neutral Hedge Return Profile—Unleveraged

HOW MUCH TO HEDGE?

Assuming that we wanted a market-neutral hedge, how did we know that 75% was the correct hedge ratio? There are two ways to derive this answer. First, we can make an estimate of where the convertible will trade given a move in the stock price. We can make this estimate based on where this particular convertible has traded in the past. If there is no history, we might look at where similar securities have traded. In our example, we assumed that the convertible would trade at 151.60% with the stock price up 50% to $150. To calculate the price sensitivity of the convertible for a change in the stock price, we look at how the convertible's parity changed. With the stock at $100 and a conversion ratio of 8, we began with a parity of $800 per bond, or 80%. With the stock at $150, parity has increased to $1,200, or 120%. We can then calculate the delta of a 50% up move in the stock as 82.55%, as follows:

$$\text{Upside delta} = \frac{\text{Current convertible price} - \begin{array}{c}\text{Convertible price after 50\%}\\ \text{increase of the underlying}\\ \text{stock price}\end{array}}{\text{Current parity} - \begin{array}{c}\text{Parity after a 50\%}\\ \text{increase of the underlying}\\ \text{stock price}\end{array}}$$

$$= \frac{118.58 - 151.60}{80 - 120}$$

$$= 82.55\%$$

For a 50% down move in the stock, price parity falls from 80% to 40% with the bonds at 93.1%. This gives a downside delta of 63.80%. To find the neutral hedge ratio, we take the midpoint of the upside and downside deltas to arrive at 73.17%, which we round up to 75%. This is a wonderful method, but it is only as effective as our ability to predict the future price behavior of the convertible with respect to the stock price. For the experienced investor this may be effective, but for the novice it is merely guessing.

The second method is to use a modeling approach. We separate the convertible into its two component parts: the bond and the warrant. Using the Black–Scholes model to value the warrant, we derive the options delta as 75.92% (see Chapter 9). This is a good starting point, but its accuracy is subject to all the limitations discussed previously.

If the investor has a view on the direction of the stock price, the hedge can be tailored to optimize this view. In the examples following, we select hedge ratios for a bull (50%) and a bear (95%) hedge that protect the investor if the stock moves against him or her but maximize the gains if the investor is correct. (See Tables 12.3, 12.4 and Figures 12.9, 12.10.)

Table 12.3 XYZ Corporation Convertible Bond
Bull Hedge: 50%
No Leverage

Strategy: Buy 1,000 bonds at 118.57% and short 4,000 shares at $100							
Stock price % change	−50%	−33%	−16%	0	+16%	+33%	+50%
Assumed stock price	50.0	66.7	83.3	100.0	116.7	133.3	150.0
Estimated cvt. price (%)	93.1	100.2	108.9	118.6	129.1	140.1	151.6
Current yield (%)	5.4	5.0	4.6	4.2	3.9	3.6	3.3
Conversion premium (%)	132.6	87.9	63.3	48.2	38.2	31.3	26.3
Parity (%)	40.0	53.3	66.7	80.0	93.3	106.7	120.0
Delta (%)	47.2	59.9	69.1	75.9	80.9	84.7	87.6
P/l convertible ('000)	−255	−183	−96	0	+105	+215	330
P/l stock ('000)	+200	+133	+67	0	−67	−133	−200
Bond interest ('000)	+50	+50	+50	+50	+50	+50	+50
Stock dividend	0	0	0	0	0	0	0
Total P/l ('000)	−5	+0	+20	+50	+88	+132	+180
Amount invested ('000)	1,185	1,185	1,185	1,185	1,185	1,185	1,185
Leverage	0	0	0	0	0	0	0
ROI (%)	−0.4	0.0	1.7	4.2	7.4	11.1	15.2
Convertible unhedged							
Convertible p/l ('000)	−205	−133	−47	+50	+155	+265	+380
ROI (%)	−17.3	−11.2	−3.9	+4.2	+13.0	+22.3	+32.1

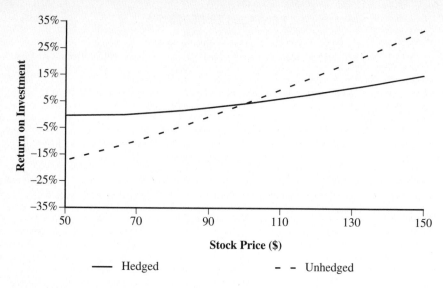

Figure 12.9 Bull Hedge Return Profile—Unleveraged

Table 12.4 XYZ Corporation Convertible Bond
Bear Hedge: 95%
No Leverage

Strategy: Buy 1,000 bonds at 118.57% and short 7,600 shares at $100							
Stock price % change	−50%	−33%	−16%	0	+16%	+33%	+50%
Assumed stock price	50.0	66.7	83.3	100.0	116.7	133.3	150.0
Estimated cvt. price (%)	93.1	100.2	108.9	118.6	129.1	140.1	151.6
Current yield (%)	5.4	5.0	4.6	4.2	3.9	3.6	3.3
Conversion premium (%)	132.6	87.9	63.3	48.2	38.2	31.3	26.3
Parity (%)	40.0	53.3	66.7	80.0	93.3	106.7	120.0
Delta (%)	47.2	59.9	69.1	75.9	80.9	84.7	87.6
P/l convertible ('000)	−255	−183	−96	0	+105	+215	330
P/l stock ('000)	+380	+253	+127	0	-127	-253	-380
Bond interest ('000)	+50	+50	+50	+50	+50	+50	+50
Stock dividend ('000)	0	0	0	0	0	0	0
Total p/l ('000)	+175	+120	+80	+50	+28	+12	+0
Amount invested ('000)	1,185	1,185	1,185	1,185	1,185	1,185	1,185
Leverage	0	0	0	0	0	0	0
ROI (%)	+14.7	+10.1	+6.7	+4.2	2.4	1.0	0.0
Convertible unhedged							
Convertible p/l ('000)	−205	−133	−47	+50	+155	+265	+380
ROI (%)	−17.3	−11.2	−3.9	+4.2	+13.0	+22.3	+32.1

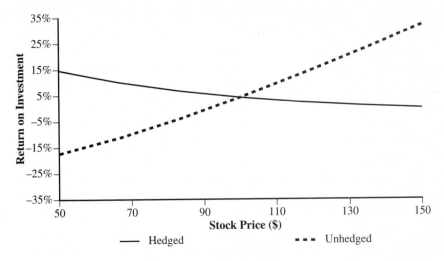

Figure 12.10   Bear Hedge Return Profile—Unleveraged

LEVERAGING THE POSITION UNDER REGULATION T (50% LEVERAGE)

The Neutral Hedge: Using 50% Leverage

In Table 12.5, we show how the returns of the neutrally hedged case change if we leverage the long position by 50%. At inception, this is the maximum leverage allowed by an investor subject to regulation T. We assume a Broker Loan Offer rate of 5.75% plus a spread of 25 basis points for an all-in-debit rate of 6.00%. It is immediately apparent that the returns are no longer symmetrical. On the downside, the return increases by 62% to 13%. On the upside, the return is actually reduced by 33% to 4.50%. The reason for this asymmetry is the variation in the total cost of the margin debt. Initially, we borrowed 50% of our position, or $592,882. When the stock price fell, we were able to transfer the profit in the short-stock account to the general account and reduce the amount of margin debt. Conversely, as the stock price rose, the short-stock account needed to be topped up by the amount of the loss. Our broker lent us this money by increasing the margin debit in our general account. The general account and the short-stock account remain segregated. We earn no interest on our short-stock proceeds and pay no stock-loan fee. At inception, leverage is 50%, or a

Table 12.5   XYZ Corporation Convertible Bond
Neutral Hedge: 75%
50% Leverage

Strategy: Buy 1,000 bonds at 118.57% and short 6,000 shares at $100							
Stock price % change	−50%	−33%	−16%	0	+16%	+33%	+50%
Assumed stock price	50.0	66.7	83.3	100.0	116.7	133.3	150.0
Estimated cvt. price (%)	93.1	100.2	108.9	118.6	129.1	140.1	151.6
Current yield (%)	5.4	5.0	4.6	4.2	3.9	3.6	3.3
Conversion premium (%)	132.6	87.9	63.3	48.2	38.2	31.3	26.3
Parity (%)	40.0	53.3	66.7	80.0	93.3	106.7	120.0
Delta (%)	47.2	59.9	69.1	75.9	80.9	84.7	87.6
P/l convertible ('000)	−255	−183	−96 0	0	+105	+215	330
P/l stock ('000)	+300	+200	+100	0	−100	−200	−300
Bond interest ('000)	+50	+50	+50	+50	+50	+50	+50
Stock dividend ('000)	0	0	0	0	0	0	0
Margin interest	−18	−24	−30	−36	−42	−48	−54
Total p/l ('000)	+77	+43	+23	+14	+13	+18	+27
Amount invested ('000)	593	593	593	593	593	593	593
Leverage	3.2	2.6	2.2	2.0	1.9	1.8	1.7
ROI (%)	13.0	7.3	3.9	2.4	2.2	2.9	4.5
Margin debt calculations ('000)							
Initial margin (50%)	−593	−593	−593	−593	−593	−593	−593
Short stock adjustment	+300	+200	+100	0	−100	−200	−300
Total margin debt	−293	−393	−493	−593	−693	−793	−893
Margin interest (@ 6%)	−18	−24	−30	−36	−42	−48	−54

gearing of two times. When the stock price moves, the margin debt changes and the gearing increases on the downside and decreases on the upside.

Figure 12.11 shows the returns from the neutral, bull, and bear hedge cases using 50% leverage. We used the same hedge ratios as in the unleveraged cases so as to contrast their relative returns. If we wanted to avoid losses in the leveraged bull and bear cases, we could fine-tune the hedge ratios to 60% and 80%, respectively.

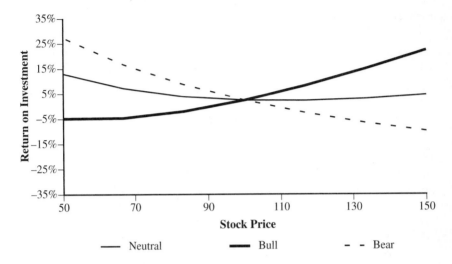

Figure 12.11 Hedge Return Profiles—50% Leveraged

MAXIMIZING LEVERAGE

Finally, we consider an investor domiciled outside the United States who is not subject to regulation T. Brokers establish their own margin requirements. Typically, the margin requirement is 30% of the un-hedged market value of the convertible. In our market-neutral example, we used a 75% hedge ratio. We calculate the unhedged portion to be one minus the hedge ratio or 25% of the convertible's current market price. Twenty-five percent of our initial investment of $1,185,764 is $296,441, and 30% of this amount is $88,932. Notice here that our original hedge ratio was calculated as a percentage of the conversion ratio. The 6,000 shares we shorted were equal to 75% of the total number of shares underlying the convertibles we purchased, or 8,000 shares. Effectively, we hedged only the equity content or parity of the convertible. If our delta calculation is correct, we have created a market-neutral position on the equity portion of the convertible.

However, the position is still at risk for the difference between the convertible price and parity. This difference is the convertible's premium. Consequently, it is customary for the broker to require additional margin equal to the lesser of the premium, or 10% of the initial margin requirement. In our example, the total premium is $385,764, representing the convertible price of 118.57% minus parity of 80%, times the size and denomination of our position. Since 10% of the initial margin is only $8,893, we add $8,893 to our original margin of $88,932 to arrive at a total margin requirement of $97,826.

THE COST OF CARRY

In the neutral, bull, and bear positions illustrated next, we assume that the stock price moves on the first day and that we immediately adjust our hedge ratio back to delta-neutral. In this manner, we capture the profit generated by the price move and illustrate the financing required to carry the position forward.

THE COST OF MARGIN DEBT

The first element in calculating the cost-of-carry is the cost of the margin debt, the total amount we can borrow. Initially, in the neutrally hedged position, the margin debt is $1,087,939. We pay interest on this amount at the London Interbank Offered Rate (LIBOR), plus a credit spread of 0.25%, for a total of 6.00%.

When the stock price rises by 50%, two things happen. First, the delta increases to 87.6% so that the unhedged portion falls to only 12.4% of the convertible's current market price of 151.60%, or $187,984. The 30% margin required on this is $56,395 plus the 10% additional margin, for a total margin requirement of $61,882. This means that we can borrow the current market value of the convertible position, $1,516,066, less the margin requirement of $61,882, or $1,454,184. Second, we have lost $300,000 on our short-stock position. The broker will lend us this amount as well, for a total margin debt of $1,754,184. Our investment in this position is our margin requirement of $61,882, resulting in a gearing of 24.5 times. It should now be apparent that as the delta approaches 100% and the premium goes to zero, the degree of leverage becomes infinite. In practice, a neutral hedge is not likely to exceed 95% of the position even if it is very deep in-the-money. This is because if the position is completely hedged, the arbitrageur will lose the spread between the borrowing and lending rates.

As the stock price falls, the delta declines and the amount of the unhedged position increases even as the convertible price falls. However, this increase in margin requirement is more than offset by the gain in the short-stock position because the stock price falls faster than the convertible price. The net effect is to reduce the cost of the margin debt as the stock price falls.

THE SHORT REBATE

The second element in calculating the cost-of-carry is the short rebate. Unlike the situation under regulation T, the prime broker relationship allows the investor to earn interest on the proceeds from the short-stock sale. The notional amount of the short sale moves up and down with the stock price. The investor earns interest on this balance at the London Interbank Bid Rate (LIBID) (5.625) less a credit spread (0.25%), and pays a stock loan fee (0.50%) to the broker. In our examples, this nets to a short rebate of 4.875%.

NEUTRAL HEDGE WITH MAXIMUM LEVERAGE

Table 12.6 shows the returns from a neutral hedge position given a 50% move in the stock price and a one-year holding period. The returns are much enhanced over the unleveraged case. The standstill rate of return now increases from 4.21% to 14.28%. If the stock falls by 50%, the return on investment rises from 8.0% to 50.7%. If the stock price rises by 50%, the return increases from 6.0% to 30.5%. Of course, these results assume that interest rates, credit spreads, volatility, and premium relationships remain stable. (See also Figure 12.12.)

BULL HEDGE WITH MAXIMUM LEVERAGE

By way of comparison, we maintain our bull hedge ratio at 50%. If we are correct, and the stock rises by 50%, we make an incredible 178% return on our investment. The standstill rate of return is a reasonable 5.15%, but if we are wrong and the stock price falls, we lose money. Again, we could tailor our hedge to minimize loss on the downside by increasing the amount of our hedge. Of course, by doing so we would also give up some of the potential gain from the trade. (See Figure 12.13.)

Table 12.6   XYZ Corporation Convertible Bond
Neutral Hedge: 75%
Maximum Leverage

Strategy: Buy 1,000 bonds at 118.57% and short 6,000 shares at $100							
Stock price % change	−50%	−33%	−16%	0	+16%	+33%	+50%
Assumed stock price	50.0	66.7	83.3	100.0	116.7	133.3	150.0
Estimated cvt. price (%)	93.1	100.2	108.9	118.6	129.1	140.1	151.6
Current yield (%)	5.4	5.0	4.6	4.2	3.9	3.6	3.3
Conversion premium (%)	132.6	87.9	63.3	48.2	38.2	31.3	26.3
Parity (%)	40.0	53.3	66.7	80.0	93.3	106.7	120.0
Delta (%)	47.2	59.9	69.1	75.9	80.9	84.7	87.6
P/l convertible ('000)	−255	−183	−96	0	+105	+215	330
P/l stock ('000)	+300	+200	+100	0	−100	−200	−300
Bond interest ('000)	+50	+50	+50	+50	+50	+50	+50
Stock dividend ('000)	0	0	0	0	0	0	0
Margin interest ('000)	−27	−40	−53	−65	−79	−92	−105
Short rebate ('000)	+15	+20	+24	+29	+34	+29	+44
Total p/l ('000)	+82	+46	+25	+14	+10	+12	+19
Amount invested ('000)	162	133	111	97	81	71	62
Leverage	5.7	7.5	9.8	12.1	15.9	19.8	24.5
ROI (%)	+50.7	+34.6	+22.3	+14.3	+12.7	+17.7	+30.5
1) Margin debt calculations ('000)	−50%	−33%	−16%	0	+16%	+33%	+50%
Assumed stock price	50.0	66.7	83.3	100.0	116.7	133.3	150.0
Cvt. market value	931	1,002	1,089	1,186	1,290	1,401	1,516
Delta (%)	47	60	69	75	81	85	88
Unhedged portion (%)	53	40	31	25	19	15	12
Amount unhedged	493	402	336	296	245	214	187
Margin @ 30%	148	121	101	89	74	64	56
Plus lesser of:							
Premium or	531	469	422	386	357	334	316
10% of margin required	15	12	10	9	7	6	5
Total margin	162	132	111	98	81	71	62
Loan amount	−768	−869	−977	−1,087	−1,209	−1,330	−1,454
Short stock adjustment	+300	+200	+100	0	−100	−200	−300
Total margin debt	−468	−669	−878	−1,088	−1,309	−1,530	−1,754
Margin interest (@ 6%)	−27	−40	−53	−65	−79	−92	−105
2) Short rebate calculation ('000)							
Proceeds	300	400	500	600	700	800	900
Rebate (@ 4.875%)	+15	+20	+24	+29	+34	+29	+44

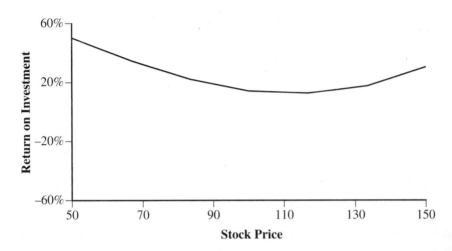

Figure 12.12   Neutral Hedge—Maximum Leverage

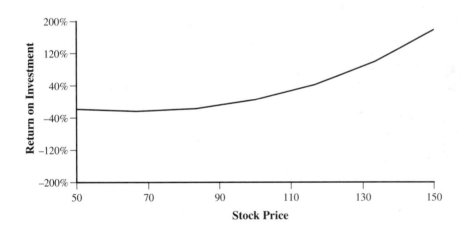

Figure 12.13   Bull Hedge—Maximum Leverage

BEAR HEDGE WITH MAXIMUM LEVERAGE

Here, we earn very attractive returns if the stock price remains flat or falls but lose money if the stock rises. Reducing the hedge to 80% from 95% would eliminate losses on the upside but reduce the maximum gain on the downside from 104.8% to 63.8%. (See Figure 12.14.)

WHEN TO ADJUST THE HEDGE?

In the previous examples we made things easy. We allowed the stock to make large movements before adjusting our hedge ratio. In practice, we would adjust the hedge more frequently to capture the volatility in the stock price. Adjusting the hedge too quickly would limit our potential gain and incur excessive transaction costs. By not adjusting the hedge soon enough, we might miss the opportunity to lock in a profit as the stock price returns to its original level. In carry trades, the need to adjust the hedge is infrequent. In volatility trades, a delta move of 5% or more is usually cause for an adjustment.

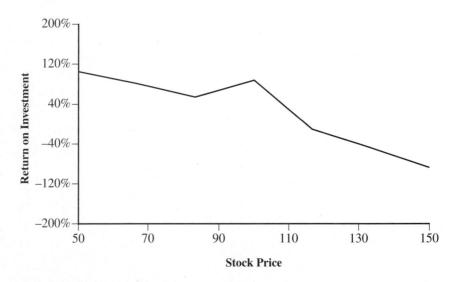

Figure 12.14   Bear Hedge—Maximum Leverage

HOW TO ADJUST THE HEDGE?

The hedge can be adjusted by either buying or selling stock or convertible bonds. If the stock price falls, and the convertible has become theoretically cheaper, it would be wiser to buy more bonds rather than buy back stock to reduce the delta of the position. Similarly, if the convertible richens as the stock price rises, it would be better to increase the hedge by selling some bonds rather than shorting more stock. Calculating the size of the adjustment is simple. If we want to sell short 5 more delta points' worth of stock, we multiply the conversion ratio by 5% and multiply this sum by the number of bonds in our position. To calculate the like number of bonds to buy back, we divide the number of shares to be sold by the conversion ratio times the current delta.

WHEN TO CLOSE OUT THE HEDGE?

If carry or volatility trades are working well, there is no need to close the position. The main reason to close a position early is if it was purchased at a deep discount to theoretical value and has since been rerated. This could happen if a catalyst occurred to improve the stock's valuation or the bond's creditworthiness. Another reason to close a position would be to reallocate capital more efficiently.

WHAT CAN GO WRONG WITH THE HEDGE?

Using a short-stock position to hedge a convertible subjects the arbitrageur to certain unique risks. The most common of these are mentioned below.

Takeover

To a convertible investor, time is an important component of a convertible's value. Not only has the investor paid in advance for the time value embedded in the call warrant, but time is required to earn the yield advantage over the common stock. A takeover bid may accelerate the investor's holding period. The worst case for the arbitrageur is a cash bid when the convertible is selling above par. In our XYZ example, let us assume that the company accepts an all-cash offer for $140—40% above the current stock price. At $140, the parity of the bond rises from 80% to 112%. The arbitrageur loses money on both the short-stock position and the convertible that had been trading at 118.6% on a 48% premium, with the stock at $100. If the bid is for stock, the time element will not be interrupted. However, the value of the convertible could fall if the acquirer's stock paid a higher dividend or had a lower volatility. Of course, a stronger credit rating would lift the convertible valuation, all else being equal. The only other time when an arbitrageur might benefit from a takeover bid is if the bond was trading substantially below par on a light hedge. If a change of control put at par was triggered, the gain in the bond price could surpass the loss on the short-stock position. A change of control is usually triggered if the bid is greater than 50% in stock. Finally, the loss of premium may be mitigated by a special clause in the prospectus that increases the conversion ratio in the event of a successful takeover. (See Chapter 3.)

Special Dividends

The payment of a special dividend can be harmful to the arbitrageur if no compensating adjustment is made to the terms of the convertible. If no adjustment is made, the arbitrageur is still obliged to pay the special dividend on the short-stock position.

Recall of Borrowed Stock

If borrowed stock is called away from the arbitrageur, the hedge position will have to be closed unless the borrow can be replaced. This may occur at an inopportune moment. Lent stock can be recalled for any number of reasons including the original owner's sale of the position, or the desire to be registered for corporate actions or dividend payments.

Other Risks

Many of the assumptions used in estimating the price path of a convertible can change, including interest rates, credit spreads, volatility, and dividend policy. Moreover, in practice there are actually three deltas: the theoretical delta established by the Black–Scholes model, the delta determined by market makers, and the empirical delta, being a measure of where the convertible actually traded. Choosing the correct delta is often more of an art than a science. If the market is disrupted such that liquidity dries up, bid-to-offer spreads widen, or premiums contract, then hedge positions using a large amount of leverage will suffer. This occurred during the October stock market crash in 1987, the Mexican peso devaluation in December 1994, the Russian debt crisis in August 1998, the NASDAQ meltdown in March 2000, and the terrorist attack on the U.S. in September 2001. For example, CEMEX, the Mexican cement company, had issued a three-year, dollar-denominated, convertible bond due in November 1997. Before the devaluation, the bonds traded on a delta-neutral hedge of 75%. In order to avoid losing money after the devaluation, a hedge of at least 125% would have been required as the investment value fell and the premium contracted. The bonds eventually traded down to fifty cents on the dollar, offering a 33% yield to maturity. For long-term investors, these bonds offered exceptional value, eventually maturing at par.

ADDITIONAL NOTES: DEEP IN-THE-MONEY HEDGING STRATEGY

One of the most popular hedging strategies is to set up a deep in-the-money convertible on a heavy hedge ratio. The purpose of this trade is to capitalize on the convertible's yield advantage. This is a carry trade because the gamma of the convertible is very low and delta hedging is irrelevant. However, the absence of any significant conversion premium allows the arbitrageur to set up the position for only the cost of borrowing the stock. Meanwhile, the convertible will continue to pay its coupon while the stock pays little or no dividend. On an unlevered basis, this trade is uninteresting yielding close to the risk-free rate. However, the returns improve markedly once leverage is applied. Being deep in-the-money, the position can be highly leveraged and the hedge proceeds provide enough cash to cover almost the entire long position. This is illustrated in Table 12.7, in which the price of XYZ stock has risen to $600 and its convertible trades at $5,018 (501.8%).

In this case, the arbitrage is nearly risk free and requires minimal capital to finance. In the last scenario, a capital requirement of 2.5%

Table 12.7 XYZ Corporation Convertible Bond
Full Hedge: 99.65%
Varying Leverage

Conversion premium: 5.54%
Funding rate: 6.0%
Rebate on XYZ shares: 5.50%
Various levels of leverage

Strategy: Buy 1 bond at 501.8% and short 7.972 shares at $600

Leverage	Cvt. Price	Capital Needed	Amount Funded	Cost of Funding	Short Proceed	Rebate	Coupon	P&L	ROE
0.0%	5,018	5,018	—	—	4,783	263	50	313	6.2%
10.0%	5,018	4,516	501	30	4,783	263	50	282	6.3%
25.0%	5,018	3,763	1,254	75	4,783	263	50	237	6.3%
50.0%	5,018	2,509	2,509	150	4,783	263	50	162	6.5%
75.0%	5,018	1,254	3,763	225	4,783	263	50	87	7.0%
90.0%	5,018	501	4,516	270	4,783	263	50	42	8.4%
95.0%	5,018	250	4,767	286	4,783	263	50	27	10.8%
97.5%	5,018	125	4,892	293	4,783	263	50	19	15.6%

permits up to 40 times leverage, generating a 15.6% return on capital with minimal risk.

Because of the high hedge ratio, the portfolio is insensitive to changes in the underlying stock price (see Table 12.8).

This strategy is applicable to most deep in-the-money convertibles and is widely used by highly leveraged hedge funds.

Table 12.8 XYZ Corporation Convertible Bond
Full Hedge: 99.65%
Portfolio Sensitivity

Stock Price % Change	−15%	0%	15%
Stock price	510.00	600.00	690.00
Market value of stock	4,065.72	4,783.20	5,500.68
Market value of cvt.	4,301.00	5,018.00	5,736.00
Value of portfolio	235.28	234.80	235.32
P&L	0.48	0.00	0.52

13

HEDGING WITH OPTIONS

INTRODUCTION

A short-stock position can also be created through the use of options. An investor can buy puts, sell calls, or combine these strategies to create a short position. One advantage for individual investors is that the premium earned from selling options against a convertible position can be used immediately. Premiums are not segregated in the margin account like the proceeds from a short-stock sale are. No margin is required as long as the number of shares sold short via the option does not exceed the number of shares underlying the convertible. Proceeds from an option sale earn interest and can be used to reduce the cost of the investment. Conversely, option premium paid adds to the cost of the investment and must be financed. Using options eliminates the need to pay any stock dividends. However, the price of the option already reflects any anticipated dividend payments.

Stock options trade in maturities from one month to five years. We consider options with terms of six months. We show both absolute and annualized returns. When annualizing returns, one assumes that the option position can be rolled over on identical terms after expiration.

This may not be possible because the various inputs to the option pricing model may have changed. Therefore, it is important to consider trades that make sense under both scenarios. All returns are based on a nonleveraged basis.

We have assumed that both the convertible and the options are fairly priced. Consequently, these strategies can change the risk profile of the position but will not enhance returns. The best results are achieved when the convertible is theoretically cheap and the options are mispriced. Equity options, being generally shorter dated than the embedded warrant in a convertible, are more sensitive to immediate changes in implied volatility. For example, if a wave of enthusiasm were to hit the gold market, the implied volatility on short-dated call options of gold mining stocks might increase twice as quickly as that of the corresponding convertibles. This would present an ideal opportunity to short expensive calls, rather than buy expensive puts or to short stock, to create a hedge.

HEDGING CONVERTIBLES WITH PUT OPTIONS: FULL HEDGE

Beginning again with our generic XYZ Corporation convertible, we consider hedging the convertible by buying 80, six-month, put options struck at-the-money. Each put option gives us the right to sell 100 shares of XYZ stock at $100 on expiration. This represents 8,000 shares, which is commensurate to the number of shares underlying our convertible position. Notice that the cost of purchasing downside protection with puts is greater than the accrued interest from the convertibles. This means that if the stock price is unchanged, or declines only marginally, we will lose money. This is in contrast to our neutral hedge with stock, which earns a positive stand-still rate of return. However, if the stock price jumps one way or the other, the option strategy is attractive. On the downside, since the stock price moves down faster than the convertible price, our gain accelerates as the stock price falls. On the upside, once the put premium is recovered, our profit increases as the stock price rises. (See Table 13.1 and Figure 13.1.)

Table 13.2 and Figure 13.2 compare the previous strategy to the alternative of buying the stock plus an equal number of at-the-money

Table 13.1   XYZ Corporation Convertible Bond
100% Hedge with At-the-Money Puts, No Leverage

Strategy 1: Buy 1,000 bonds at 118.57% and buy 80 puts struck at $100							
Buy 1,000 bonds at 118.57%					= $1,185,700		
Buy 80 puts struck at $100 for $9.75 per option					= $ 78,000		
Total investment					= $1,263,700		

Puts expire in 182 days Stock price % change	−50%	−33%	−16%	0	+16%	+33%	+50%
Assumed stock price	50.0	66.7	83.3	100.0	116.7	133.3	150.0
Estimated cvt. price (%)	93.1	100.2	108.9	118.6	129.1	140.1	151.6
Current yield (%)	5.4	5.0	4.6	4.2	3.9	3.6	3.3
Conversion premium (%)	132.6	87.9	63.3	48.2	38.2	31.3	26.3
Parity (%)	40.0	53.3	66.7	80.0	93.3	106.7	120.0
Delta (%)	47.2	59.9	69.1	75.9	80.9	84.7	87.6
P/l convertible ('000)	−255	−183	−96	0	+105	+215	330
P/l put ('000)	+322	+189	+55	−78	−78	−78	−78
Interest paid (@ 5.75)	−2	−2	−2	−2	−2	−2	−2
Bond interest ('000)	+25	+25	+25	+25	+25	+25	+25
Stock dividend ('000)	0	0	0	0	0	0	0
Total p/l ('000)	+90	+28	−18	−55	+49	+160	+275
Amount invested ('000)	1,264	1,264	1,264	1,264	1,264	1,264	1,264
Leverage	0	0	0	0	0	0	0
ROI	+7.1	+2.2	−1.5	−4.4	+3.9	+12.7	+21.7
ROI (annualized)	+14.7	+4.5	−2.9	−8.6	+7.9	+27.0	+48.4

puts. Although the latter strategy outperforms on the upside, it provides little downside support and is expensive to implement.

HEDGING CONVERTIBLES WITH PUT OPTIONS: PARTIAL HEDGE

Bull investors can reduce the number of puts purchased. In Table 13.3 we purchase only 50 puts for a hedge ratio of 62.50%. As expected, this strategy reduces the loss on a stand-still basis, permits modest losses on the downside, and increases returns on the upside. (See also Figure 13.3.)

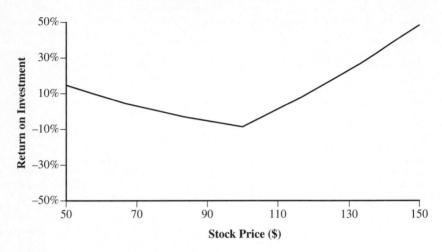

Figure 13.1 Full Hedge: Buy 80 ATM Puts, Unleveraged

Table 13.2 Long Stock Plus Long Puts

Buy 8,000 shares at $100 and buy 80 puts struck at $100 for $9.75 each							
Buy 8,000 shares at $100					= $800,000		
Buy 80 puts struck at $100 for $9.75 per option					= $ 78,000		
Total investment					= $878,000		
Stock price % change	−50%	−33%	−16%	0	+16%	+33%	+50%
Assumed stock price	50.0	66.7	83.3	100.0	116.7	133.3	150.0
Stock p/l	−400	−267	−133	0	+133	+267	+400
Put p/l	+322	+189	+55	−78	−78	−78	−78
Interest paid (@ 5.75)	−2	−2	−2	−2	−2	−2	−2
Total p/l	−79	−79	−79	−79	+53	+187	+320
ROI	−9.1	−9.1	−9.1	−9.1	+6.1	+21.2	+36.5
ROI (annualized)	−17.4	−17.4	−17.4	−17.4	+12.6	+47.2	+86.5

HEDGING CONVERTIBLES WITH CALL OPTIONS: FULL HEDGE

In Table 13.4 we sell 80 calls struck at-the-money. The best circumstance is if the stock price remains unchanged and the option premium enhances our income and reduces our initial investment. As the stock price moves up, we start to get squeezed as the loss on our short-call position begins to catch up with the premium earned, and the gain on the

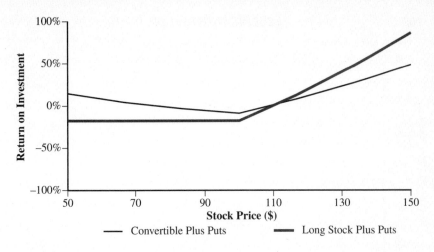

Figure 13.2   Long Stock Plus 80 Puts versus Long Convertible Plus 80 Puts

Table 13.3   XYZ Corporation Convertible Bond
62.50% Hedge with At-the-Money Puts, No Leverage

Strategy 2: Buy 1,000 bonds at 118.57% and buy 50 puts struck at $100						

Buy 1,000 bonds at 118.57%	= $1,185,700
Buy 50 puts struck at $100 for $9.75 per option	= $ 48,750
Total investment	= $1,234,450
Puts expire in 182 days	

Stock price % change	−50%	−33%	−16%	0	+16%	+33%	+50%
Assumed stock price	50.0	66.7	83.3	100.0	116.7	133.3	150.0
Estimated cvt. price (%)	93.1	100.2	108.9	118.6	129.1	140.1	151.6
Current yield (%)	5.4	5.0	4.6	4.2	3.9	3.6	3.3
Conversion premium (%)	132.6	87.9	63.3	48.2	38.2	31.3	26.3
Parity (%)	40.0	53.3	66.7	80.0	93.3	106.7	120.0
Delta (%)	47.2	59.9	69.1	75.9	80.9	84.7	87.6
P/l convertible ('000)	−255	−183	−96	0	+105	+215	330
P/l put ('000)	+201	+118	+35	−49	−49	−49	−49
Interest paid (@ 5.75)	−1	−1	−1	−1	−1	−1	−1
Bond interest ('000)	+25	+25	+25	+25	+25	+25	+25
Stock dividend ('000)	0	0	0	0	0	0	0
Total p/l ('000)	−30	−42	−39	−25	+80	+190	+305
Amount invested ('000)	1,234	1,234	1,234	1,234	1,234	1,234	1,234
Leverage	0	0	0	0	0	0	0
ROI	−2.4	−3.4	−3.1	−2.0	+6.4	+15.4	+24.7
ROI (annualized)	−4.8	−6.7	−6.2	−4.0	+13.3	+33.3	+55.7

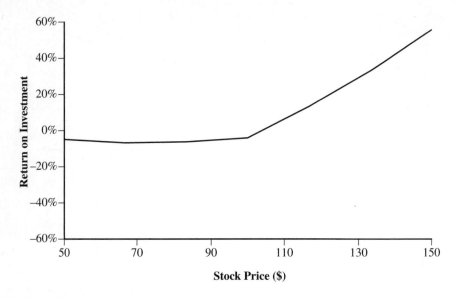

Figure 13.3   Partial Hedge: Buy 50 ATM Puts, Unleveraged

convertible. On the downside, the premium earned cushions the blow as the stock price falls, but provides no real support. (See Figure 13.4.)

HEDGING CONVERTIBLES WITH CALL OPTIONS: PARTIAL HEDGE

The bull investor can change the return profile by selling fewer calls or by selling calls struck out-of-the-money. In Table 13.5 and Figure 13.5, we sell only 50 calls struck 10% out-of-the-money at $110.

In Table 13.6 and Figure 13.6, we contrast the payoffs from Table 13.5 and Figure 13.5 with a long stock position hedged by selling out-of-the-money calls. The convertible hedge strategy outperforms on both the upside and the downside.

HEDGING CONVERTIBLES WITH PUTS AND CALLS: NEUTRAL HEDGE

The previous examples illustrate what we already know about options. If we buy puts and pay a premium, we want the market to

Table 13.4 XYZ Corporation Convertible Bond
100% Hedge with At-the-Money Calls, No Leverage

Strategy 3: Buy 1,000 bonds at 118.57% and sell 80 calls struck at $100	
Buy 1,000 bonds at 118.57%	= $1,185,700
Sell 80 calls struck at $100 for $12.54 per option	= −$100,320
Total investment	= $1,085,380
Calls expire in 182 days	

Stock price % change	−50%	−33%	−16%	0	+16%	+33%	+50%
Assumed stock price	50.0	66.7	83.3	100.0	116.7	133.3	150.0
Estimated cvt. price (%)	93.1	100.2	108.9	118.6	129.1	140.1	151.6
Current yield (%)	5.4	5.0	4.6	4.2	3.9	3.6	3.3
Conversion premium (%)	132.6	87.9	63.3	48.2	38.2	31.3	26.3
Parity (%)	40.0	53.3	66.7	80.0	93.3	106.7	120.0
Delta (%)	47.2	59.9	69.1	75.9	80.9	84.7	87.6
P/l convertible ('000)	−255	−183	−96	0	+105	+215	330
P/l calls ('000)	+100	+100	+100	+100	−133	−267	−400
Interest earned (@ 5.75)	+3	+3	+3	+3	+3	+3	+3
Bond interest ('000)	+25	+25	+25	+25	+25	+25	+25
Stock dividend ('000)	0	0	0	0	0	0	0
Total p/l ('000)	−127	−55	+31	+128	0	−24	−42
Amount invested ('000)	1,085	1,085	1,085	1,085	1,085	1,085	1,085
Leverage	0	0	0	0	0	0	0
ROI	−11.7	−5.1	+2.9	11.8	0.0	−2.2	−3.8
ROI (annualized)	−22.0	−9.9	+5.8	+25.1	0.0	−4.3	−7.6

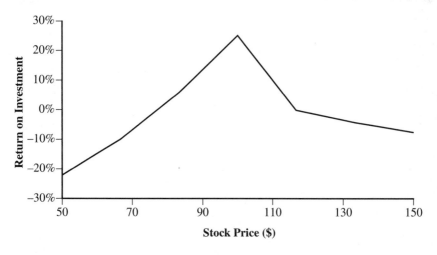

Figure 13.4 Full Hedge: Sell 80 ATM Calls, Unleveraged

Table 13.5 XYZ Corporation Convertible Bond
Partial Hedge with Out-of-the-Money Calls, No Leverage

Strategy 4: Buy 1,000 bonds at 118.57% and sell 50 calls struck at $110		
Buy 1,000 bonds at 118.57		= $1,185,700
Sell 50 calls struck at $110 for $8.49 per option		= −$42,450
Total investment		= $1,143,250
Calls expire in 182 days		

Stock price % change	−50%	−33%	−16%	0	+16%	+33%	+50%
Assumed stock price	50.0	66.7	83.3	100.0	116.7	133.3	150.0
Estimated cvt. price (%)	93.1	100.2	108.9	118.6	129.1	140.1	151.6
Current yield (%)	5.4	5.0	4.6	4.2	3.9	3.6	3.3
Conversion premium (%)	132.6	87.9	63.3	48.2	38.2	31.3	26.3
Parity (%)	40.0	53.3	66.7	80.0	93.3	106.7	120.0
Delta (%)	47.2	59.9	69.1	75.9	80.9	84.7	87.6
P/l convertible ('000)	−255	−183	−96	0	+105	+215	330
P/l calls ('000)	+42	+42	+42	+42	−33	−117	−200
Interest earned (@ 5.75)	+1	+1	+1	+1	+1	+1	+1
Bond interest ('000)	+25	+25	+25	+25	+25	+25	+25
Stock dividend ('000)	0	0	0	0	0	0	0
Total p/l ('000)	−187	−115	−28	+69	+97	+125	+156
Amount invested ('000)	1,143	1,143	1,143	1,143	1,143	1,143	1,143
Leverage	0	0	0	0	0	0	0
ROI	−16.3	−10.0	−2.5	+6.0	+8.5	+10.9	+13.7
ROI (annualized)	−30.0	−19.1	−4.9	+12.4	+17.8	+23.1	+29.3

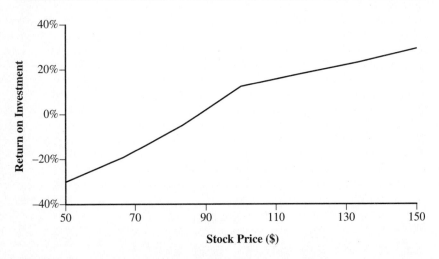

Figure 13.5 Partial Hedge: Sell 50 OTM Calls, Unleveraged

Table 13.6 Long Stock Plus Short Calls

Buy 8,000 shares at $100 and sell 80 calls struck at $110 for $8.49 each

Stock price % change	−50%	−33%	−16%	0	+16%	+33%	+50%
Assumed stock price	50.0	66.7	83.3	100.0	116.7	133.3	150.0
Stock p/l	−400	−267	−133	0	+133	+267	+400
Call p/l	+68	+68	+68	+68	−53	−187	−320
Interest earned (@ 5.75)	+2	+2	+2	+2	+2	+2	+2
Total p/l	−330	−197	−63	+69	+82	+82	+82
ROI	−45.2	−26.9	−8.7	+9.5	+11.2	+11.2	+11.2
ROI (annualized)	−70.1	−46.7	−16.7	+20.1	+23.8	+23.8	+23.8

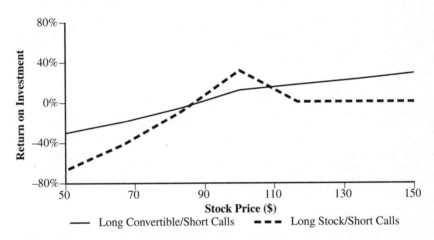

Figure 13.6 Long Stock/Short Calls versus Long Convertible/Short Calls

move. If we earn a premium by selling calls, we want the market to stand still. By buying puts and selling calls, we can combine the attributes of both. In Table 13.7 and Figure 13.7 we illustrate the payoff from hedging the long convertible position by selling 50 calls and buying 50 puts, both struck at-the-money. This generates a payoff similar to the neutral stock hedge we created in Table 13.2. By altering the number of options and their strike prices, we can modify the return profile to match our view of the market.

Table 13.7 XYZ Corporation Convertible Bond
Partial Hedge with ATM Puts and Calls, No Leverage

Strategy 5: Buy 1,000 bonds at 118.57%, sell 50 calls and buy 50 puts, both struck at $100

Buy 1,000 bonds at 118.57%	= $1,185,700
Sell 50 calls struck at $100 for $12.54 per option	= −$62,700
Buy 50 puts struck at $100 for $9.72 per option	= $48,600
Total investment	= $1,171,600
Options expire in 182 days	

Stock price % change	−50%	−33%	−16%	0	+16%	+33%	+50%
Assumed stock price	50.0	66.7	83.3	100.0	116.7	133.3	150.0
Estimated cvt. price (%)	93.1	100.2	108.9	118.6	129.1	140.1	151.6
Current yield (%)	5.4	5.0	4.6	4.2	3.9	3.6	3.3
Conversion premium (%)	132.6	87.9	63.3	48.2	38.2	31.3	26.3
Parity (%)	40.0	53.3	66.7	80.0	93.3	106.7	120.0
Delta (%)	47.2	59.9	69.1	75.9	80.9	84.7	87.6
P/l convertible ('000)	−255	−183	−96	0	+105	+215	330
P/l calls ('000)	+63	+63	+63	+63	−83	−167	−250
Interest earned (@ 5.75)	+2	+2	+2	+2	+1	+2	+2
P/l puts ('000)	+201	+118	+35	−49	−49	−49	−49
Interest paid (@ 5.75)	−1	−1	−1	−1	−1	−1	−1
Bond interest ('000)	+25	+25	+25	+25	+25	+25	+25
Stock dividend ('000)	0	0	0	0	0	0	0
Total p/l ('000)	+34	+22	+25	+39	−2	+25	+57
Amount invested ('000)	1,172	1,172	1,172	1,172	1,172	1,172	1,172
Leverage	0	0	0	0	0	0	0
ROI	+2.9	+1.9	+2.2	+3.4	+0.0	+2.2	+4.9
ROI (annualized)	+5.9	+3.9	+4.4	+6.7	+0.0	+4.4	+10.0

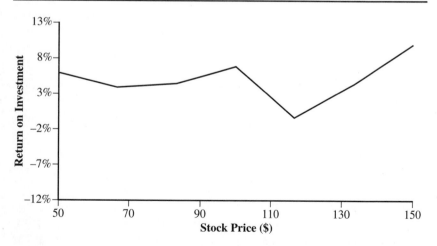

Figure 13.7 Partial Hedge: Sell ATM Calls/Buy ATM Puts, Unleveraged

14

HEDGING INTEREST RATE AND DEFAULT RISK

HEDGING INTEREST RATE RISK

In Chapter 9, we explained how to calculate the price sensitivity of a convertible bond with respect to a change in interest rates (rho). A shift in interest rates affects the convertible's investment value and its warrant value. The investment value is inversely proportional to the movement in interest rates, while the warrant price is directly proportional. In convertible securities, a change in interest rates also affects the warrant's exercise price, which is tied to the investment value. Convertibles that are deep in-the-money have very low interest-rate sensitivity compared to those deep out-of-the-money, because the former behave like equity and the latter like debt.

In Chapter 9, we determined that the implied duration of our generic XYZ convertible was approximately 0.89 years. Knowing this duration, how can we hedge for a change in interest rates?

THE CASH HEDGE: SHORTING TREASURIES

The first method is to short a U.S. Treasury security with a similar duration. If the duration is not identical, we can sell short a ratio-adjusted proportion of Treasuries to hedge our position. For example, on 14 April 2000, the current on-the-run, five-year Treasury note, the 5.875% of November 2004, sold at 99.0781% and had a duration of 3.97 years. All U.S. Treasury notes have a denomination of $1,000. Thus, to hedge our original long convertible position of $1,185,700 (see Chapter 12), we should sell short $265,812 worth of the current five-year Treasury note, or 268 notes.

$$\text{Cash hedge ratio} = \frac{\dfrac{\text{Duration of the convertible}}{\text{Duration of the hedging instrument}} \cdot \text{Market value of the convertible}}{\text{Market price of the hedging instrument}}$$

$$= \frac{\dfrac{0.89}{3.97} \cdot \$1,185,700}{\$990.78}$$

$$= \frac{\$265,812}{\$990.78}$$

$$= 268.29 \text{ notes}$$

The Treasury yield curve is not linear, so this hedge will work only for small changes in interest rates. The hedge must be monitored and adjusted after larger interest rate movements. The hedge also assumes a parallel shift in interest rates. If short rates rise while long rates remain unchanged, the duration of the convertible will decline relative to the hedging instrument and create a mismatch. Finally, shorting Treasuries is not free. The hedger must pay the lender the coupon on the Treasury. In return, the hedger earns interest on the cash proceeds from the short sale (the reverse repurchase rate). This results in a negative spread of typically 1%, but may vary depending on the available supply of Treasuries. After the stock market crash in October 1987, few institutions were prepared to lend Treasuries because they feared their counterparty's credit-worthiness. Under these circumstances, the reverse repurchase rate went to 0% and stayed there for more than six weeks. This was the worst possible situation for anyone short Treasuries because they had to pay away the full coupon but received no interest on the cash proceeds from the short sale.

THE FUTURES HEDGE

The Markets

Since their origin in 1975, financial futures markets in the United States have grown rapidly. Currently, there are futures contracts on a number of financial instruments including three-month eurodollar deposits, three-month domestic certificates of deposit, ninety-day U.S. Treasury bills, U.S. Treasury notes and bonds, and Government National Mortgage Association (GNMA) securities. Financial futures contracts are also available on a host of both short- and long-dated foreign instruments. Today, because of the many uses of financial futures in portfolio management, it is not surprising that the market value of these contracts far exceeds the actual value of cash instruments traded on a daily basis.

THE U.S. TREASURY BOND FUTURES CONTRACT

One of the most liquid futures contracts is the Treasury bond futures contract that is traded on the Chicago Board of Trade (CBOT).

Conventions

Treasury bond prices, and their futures contracts, are quoted in dollars and thirty-seconds of a dollar. A quote of 100-16 indicates a price of $100^{16}/_{32}$, or $100.50 in decimal form. The denomination of a Treasury bond is $1,000. Each futures contract calls for the delivery of 100 Treasury bonds for a contract value of $100,000. If the price of the futures contract increases by $1, the value of the futures contract will rise by $1,000. The minimum price movement on the contract is $31.25 because the smallest price change is $1/_{32}$. Delivery can be made at any time during the delivery month. All financial futures contracts have a March, June, September, December delivery cycle. The nearby futures contract may be delivered in a range from one to approximately 90 days, while the longest dated contracts may extend some 30 months into the future.

The Treasury bond futures contract calls for delivery of a 20-year government bond with a 6% coupon. Since such a bond is unlikely to exist on the delivery date, any government bond with more than 15 years to maturity (and not callable before 15 years) may be delivered. The party who holds the short position in the contract chooses which bond to deliver.

The Cheapest to Deliver Treasury

Determining the cheapest to deliver Treasury is important for two reasons. First, it is the bond that is used to calculate the futures price. Second, it is the duration of this bond that is used to calculate the interest rate hedge ratio.

The cheapest to deliver Treasury is the eligible Treasury with the highest implied repo rate. The implied repo rate is the assumed financing rate in the futures price equation that causes the cash plus carry to equate to the observed price of the futures contract. In other words, it is the break-even financing rate for cash/futures arbitrage. If the implied repo rate is higher than the cost of financing, the investor should buy the cash instrument and sell the futures contract. This is known as a "cash and carry" trade. If the implied repo rate is lower than the cost of financing, then the investor should sell the cash and buy the futures contract. In equilibrium, the implied repo rate will equal the financing rate.

The Conversion Factor

The conversion factor equates the bond to be delivered with the nominal 6% coupon bond called for in the futures contract. To replicate the notional bond as closely as possible, the CBOT stipulates what settlement and maturity dates to use on the deliverable bond. The settlement date is the first day in the delivery month of the futures contract. The maturity date is the first delivery date of the contract that expires closest to the maturity of the bond. The conversion factor is calculated by setting the yield to maturity of the Treasury bond to be delivered equal to 6%, and dividing this price by 100. On 14 April 2000, the cheapest to deliver Treasury bond for the December 2000 contract was the 8.875% of 15-August-17 trading at 128.125%. Its conversion factor of 1.2985 is calculated next.

U.S. Treasury bond 8.875% due 15-Aug-17	
Coupon	8.875%
Settlement date (t plus 3 days)	17-Apr-00
Maturity date	15-Aug-17
Price	128.125
Yield to maturity	6.20%
Adjusted settlement date	01-Dec-00
Adjusted maturity date	1-Jun-17
Adjusted yield to maturity	6.0%
New price	129.850
Conversion factor	1.2985

The conversion factor tells us that the cheapest to deliver bond is equivalent to 1.2985 of the nominal 6% bond underlying the contract. The conversion factor is greater than 1 because the coupon on the cheapest to deliver bond is greater than 6%. To satisfy the contract, we need to deliver only 0.7701 (1.000/1.2985) of the cheapest to deliver bond for every Treasury underlying the futures contract, or 77 bonds (0.7701 · 100 = 77 bonds). Any fractional amounts are rounded.

CALCULATING THE U.S. TREASURY BOND CASH FUTURES PRICE

The Treasury bond cash futures price (F) is calculated according to the following formula:

$$F = (S - I) \cdot e^{r(T-t)}$$

where S = cash value of the cheapest to deliver bond at time t
I = present value of any coupon payments due the bond holder
T = maturity date of the futures contract
t = current time period
r = risk-free rate of interest

Cash Value of the Cheapest to Deliver Treasury Bond

The cash value of the bond (S) is equal to its quoted price plus any accrued interest since the last coupon date. In the preceding example the cash price of the cheapest to deliver bond is $129.637.

Current price	128.125
Coupon	8.875%
Payment frequency	Semiannually
Day count	Actual/actual
Last coupon payment	15-Feb-00
Settlement date	17-Apr-00
Number of days accrued	62

$$\text{Cash price} = \$128.125 + \left(\frac{62}{182} \cdot \frac{8.875}{2} \right)$$
$$= \$128.125 + \$1.512$$
$$= \$129.637$$

Present Value of Interest Due to the Bond Holder

The next coupon payment of 4.4375% will be made in 120 days (0.3287 years). The present value of this payment assuming a risk-free rate of 6.0% is 4.351.

$$0.44375 \cdot e^{-0.3287 \cdot .06} = 4.351$$

Term of the Cash Futures Contract ($T - t$)

The last delivery day for the December 2000 contract is 29 December 2000. The contract will remain outstanding for 256 days (0.7013 years). (See Figure 14.1.)

Cash Futures Price

Thus, the cash futures price, if the contract were written on the cheapest to deliver 8.875% Treasury bond, would be 130.671.

$$F = (S - I) \cdot e^{r(T-t)}$$
$$= (129.637 - 4.351) \cdot e^{0.7013 \cdot .06} = 130.671$$

QUOTED FUTURES PRICE

Adjusting for Accrued Interest

At delivery, there are 136 days of accrued interest equal to 3.279. The quoted futures price is the cash futures price less the accrued interest, or 127.391 (130.671 − 3.279 = 127.391).

Adjusting for the Nominal Bond

This price is based on the cheapest to deliver bond, the 8.875% of 15-August-17. However, the Treasury bond futures contract is based on the nominal 6% bond. To calculate the correct futures price, we must adjust the above price by the conversion factor. The correct futures price is 98.106 (127.391/1.2985 = 98.106). We round this figure up to the next thirty-second of a point, or 98-4 (98.125).

CONSTRUCTING THE FUTURES HEDGE

Returning to our original XYZ convertible example, we are long 1,000 bonds at 118.57%, or $1,185,700. The convertible has an implied duration of 0.89 years. The December Treasury bond futures price is 98-4

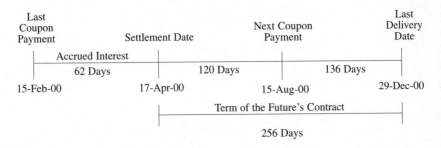

Figure 14.1 Treasury Bond Future's Price: Time Line

or $98,125 per contract. The cheapest to deliver Treasury bond has a duration of 9.7 years. The duration-based hedge ratio is calculated as follows:

$$\text{Futures hedge ratio} = \frac{\dfrac{\text{Duration of the convertible}}{\text{Duration of the hedging instrument}} \cdot \text{Market value of the convertible}}{\text{Market price of one unit of the hedging instrument}}$$

$$= \frac{\dfrac{0.89}{9.7} \cdot \$1,185,700}{\$98,125}$$

$$= \frac{\$108,791}{\$98,125}$$

$$= 1.108 \text{ futures contracts}$$

Therefore, to hedge our position we would sell one December 2000 Treasury bond contract.

THE OPTION HEDGE

Options are also available on many futures contracts. We can hedge interest-rate risk by buying puts or selling calls on the Treasury bond futures contract. Once we know how many futures contracts to sell, we can easily calculate the number of options we would need to duplicate that position. Consider the December 2000 Treasury bond put option with a strike price of 98. The delta of this option is 47%. Instead of shorting 1.108 futures contracts with a delta of 100%, we could alternatively buy 2 put options (1.108/.47 = 2.35).

HEDGING DEFAULT RISK

Although we can immunize the convertible from changes in the absolute level of interest rates, we are still at risk for deteriorating credit quality. Declining credit quality will widen the credit spread and lower the investment value. One way to eliminate both credit risk and interest rate risk is to short a straight bond of the issuer. Unfortunately, this debt may not exist, borrowing it may be impossible, or the cost of carry may be prohibitive. An alternative way to hedge the issuer's default risk is with a callable asset swap.

THE ASSET SWAP MARKET

In a callable asset swap, the hedger sells the convertible to another counterparty, usually a broker or an investment bank, in exchange for cash and an over-the-counter American-style call option. The cash component is equal to the investment value of the convertible. The call option gives the hedger the right to call the convertible from the broker at its investment value, subject to certain adjustments. Having sold the convertible's straight-bond component, the hedger has immunized the default risk and is left holding only the embedded call warrant. In Figure 14.2 we refer once again to our generic XYZ convertible.

As long as the swap remains outstanding, the hedger is exposed to interest rates only as they affect the price of the warrant. If the convertible is called, the hedger has the right to terminate the asset swap early and call the convertible from the broker. The credit spread remains fixed once the convertible's investment value is determined. Any change in the issuer's credit quality will not affect the hedger. The hedger's credit risk has been transferred from the convertible is-

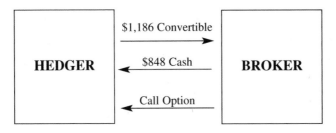

Figure 14.2 Callable Asset Swap: Hedger/Broker: Initial Cash Flows (Step One)

suer to the broker, since the broker is obliged to return the original convertible security to the hedger.

THE MECHANICS: INITIATING THE ASSET SWAP

In Figure 14.3 (step two), the hedger sells the convertible to the broker at a price of $1,186 (118.6%) in exchange for cash equal to the convertible's investment value ($848 or 84.8%) plus a call option. The investment value is determined by the yield to maturity, which is a function of interest rates and the issuer's credit quality. In this case, the investment value is 84.8%, representing a yield to maturity of 8.83% (see Chapter 8). This means that the balance of the convertible's price, or 33.8%, is the implied value of the embedded call warrant.

In step two, the broker immediately sells the convertible (without its conversion rights) to a straight-bond investor at par (100%). The straight-bond investor is usually an insurance company or a bank that funds itself on a floating-rate basis. Floating rates are usually set off the London Interbank Offered Rate (LIBOR), which is the rate at which banks are willing to trade deposits of varying maturities with one another. The extra cash received up front by the broker from sell-

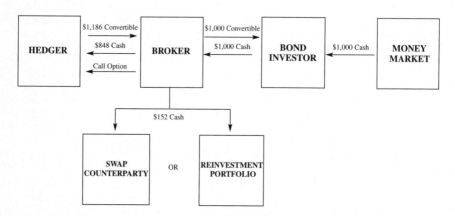

Figure 14.3 Callable Asset Swap: Hedger/Broker/Swap Counterparty/Bond Investor: Cash Flows (Step Two)

ing the bond at 100% ($152 or 15.2%) must be reinvested in order to earn the difference between the convertible's 5% coupon and its 8.83% yield to maturity.

CALLABLE ASSET SWAP: CASH FLOWS

Figure 14.4 illustrates the cash flows of the asset swap while it remains outstanding. The bond investor is content. Via an interest rate swap, a fixed-rate asset (the bond) has been converted into a floating-rate asset paying a 1.75% spread. The investor receives the 5% coupon on the bond and pays away only 3.25% to the broker. The 1.75% spread is locked in (5.00% − 3.25% = 1.75%). No matter what happens to interest rates, the investor will earn this spread over his or her cost of funds (LIBOR). Both fixed- and floating-rate cash flows are made semiannually as the bond coupon is paid and the LIBOR reference rate is reset.

The broker hedges his or her interest rate risk by entering into an interest rate swap with a counterparty. In this swap, the broker receives LIBOR and makes a fixed-rate payment. Here, the broker has a choice. He or she can manage the reinvestment risk on the extra cash

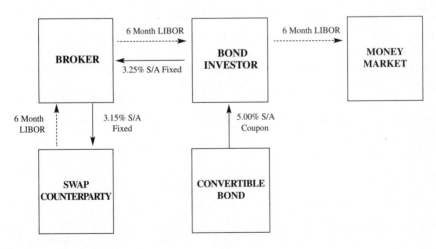

Figure 14.4   Callable Asset Swap: Broker/Bond Investor, No Reinvestment Risk

received from the bond investor ($152); or the broker can pass it on to his or her swap counterparty and make a lower fixed-rate payment. If he or she chooses the latter, the broker will pay 3.15% semiannually retaining 0.10% as the profit. For the broker, the swap is an off-balance-sheet transaction.

If the broker elects to manage the reinvestment of the extra cash, he or she will enter into an interest-rate swap at prevailing market rates. The swap rate is a function of the current level of interest rates plus a swap spread. In Figure 14.5, the five-year Treasury yield is 5.75%, and the five-year swap spread is 50 basis points (0.50%). Thus, the all-in-five-year swap rate is 6.25%. The swap spread reflects the general level of credit risk in the interbank market, which is perceived to be single A. This spread may change owing to supply and demand, or due to perceived changes in credit risk. During the Russian debt crisis of August 1998, five-year swap spreads rose to greater than 1.25%.

In Figure 14.5, the broker now has a negative mismatch in fixed-rate cash flows. He or she receives a 3.25% payment from the bond investor, but must pay out 6.25% in the interest-rate swap. How does the broker make up for the 3.00% shortfall and still make a 0.10% profit? Fundamentally, we know the math must work out. The difference between the yield to maturity on the convertible's investment value (8.83%), and its 5% coupon is 3.83%. This means that the broker can cover the complete shortfall of 3.00% and still be left with 0.83% of profit per annum. Unfortunately, to accomplish this, the broker must invest the excess cash in an asset with the same payment dates and credit quality (yield) as the convertible (B+). Alternatively, the broker can eliminate the reinvestment risk by purchasing zero-coupon Treasury strips. In Table 14.1, we show how the excess cash can be reinvested to cover the 3% per annum shortfall (1.50% semiannually) and still lock in a profit of 0.50%. The cash invested is $152 per $1,000 face amount of the asset swap.

CALLING THE SWAP

Figure 14.6 illustrates the cash flows if the hedger decides to terminate the asset swap early. The hedger is required to pay the broker a penalty that is passed on to the bond investor. This penalty, or

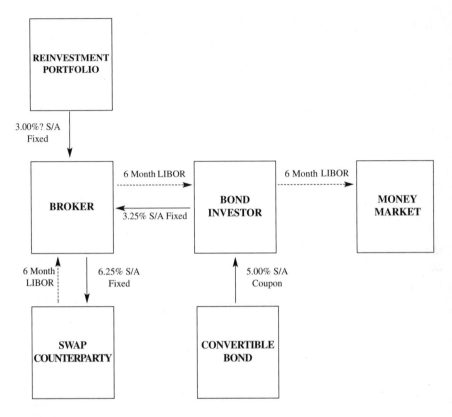

Figure 14.5   Callable Asset Swap: Broker/Bond Investor, Reinvestment Risk

make-whole agreement, is designed to compensate the bond investor for the loss of future income. Generally, it applies only during the first six months of the transaction. Swap payments are usually made semiannually. If the swap is called after three months, the hedger must pay the bond investor (via the broker) a penalty equal to the present value of the spread due the bond investor on the fixed-rate leg of the swap for the remaining three-month period. Moreover, since the bond investor must break the six-month LIBOR funding arrangement early and replace it with a three-month LIBOR deposit (he or she receives cash in exchange for returning the bond to the broker), the hedger must compensate the bond investor for any loss incurred. If the three-month LIBOR is lower than the

Table 14.1   Callable Asset Swap: Broker's Reinvestment Risk

Cash flow per $1,000 invested

	Percent	Cash Flow		
Cash inflow (P/A)	3.25%	$32.50	Interest rate	5.75%
Swap outflow (P/A)	−6.25%	−$62.50	Periods per year	2
Reinvested cash flow (P/A)	3.00%	$30.00	Yield curve slope (S/A)	0.10%
(a) Cash received from the bond investor			$152.00	
(b) Present value of reinvested cash flow			$130.89	
Difference (a–b)			$21.11	
Semiannual profit			0.25%	
Annual profit			0.50%	

Period	(1) Cash Inflow	(2) Swap Outflow	(1–2) Deficit	(3) Reinvested Cash Flow	Discount Rate	Present Value of (3)
1	$16.25	−$31.25	−$15.00	$15.00	1.975%	$14.71
2	$16.25	−$31.25	−$15.00	$15.00	2.075%	$14.40
3	$16.25	−$31.25	−$15.00	$15.00	2.175%	$14.06
4	$16.25	−$31.25	−$15.00	$15.00	2.275%	$13.71
5	$16.25	−$31.25	−$15.00	$15.00	2.375%	$13.34
6	$16.25	−$31.25	−$15.00	$15.00	2.475%	$12.95
7	$16.25	−$31.25	−$15.00	$15.00	2.575%	$12.55
8	$16.25	−$31.25	−$15.00	$15.00	2.675%	$12.14
9	$16.25	−$31.25	−$15.00	$15.00	2.775%	$11.72
10	$16.25	−$31.25	−$15.00	$15.00	2.875%	$11.30
Total	$162.50	−$312.50	−$150.00	$150.00		$130.89

previous six-month rate, the hedger will have to pay the bond investor the present value of this difference. If rates have risen, the bond investor generally enjoys the benefit of the higher deposit rate. If the swap is called after the initial six-month period, typically only a LIBOR rate adjustment is required, but no further make-whole payment is made.

Finally, the broker's interest rate swap must be unwound. If in-

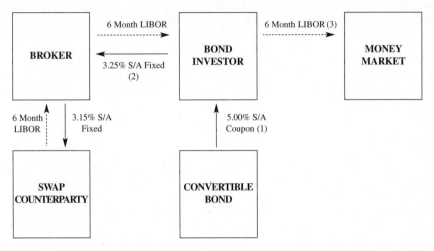

Note:
Hedger pays a penalty to the bond investor (via the broker) as follows:

a) Present value of the 1.75% spread on the national amount of the bond for three-months (1-2) plus
b) Present value of the loss (if any) on replacing the bond investor's floating rate funding until the next reset period (3).

Figure 14.6 Callable Asset Swap: Calling the Swap before the First Reset Date

terest rates have fallen, unwinding the swap will cost the hedger money. This is because the fixed-rate receiver (the broker's interest-rate swap counterparty) is able only to replace the broken swap with a lower fixed-rate payment. The hedger must pay the broker the present value of the difference between these two rates over the remaining life of the swap. On the floating-rate leg of the swap, the hedger gains the present value of the difference between the original floating-rate payment and the lower replacement rate until the next reset date. This works out well for the hedger. The gain on the floating-rate leg of the swap is commensurate to the adjustment due the bond investor. The loss on the fixed-rate leg of the swap is compensated for by a gain in the convertible's investment value. The hedger realizes this gain when he or she calls the swap and recovers the convertible. Conversely, if interest rates rise, the gain on breaking the fixed-rate leg of the swap is offset by the loss on the investment value. The hedger must pay the loss on the floating-rate

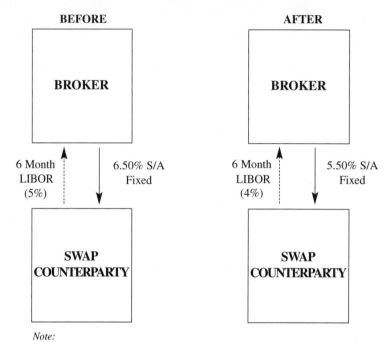

Note:

Effect on the Fixed-Rate Leg of the Interest Rate Swap

The hedger pays the broker, (who pays his swap counterparty), the present value of 1% times the notional amount of the swap, over its remaining term. The hedger's loss is mitigated by the gain in the convertible's investment value.

Effects on the Floating-Rate Leg of the Interest Rate Swap

The broker gains the present value of 1% times the notional amount of the swap until the next LIBOR reset period. This gain is passed on to the bond buyer.

Figure 14.7 Callable Asset Swap: Effect of an Early Call on the Broker's Swap Counterparty: Interest Rates Fall by 1%

leg of the swap since the bond investor usually retains this benefit. (See Figures 14.7 and 14.8.)

The end result is the same regardless of how the broker structured the transaction. If the broker invested the excess cash, the gain on the Treasury strips due to a decline in interest rates would be netted against the negative adjustment on the fixed-rate leg of

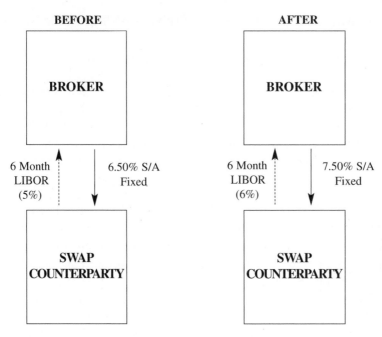

BEFORE

AFTER

Note:

Fixed Leg of the Interest Rate Swap

The broker receives from the swap counterparty, (and pays to the hedger), the present value of 1% times the notional amount of the swap over its remaining term. The hedger's gain is mitigated by the loss in the convertible's investment value.

Floating Leg of the Interest Rate Swap

The hedger pays the broker, who pays the swap counterparty, the present value of 1% times the notional amount of the swap until the next LIBOR reset period. The hedger receives no compensation from the bond investor.

Figure 14.8 Callable Asset Swap: Effect of an Early Call on the Broker's Swap Counterparty: Interest Rates Rise by 1%

the swap. Conversely, if interest rates rose, the loss on the Treasuries would be netted against the gain on breaking the swap transaction. If the broker avoided the reinvestment risk by paying the cash to the swap counterparty, the amount of cash returned to the broker upon termination of the swap would likewise reflect any change in interest rates.

CALLABLE ASSET SWAPS: BENEFITS AND DRAWBACKS

The first benefit is to eliminate the default risk of the issuer. Once the asset swap price has been agreed upon (the convertible's investment value determined), the credit spread is locked in. Guaranteeing the price of the investment value is of great worth to the hedger. He or she has succeeded in isolating the cheap volatility of the convertible's embedded call warrant. The bond investor now accepts the default risk of the issuer. This does not mean that the hedger is void of default risk. He or she has replaced the default risk of the issuer with that of the broker, who must return the convertible if called upon to do so. The second benefit of separating the warrant from the bond is that less capital is required to set up a hedge position. The broker will accept the call option on the asset swap, which he or she has written, as collateral against the hedger's short-stock position. This trade maximizes the hedger's return on capital.

The first drawback is that asset swaps may be available only on investment grade credits and not on speculative credits where the hedger would most like to lay off the credit risk. Table 14.2 illustrates the typical pricing of secondary market convertible asset swaps.

The second drawback is that the hedger is not immune from changes in interest-rate swap spreads. The hedger has a mismatch between corporate bond spreads and swap spreads. If swap spreads fall (rise) faster (slower) than corporate bond spreads, the hedger will lose money in an unwind.

Finally, if the convertible that is being asset swapped is out-of-the-money, there will be a close correlation between its price and the value of the broker's swap position for any given change in interest

Table 14.2   Callable Asset Swaps: Bid Levels

Issuer	Credit Rating	Level
Allianz	AAA	LIBOR + 30 basis points
France Telecom	A–	LIBOR + 120 basis points
Siemens	AA	LIBOR + 50 basis points
Vivendi	BBB	LIBOR +110 basis points
Roche	NR	LIBOR + 65 basis points

Source: Merrill Lynch, May 2001

rates. If the swap is called, any gain (loss) in the swap will be offset by a loss (gain) in the investment value. However, if the convertible is deep in-the-money, its price will not be affected by changing interest rates, while the broker's swap position will be. This creates a mismatch. If rates rise, and the convertible price remains unchanged, the hedger will make a net gain when the broker's swap is unwound. Conversely, if rates fall, the hedger will be required to make the broker whole for terminating the swap, but will not be compensated by a commensurate gain in the convertible price. Since hedgers trading volatility favor equity-sensitive call warrants (in-the-money), which are more likely to be called, the latter case poses a real threat. To eliminate this risk, the hedger needs to buy a Treasury security, or derivative product, to match the duration of the swap. Executing such a hedge reduces the profitability of the trade since it either requires the use of capital (purchasing Treasuries) or costs money (pays an option premium or puts up a futures margin).

CREDIT DEFAULT SWAPS

A credit default swap (CDS) is a bilateral contract that enables a bond investor to buy protection against the risk of default. The protection buyer makes a fixed periodic payment, typically expressed in basis points per annum, over the life of the agreement. The protection seller makes no payments unless a specific credit event occurs. Credit events are defined in the 1999 International Swap Dealers Association (ISDA) Credit Derivative definitions. These events include bankruptcy, failure to pay, obligation acceleration or default, repudiation or moratorium, and restructuring. Following a credit event, a default swap is settled in two ways. In a physical settlement, the protection buyer delivers the defaulted security to the protection seller in return for its par value in cash. In a cash settlement, the protection buyer receives par minus the default price of the underlying security paid in cash. The default price is established once the recovery value of the security has stabilized. Physical settlement is most commonly used (see Figure 14.9).

The fee paid for protection is called the default swap spread, which is linked to the credit quality of the underlying asset. This spread is closely linked to credit spreads in the cash market. However,

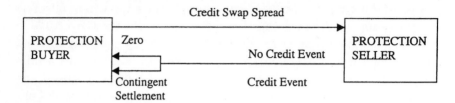

Figure 14.9   Mechanics of a Credit Default Swap

because CDSs are tradable securities, market forces including liquidity and supply and demand affect their prices. The spread, or basis, between the cash market and the default swap market is largely determined by the cost of financing the underlying security (repo rate). In theory, in order to avoid arbitrage, the default swap spread is equal to the spread earned on the asset less the financing cost. The spread earned on the asset and the cost of financing are both expressed as a spread over LIBOR.

In recent years, the credit default swap market has become the most liquid credit derivative instrument. Starting from a notional value of just USD 50 billion in 1996, the credit derivative market has grown to over USD 1 trillion as of the end of 2000. Credit default swaps comprise about 38% of this market. In the U.S. convertible market, credit default swaps constitute about 90% of the market for default protection versus only 10% for asset swaps. In Europe, credit

Table 14.3   Differences between Asset Swaps and Credit Default Swaps

Credit Default Swaps	Asset Swaps
• Standard contracts	• Nonstandard contracts
• Not callable	• Callable
• Hedges spread risk	• Hedges spread and rate risk
• No leverage	• Leverage
• Easier to assign	• Difficult to assign
• No fixed income optionality	• Credit spread option struck at the recall spread
• Lower spread over LIBOR	• Higher spread over LIBOR

Source: Deutsche Bank

default swaps are growing in popularity; they now make up about 60% of the market.

The major differences between credit default swaps and asset swaps are summarized in Table 14.3. There are two main differences. First, in an asset swap the hedger receives an up-front cash payment in exchange for selling the investment value of the convertible to the bond buyer. This frees up capital for the hedger and provides more leverage. In a credit default swap there is no up-front cash payment, so leverage is unchanged. Second, the hedger has the right to call an asset swap, while credit default swaps are not callable. In an asset swap, the hedger can benefit from an improvement in the credit quality of the underlying asset as spreads tighten. The default swap buyer enjoys no such option. Consequently, default swap spreads tend to be lower than asset swap spreads.

15

HEDGING CURRENCY RISK

The convertible market is a global market (see Chapter 4). Domestic convertible investors who invest internationally are subject to currency risk. This risk can be substantial. There are four different cases of currency exposure. We will identify each case and how it affects both the outright and hedged convertible investor. Each example is explained from the point of view of a U.S. dollar based investor. Before proceeding, a brief explanation of the foreign exchange market follows.

THE FOREIGN EXCHANGE MARKET

The foreign exchange market is a large market trading hundreds of billions of dollars worth of currencies daily. There is no central market. Transactions are executed over the phone or via other electronic means. The principal dealers are the large commercial and investment banks.

QUOTATION CONVENTIONS

Indirect Quotes (Foreign Currency Per Dollar)

Generally, exchange rates are quoted in the number of units of foreign currency required to purchase one U.S. dollar. This is known as an indirect quote. For example, a dollar/yen rate of 100 means that you can buy 100 yen with one dollar. If the yen were to depreciate 10% against the dollar, it would take more yen to buy one dollar. We would then expect a quote of 110 yen to the dollar and vice versa.

Direct Quotes (Dollars Per Foreign Currency)

To make life more interesting, some currencies are quoted in exactly the opposite manner. For example, the British pound and the euro are quoted in the number of dollars you can buy with one unit of the foreign currency. This is known as a direct quote. A euro/dollar rate of 1.05 means that you can buy 1.05 dollars with one euro. If the euro were to depreciate against the dollar, one euro would buy fewer dollars so the quote would fall to, say, .95 euros to the dollar.

When quoting currencies, we mention first the currency that remains unitary. Thus, we say dollar/yen rather than yen/dollar.

CROSS CURRENCY RATES

Cross currency rates are derived through the U.S. dollar. For example, the euro/yen rate is calculated from the euro/dollar rate and the dollar/yen rate. Changes in either of these two rates will affect the cross rate. The euro/yen rate is a direct quote. It indicates the amount of yen that can be purchased with one euro. Assume that the current euro/yen rate is 99.75. If this rate increases 10% to 109.73, it means that one euro now buys more yen. In other words, the yen has weakened (depreciated) against the euro. In a cross currency calculation, this can happen by either (1) a 10% devaluation in the dollar/yen rate, (2) a 10% appreciation in the euro/dollar rate, or (3) some combination of the two. Table 15.1 illustrates how the euro/yen rate is calculated if one leg of the cross currency rate moves while the other remains constant.

Table 15.1   Euro/Yen Cross Rate Calculation

Euro/yen rate = Dollar/yen rate · Euro/dollar rate

Yen depreciates 10%, Euro unchanged	Before	After
Dollar/yen · euro/dollar	105 · 0.95	115.50 · 0.95
Euro/yen	99.75	109.73

Euro appreciates 10%, yen unchanged	Before	After
Dollar/yen · Euro/dollar	105 · 0.95	105 · 1.045
Euro/yen	99.75	109.73

SPOT AND FORWARD MARKETS

The foreign exchange market is separated into a spot and forward market. The spot market (or cash market) is for immediate delivery, which usually means two days. The forward market is for future delivery. Transactions in the forward market can be tailored to meet the size and maturity requirements of the customer. This differs from organized futures and options markets, which offer standardized contracts on a limited number of currencies with specific settlement dates for future delivery.

FORWARD EXCHANGE RATES

Interest Rate Parity

Forward exchange rates are determined by interest rate differentials. This principle, known as interest rate parity, states that there should be no risk-free arbitrage between currency markets. For example, if interest rates are higher in the United States (5.75%) than in Euroland (4.75%), it should not be possible to make a risk-free profit by borrowing in the low interest rate currency and investing in the high interest rate currency.

MONEY MACHINE?

Consider the following steps:

1. Borrow 1,000,000 euros for one year at 4.75% (4.6406% continuously compounded), which will accrue to 1,047,500 euros.
2. Convert the euros' spot to dollars at a rate of 1:1 for $1,000,000.
3. Invest the dollars for one year at 5.75% (5.5908% continuously compounded), which will accrue to $1,057,500.
4. Lock in the interest rate differential of 1% (or 10,000 euros) by selling $1,057,500 one year forward in exchange for 1,057,500 euros at a rate of 1:1.
5. Repay the 1,047,500 euro loan.
6. Make a 10,000 euro risk-free profit.

To preclude this from being a virtual money machine, the rate at which dollars can be sold one year forward for euros must be less than the current exchange rate of 1:1. In other words, the dollar depreciates against the euro in the forward market in order to eliminate any risk-free profit. The forward rate is given by the following formula:

$$F = Se^{(r-r^*) \cdot T}$$

where F = forward rate
S = current price in the local currency (USD) of one unit of foreign currency (euro)
r = annual risk-free rate of interest (continuously compounded) in the local currency (USD)
r^* = annual risk-free rate of interest (continuously compounded) in the foreign currency (euro)
T = time to maturity in years

Solving for the euro/dollar forward rate (F), we get a value of 1.009547 dollars per euro. The dollar has depreciated against the euro one year forward because it now requires more dollars (1.009547 versus 1.000000) to buy one euro. The euro/dollar forward rate sells at a premium to the spot rate.

$$F = \cdot\ e^{(5.5908\%-4.606\%)\cdot 1}$$
$$= 1.009547 \text{ \$ per euro}$$

Returning to our money machine example, the $1,057,500 deposit in step 4 would be sold forward at a rate of 1.009547 dollars per euro. This exactly equals the amount of our euro loan in step 1 or 1,047,500 euros ($1,057,500/1.009547). The arbitrage profit is eliminated. The two investments are identical, which makes sense because they are both risk free.

FISHER'S THEOREM

As illustrated previously, higher interest rate currencies sell at a discount to their spot rates in the forward market while lower interest rate currencies sell at a premium. This is logical because countries with higher (lower) interest rates usually have higher (lower) inflation rates. The interest rate differential among currencies reflects the expected difference in inflation rates. Economist Irving Fisher formulated this theory in 1930. The United States has higher interest rates than Euroland (5.75% versus 4.75%). Currently, inflation rates in the United States are also higher (3% versus 2%). Adjusted for inflation, we would expect the returns in either currency to be equal. In other words, the real rates of return are the same (2.75%). The real rate of interest is defined as the nominal rate (the observable rate) less the inflation rate.

FORWARD POINTS: DISCOUNT OR PREMIUM?

The forward rate is quoted in points (basis points) versus the spot rate. In our example, the euro/dollar forward rate might be quoted as 100/105. When the smaller number is quoted first, the points are added to the spot rate. The quote 100/105 indicates that .01 would be added to the spot bid and .0105 to the spot offer to create a forward market of 1.0100/1.0105 dollars per euro. In other words, I will pay you 1.0100 dollars for one euro or sell you one euro for 1.0105 dollars. When the higher number precedes the second number, the points are subtracted from the spot rate.

The forward premium or discount reflects the interest rate differential, which in turn reflects the difference in *expected* inflation rates. In our euro/dollar deposit example, we saw that the current interest rate differential (1.0%) exactly reflected the current and expected inflation differential (1.0%). This does not have to be the case. Suppose the interest rate differential remained unchanged, but the inflation differential was only half a percent because inflation in Euroland was 2.50%. The forward market is anticipating that inflation will (1) fall by half a percent in Euroland, (2) rise by half a percent in the United States, or (3) some combination of the two. If nothing happens, we will make a real profit of half a percent on our covered interest rate arbitrage even though the nominal cash flows remain unchanged. This is because, in real terms, the dollars we earned in step 4 will be worth half a percent more, since inflation remained at three percent and did not rise to three-and-a-half percent as anticipated. Or conversely, the euro loan liability we must repay from step 1 is worth half a percent less, since inflation remained at two-and-a-half percent and did not fall to two percent. In short, to profit from covered currency arbitrage, you must correctly anticipate whether or not the current interest rate differential, and thus the forward points, accurately reflects future inflation rates.

HEDGING CURRENCY RISK

In our XYZ convertible bond example, both the bond and the underlying equity were priced in U.S. dollars. There was no currency risk for a dollar based investor. However, a domestic investor can be faced with four different combinations of currency risk. In each case, we explain this risk from the point of view of a dollar based investor who is (1) neutrally hedged with stock and (2) outright long the convertible with no stock hedge. In each case, we start with the same convertible and stock price used in our original XYZ convertible bond example. The XYZ convertible is a five-year, 5%, noncallable, convertible bond selling at 118.60%. Each bond is convertible into eight shares at a unit price of 125. The current stock price is 100. Each example begins with the purchase of 1 million face amount of bonds (1 thousand bonds each with a 1 thousand denomination). Where relevant, a neutral stock hedge of 75% is employed. Initially, the stock hedge is valued at 600 thousand (1 thousand bonds times the conversion ratio of eight shares per bond times the hedge ratio of 75% times the current stock price of 100.). In the examples that follow, the currency denomination of either the bond or the stock may change to reflect the case being illustrated. The four combinations of currency risk are summarized in Table 15.2.

Table 15.2 Four Cases of Currency Risk

Case	Investor's Currency	Convertible Currency	Stock Currency
I	Local	Foreign	Foreign
II	Local	Local	Foreign
III	Local	Foreign	Local
IV	Local	Foreign	Different foreign

CASE I: FOREIGN CURRENCY CONVERTIBLE WITH FOREIGN CURRENCY STOCK

Investor's Currency	Convertible Currency	Stock Currency
Local	Foreign	Foreign
USD	Euro	Euro

The Investor Hedged with Stock

We define the current foreign exchange rate between the euro (EUR) and the dollar (USD) as $X(t)$ so that:

$$USD = X(t) \cdot EUR$$

We assume that $X(t)$ follows a Wiener process (see Chapter 12).

The delta hedged investor is holding a portfolio Π consisting of being long the convertible and short the delta neutral amount of stock. The euro value of this portfolio is defined as follows:

$$\Pi^{EUR} = CB^{EUR} - CR \cdot \Delta \cdot S^{EUR}$$

where CB^{EUR} = convertible bond in euros
CR = conversion ratio
Δ = delta of the warrant
S^{EUR} = stock price in euros

Because our investor is U.S. dollar based, after funding the positions, the USD value of the portfolio is expressed below.

$$\Pi^{USD} = X \cdot CB^{EUR} - X \cdot CR \cdot \Delta \cdot S^{EUR}$$

In Chapter 8, we defined the value of a convertible bond as being the sum of a straight bond plus a call warrant. Assuming no dilution, we can express the value of the euro-denominated bond as follows:

$$CB^{EUR} = B^{EUR} + CR \cdot C^{EUR}$$

where B^{EUR} = investment value in euros
    C^{EUR} = warrant value in euros

Recalling the Black–Scholes options pricing formula (see Chapter 7), the value of the euro-denominated warrant is given by the following formula.

$$C^{EUR} = S^{EUR} \cdot e^{-qt} \cdot N(d_1) - K \cdot e^{-r^{EUR}t} \cdot N(d_2)$$

and $K = \dfrac{B^{EUR}}{CR}$

The delta of the warrant is given by:

$$\Delta = \frac{\delta C}{\delta S^{EUR}}$$
$$= e^{-qt} \cdot N(d_1)$$

Replacing the value of the warrant by its implicit expression, the dollar value of the portfolio is now:

$$\Pi^{USD} = X \cdot B^{EUR} + X \cdot CR \cdot S^{EUR} \cdot e^{-qt} \cdot N(d_1)$$
$$- X \cdot CR \cdot K \cdot e^{-r^{EUR}t} \cdot N(d_2) - CR \cdot \Delta \cdot X \cdot S^{EUR}$$

Given a change fX in the euro/dollar exchange rate, the partial derivative of the portfolio is:

$$\frac{\delta\Pi^{USD}}{\delta X} = B^{EUR} + CR \cdot S^{EUR} \cdot e^{-qt} \cdot N(d_1) - CR \cdot K \cdot e^{-r^{EUR}t} \cdot N(d_2) - CR \cdot \Delta \cdot S^{EUR}$$

$$= B^{EUR} + CR \cdot C^{EUR} - CR \cdot \Delta \cdot S^{EUR}$$

$$= CB^{EUR} - CR \cdot \Delta \cdot S^{EUR}$$

$$= \Pi^{EUR}$$

Therefore, to hedge the currency risk, the dollar based delta-neutral investor must sell forward the difference between the convertible investment (CB^{EUR}) and the proceeds from the hedge $(CR \cdot \Delta \cdot S^{EUR})$.

Table 15.3 transforms the original XYZ convertible and its underlying shares into euros. The convertible is neutrally hedged on a 75% delta. The example shows the effect of a 10% devaluation of the euro without a currency hedge, given the following assumptions:

$$X(t) = 1$$

Table 15.3 Foreign Currency Convertible (i.e., Euro) with Foreign Currency Stock (i.e., Euro)
Investor Neutrally Hedged with Stock
Euro Devalues 10%, No Currency Hedge

FX Rate	Cvt. Price (%)	Long Convertible (in euros)	(1) Long Convertible (in dollars)	Short Stock (in euros)	(2) Short Stock (in dollars)	('000) (1+2) Net
1.00	118.6	1,186	1,186	−600	−600	586
0.90	118.6	1,186	1,067	−600	−540	
% Change		0.0	−10.0	0.0	+10.0	
P/l ($)		0	−119	0	+60	−59

$$X(t + \delta t) = 0.9$$
$$\Delta = 75\%$$
$$CR = 8$$
$$S^{EUR} = 100$$

Thus
$$CB^{EUR} = B^{EUR} + CR \cdot C^{EUR}$$
$$= 848 + 8 \cdot 42.5$$
$$= 1,186$$

As the value of the euro declines versus the dollar, the price of the convertible in euros remains unchanged. However, expressed in dollar terms the value of the convertible falls by 10%. The hedger's short-stock position partially offsets the currency impact on the convertible. If the euro devalues, it takes fewer dollars to buy back the original short-stock position resulting in a profit in dollars. An appreciation of the euro versus the dollar would result in an equal but opposite outcome. Since we are using a neutral stock hedge of 75%, the value of the short-stock position is insufficient to cover the total cash value of the convertible investment. To fully neutralize the remaining currency exposure, we must hedge the difference between the long and short position.

$$\text{Or } \frac{\delta \Pi^{USD}}{\delta X} = CB^{EUR} - CR \cdot \Delta \cdot S^{EUR}$$
$$= 1,186 - 8 \cdot 0.75\% \cdot 100$$
$$= 586 \text{ EUR}$$

This can be accomplished by selling the euro balance forward against dollars (see earlier explanation of a currency forward contract). The currency hedge needs to be adjusted for any change in the net value of the long and short positions including accrued interest. (See Table 15.4.) Alternatively, the hedger could borrow euros, rather than dollars, to purchase the convertible.

Table 15.4 Foreign Currency Convertible (i.e., Euro) with Foreign Currency Stock (i.e., Euro)
Investor Neutrally Hedged with Stock
Euro Declines 10% with Currency Hedge

FX Rate	Cvt. Price (%)	(1) Long Convertible (in euros)	Long Convertible (in dollars)	Short Stock (in euros)	(2) Short Stock (in dollars)	(3) FX Hedge	('000) (1+2+3) Net
1.00	118.6	1,186	1,186	−600	−600	−586	0
0.90	118.6	1,186	1,067	−600	−540	−527	
% Change		0.0	−10.0	0.0	+10.0	+10.0	
P/l ($)		0	−119	0	+60	+59	0

The Outright Investor

The outright investor is holding only the convertible. His or her portfolio is then:

$$\Pi^{EUR} = CB^{EUR}$$
$$\Pi^{USD} = X \cdot CB^{EUR}$$

Given a change fX in the euro/dollar exchange rate, the partial derivative of the portfolio is:

$$\frac{\delta\Pi^{USD}}{\delta X} = CB^{EUR}$$

If the investor has not shorted stock against the convertible, the entire position is exposed to currency risk. A 10% depreciation of the euro versus the dollar results in a 10% loss in dollars and vice versa. To hedge the currency risk, the outright investor must sell forward versus dollars the full value of the convertible investment. The term of the forward contract should match the holding period of the investment. If there is a mismatch, the contract can be rolled forward as required. The currency hedge needs to be adjusted for any change in the value of the position including accrued interest.

CASE II: LOCAL CURRENCY CONVERTIBLE WITH FOREIGN CURRENCY STOCK

Investor's Currency	Convertible Currency	Stock Currency
Local	Local	Foreign
USD	USD	Euro

The Investor Hedged with Stock

In Case II, we start with our original dollar denominated XYZ convertible, but this time the underlying stock is priced in euros. In this circumstance, the dollar based hedger is not exposed to currency risk. This is because only the warrant value, which is neutrally hedged, is affected by a change in exchange rates. The investment value is in dollars and is unaffected. Any loss in the warrant value will be compensated for by a gain in the short-stock position and vice versa.

From the point of view of the dollar based investor, the portfolio is expressed as follows:

$$\Pi^{USD} = CB^{USD} - CR \cdot \Delta \cdot X \cdot S^{EUR}$$

However, in this case the warrant price depends on the foreign exchange rate $X(t)$. The stock price is in euros, but since the convertible is in USD, both the investment value and the strike price of the warrant are set in USD.

The definition of the payout of the call warrant at maturity is:

$$C^{USD} = \max\left(S^{EUR} \cdot X - \frac{B^{USD}}{CR}, 0 \right)$$

$S^{EUR}(t)$ follows a Markov process of volatility σ_{sEUR}. $X(t)$ follows a Markov process of volatility σ_X. ρ is the correlation between $S^{EUR}(t)$ and $X(t)$. Therefore, $S^{EUR}(t) \cdot X(t)$ also follows a Markov process with a volatility defined as:

$$\sigma_{xs} = \sqrt{\sigma_x^2 + \sigma_s^2 + 2\rho\sigma_x\sigma_s}$$

The Black–Scholes valuation of the warrant is then:

$$C^{USD} = S^{EUR} \cdot X \cdot e^{-qt} \cdot N(d_1) - K^{USD} \cdot e^{-r^{USD}t} \cdot N\left(d_1 - \sigma_{xs}\sqrt{t}\right)$$

and $K^{USD} = \dfrac{B^{USD}}{CR}$

with $d_1 = \dfrac{\ln\left(\dfrac{X \cdot S^{EUR}}{K^{USD}}\right) + \left(r^{USD} - q + \dfrac{\sigma_{xs}^2}{2}\right) \cdot t}{\sigma_{xs} \cdot \sqrt{t}}$

$$\Delta = e^{-qt} \cdot N(d_1)$$

The explicit valuation of the portfolio is then:

$$\Pi^{USD} = B^{USD} + CR \cdot S^{EUR} \cdot X \cdot e^{-qt} \cdot N(d_2) - CR \cdot K^{USD} \cdot e^{-r^{USD}t}$$
$$\cdot N\left(d_2 - \sigma_{xs}\sqrt{t}\right) - CR \cdot \Delta \cdot X \cdot S^{EUR}$$

Given a change fX in the euro/dollar exchange rate, the partial derivative of the portfolio is:

$$\frac{\delta\Pi}{\delta X} = CR \cdot S^{EUR} \cdot e^{-qt} \cdot N(d_2) - CR \cdot \Delta \cdot S^{EUR}$$
$$= CR \cdot S^{EUR} \cdot e^{-qt} \cdot N(d_2) - CR \cdot e^{-r^{USD}t} \cdot N(d_2) \cdot S^{EUR}$$
$$= 0$$

The delta neutral investor in this case is hedged against the currency risk.

In Table 15.5, the euro devalues by 10%. The price of the convertible falls by $60, which is due to the fall in the warrant value. The investment value remains unchanged at $848. Since the warrant is delta neutrally hedged, the decline in its value is recovered by an offsetting gain in the short-stock position (see column 2 in Table 15.5). The net result to the dollar based hedger is zero.

The Outright Investor

Currency risk affects only the value of the warrant, since the investment value is in dollars. This can be hedged by selling forward

Table 15.5   Local Currency Convertible (i.e., USD) with Foreign Currency Stock
(i.e.,Euro)
Investor Neutrally Hedged with Stock
Euro Declines 10%, No Currency Hedge

FX Rate	(1) Long Cvt. (USD)	Long Bond (USD)	Long Warrant (USD)	Long Warrant Per Share (USD)	Short Stock (euros)	(2) Short Stock (USD)	Short Stock Per Share (USD)	(1+2) Net
1.00	1,186	848	338	42.25	−600	−600	100	
0.90	1,126	848	278	34.75	−600	−540	90	
% Change	−5.0	0.0	−17.8	−17.8	0.00	+10	+10	
P/l ($)	−60	0	−60	−7.5	0	+60	+10	0

the foreign currency amount equal to the delta neutral hedge of the warrant.

The portfolio is then as follows:

$$\Pi^{USD} = CB^{USD}$$

We replace the warrant by its implicit expression:

$$\Pi^{USD} = B^{USD} + CR \cdot S^{EUR} \cdot X \cdot e^{-qt} \cdot N(d_1) - CR \cdot K^{USD}$$
$$\cdot e^{-r^{USD}t} \cdot N\!\left(d_1 - \sigma_{xs}\sqrt{t}\right)$$

Given a change fX in the euro/dollar exchange rate, the partial derivative of the portfolio is:

$$\frac{\delta\Pi^{USD}}{\delta X} = CR \cdot S^{EUR} \cdot e^{-qt} \cdot N(d_1)$$
$$= CR \cdot S^{EUR} \cdot \Delta$$
$$= 8 \cdot 100 \cdot 75\%$$
$$= 600 \text{ EUR}$$

Therefore, the investor must sell forward 600 EUR to fully immunize the currency risk.

CASE III: FOREIGN CURRENCY CONVERTIBLE WITH LOCAL CURRENCY STOCK

Investors Currency	Convertible Currency	Stock Currency
Local	Foreign	Local
USD	Euro	USD

Table 15.6 illustrates the effect of a 10% devaluation of the euro. In euro terms, the investment value of the convertible remains unchanged. However, expressed in dollars, its price falls to $763 (848 EUR · 0.9 = $763). At the same time, the warrant price rises even though the stock price remains unchanged at $100. In Table 15.6, we demonstrate how the net result of the currency movement generates a portfolio loss of $57,500.

Hedger and Outright Investor

The hedger and the outright investor are faced with the same currency risk because the short-stock position is in dollars and has no influence on the position from a currency point of view. Consequently, the theoretical currency hedge is the same for both investors. Thus, we calculate the hedge from the point of view of a neutrally hedged investor.

Table 15.6 Foreign Currency Convertible (i.e., Euro) with Local Currency Stock (i.e., USD)
Investor Neutrally Hedged with Stock
Euro Devalues 10%, No Currency Hedge

FX Rate	Cvt. Price (%)	Cvt. (euro)	Bond (euro)	Warrant (euro)	(1) Cvt. (USD)	Bond (USD)	Warrant (USD)	('000) (2) Stock (USD)	(1+2) Net (USD)
1.00	118.6	1,186	848	338	1,186	848	338	−600	586
0.90	125.4	1,254	848	406	1,129	763	366	−600	
% Change	+5.7	+5.7	0	+20	−4.8	−10	+8	0	
P/l	+68	+0	+68	−57.5	−85	+27.5	0	−57.5	

The neutrally hedged investor is holding the following portfolio:

$$\Pi^{USD} = X \cdot CB^{EUR} - CR \cdot \Delta \cdot S^{USD}$$
$$= X \cdot B^{EUR} + CR \cdot X \cdot C^{EUR} - CR \cdot \Delta \cdot S^{USD}$$

Considering the inverse foreign exchange rate $X' = \dfrac{1}{X}$, we then need to evaluate C^{EURO}, the euro value of a call warrant struck in euros with the underlying stock in dollars:

$$C^{EUR} = \text{Max}\left(S^{USD} \cdot X' - \frac{B^{EUR}}{CR}, 0 \right)$$
$$= \text{Max}\left(S^{USD} \cdot X' - K^{EUR}, 0 \right)$$

$S^{EUR}(t)$ follows a Markov process of volatility $\sigma_{S^{EUR}}$. $X(t)$ follows a Markov process of volatility σ_X. ρ is the correlation between $S^{EUR}(t)$ and $X(t)$. Therefore, $S^{EUR}(t) \cdot X(t)$ also follows a Markov process with a volatility defined as:

$$\sigma_{xs} = \sqrt{\sigma_x^2 + \sigma_s^2 + 2\rho\sigma_x\sigma_s}$$

The Black–Scholes valuation of the warrant is then:

$$C^{EUR} = S^{USD} \cdot X' \cdot e^{-qt} \cdot N(d_1) - K^{EUR} \cdot e^{-r^{EUR}t} \cdot N\left(d_1 - \sigma_{xs}\sqrt{t}\right)$$

$$\text{with } d_1 = \frac{\ln\left(\dfrac{S^{USD}}{X \cdot K^{EUR}}\right) + \left(r^{EUR} - q + \dfrac{\sigma_{xs}^2}{2}\right) \cdot t}{\sigma_{xs} \cdot \sqrt{t}}$$

and $\Delta = e^{-qt} \cdot N(d_1)$

The explicit valuation of the portfolio is then:

$$\Pi^{USD} = X \cdot B^{EUR} + X \cdot CR \cdot X' \cdot S^{USD} \cdot e^{-qt} \cdot N(d_1) - X \cdot CR \cdot K^{EUR}$$
$$\cdot e^{-r^{EUR}t} \cdot N\left(d_1 - \sigma_{xs}\sqrt{t}\right) - CR \cdot \Delta \cdot S^{USD}$$
$$= X \cdot B^{EUR} + CR \cdot S^{USD} \cdot e^{-qt} \cdot N(d_1) - X \cdot CR \cdot K^{EUR}$$
$$\cdot e^{-r^{EUR}t} \cdot N\left(d_1 - \sigma_{xs}\sqrt{t}\right) - CR \cdot \Delta \cdot S^{USD}$$

Given a change fX in the euro/dollar exchange rate, the partial derivative of the portfolio is:

$$\frac{\delta \Pi^{USD}}{\delta X} = B^{EUR} - CR \cdot K^{EUR} \cdot e^{-r^{EUR}t} \cdot N(d_1 - \sigma_{xs}\sqrt{t})$$

$$= B^{EUR} - CR \cdot \frac{B^{EUR}}{CR} \cdot e^{-r^{EUR}t} \cdot N(d_1 - \sigma_{xs}\sqrt{t})$$

$$= B^{EUR} \cdot \left(1 - e^{-r^{EUR}t} \cdot N(d_1 - \sigma_{xs}\sqrt{t})\right)$$

$$\neq 0$$

Therefore, in order to fully immunize the currency risk, both the outright and hedged investor must sell an amount of euros equal to

$$B^{EUR} \cdot \left(1 - e^{-r^{EUR}t} \cdot N\left(d_1 - \sigma_{xs}\sqrt{t}\right)\right)$$

In Table 15.7 we derive the amount of euros to be sold as follows:

$$B^{EUR} \cdot \left(1 - e^{-r^{EUR}t} \cdot N(d_1 - \sigma_{xs}\sqrt{t})\right) = 848 \cdot \left(1 - e^{-5.75\% \cdot 5} \cdot N(d_1 - \sigma_{xs}\sqrt{t})\right)$$

$$= 848 \cdot (1 - 0.7502 \cdot 0.4285)$$

$$= 575.4 \text{ EUR}$$

When the euro devalues, it requires fewer USD to cover the short euro stock position resulting in a gain of \$57.5 (see 2 in Table 15.7). This gain covers the currency loss from the original portfolio.

Table 15.7 Foreign Currency Convertible (i.e., Euro) with Local Currency Stock (i.e., USD)
Investor Neutrally Hedged with Stock
Euro Devalues 10% with Currency Hedge

FX Rate	Cvt. Price	Cvt. (euro)	Bond (euro)	Warrant (euro)	(1) Cvt. (USD)	Bond (USD)	Warrant (USD)	(2) FX Hedge (USD)	Stock (USD)	('000) (1+2) Net (USD)
1.00	118.6	1,186	848	338	1,186	848	338	–575	–600	
0.90	125.4	1,254	848	406	1,129	763	365.5	–518	–600	
% Change	+5.7	+5.7	0	+20	–4.8	–10	+8	+11.1	0.0	
P/L		+68	0	+68	–57.5	–85	+27.5	+57.5	0	0

FX Rate	FX Hedge (Euro)	FX Hedge (USD)
1.00	–575	575
0.90	–575	517.5

212

CASE IV: FOREIGN CURRENCY CONVERTIBLE WITH A DIFFERENT FOREIGN CURRENCY STOCK

Investor's Currency	Convertible Currency	Stock Currency
Local	Foreign	Different Foreign
USD	Euro	Yen

We define the foreign exchange rate between euro (EUR) and yen (YEN) as $Y(t)$ so that:

$$EUR = Y(t) \cdot YEN$$

The Investor Hedged with Stock

To consider the overall currency exposure, we assume that the investor wants to use EUR as the pivot currency to hedge the portfolio. For the delta hedged investor, this results in the same portfolio as described in case II.

$$\Pi^{EUR} = B^{EUR} + CR \cdot S^{YEN} \cdot Y \cdot e^{-qt} \cdot N(d_1) - CR \cdot K \cdot e^{-r^{EUR}t}$$
$$\cdot N\left(d_1 - \sigma_{xs}\sqrt{t}\right) - CR \cdot \Delta \cdot Y \cdot S^{YEN}$$

As the investor converted the proceeds from the yen hedge into euros to reflect the pivotal currency, we have already demonstrated from case II that:

$$\frac{\delta \Pi^{EUR}}{\delta Y} = 0$$

The investor will now look at its EUR hedge portfolio as a USD investor.

Let's state:

$$\Pi^{USD} = X \cdot \Pi^{EUR} = X \cdot Y\Pi^{YEN}$$
$$= X \cdot B^{EUR} + X \cdot CR \cdot S^{YEN} \cdot Y \cdot e^{-qt} \cdot N(d_1) - X \cdot CR \cdot K^{EUR}$$
$$\cdot e^{-r^{EUR}t} \cdot N\left(d_1 - \sigma_{ys\,YEN}\sqrt{t}\right) - X \cdot CR \cdot \Delta \cdot Y \cdot S^{YEN}$$

Given a change fX in the euro/dollar exchange rate, the partial derivative of the portfolio is:

$$\frac{\delta\Pi^{USD}}{\delta X} = B^{EUR} + CR \cdot S^{YEN} \cdot Y \cdot e^{-qt} \cdot N(d_1) - CR \cdot K^{EUR} \cdot e^{-r^{EUR}t}$$

$$\cdot N(d_1 - \sigma_{ys\,YEN}\sqrt{t}) - CR \cdot \Delta \cdot S^{YEN}$$

$$= \Pi^{EUR}$$

Given a change fX in the euro/yen exchange rate, the partial derivative of the portfolio is:

$$\frac{\delta\Pi^{USD}}{\delta Y} = X \cdot CR \cdot S^{YEN} \cdot e^{-qt} \cdot N(d_1) - X \cdot CR \cdot \Delta \cdot S^{YEN}$$

$$= X \cdot CR \cdot S^{YEN} \cdot e^{-qt} \cdot N(d_1) - X \cdot CR \cdot e^{-qt} \cdot N(d_1)$$

$$= 0$$

Therefore, after hedging the portfolio's yen exposure by selling yen versus euro, and then buying euros versus dollars to fund the residual balance of the position, the delta neutral investor must sell forward the Π^{EUR} amount of euro versus dollar to immunize the currency risk. (See Table 15.8.)

Table 15.8   Foreign Currency Convertible (i.e., Euro) with a Different Foreign Currency Stock (i.e., Yen)
Investor Neutrally Hedged with Stock
Yen Devalues 10% versus Euro; Euro Devalues 20% versus Dollar with Currency Hedge

	CVT Price (%)	CVT Value	Bond Value	WT Value	Short Stock	Net Cash Balance	('000) FX Hedge
Phase 1: $X = 1$ and $Y = 1$ and $X \cdot Y = 1$							
YEN	118.6	1,186	848	338	−600	0	0
EURO	118.6	1,186	848	338	−600	0	−586
USD	118.6	1,186	848	338	−600	−586	586
Phase 2: $X = 0.8$ and $Y = 0.9$ and $X \cdot Y = 0.72$							
YEN	125.1	1,251	942	308	−600	0	0
EURO	112.6	1,126	848	278	−540	0	−586
USD	90	900	678	222	−432	−586	468
USD							
P/l		−286	−170	−116	+168	+118	0*

*−286 + 168 + 118 = 0

Table 15.9   Summary of Currency Risk Situations

Case (cvt/stock)	Outright Investor	Delta Neutral Hedger
I EUR/EUR	Sell forward CB^{EUR} EUR/USD	Sell forward $CB^{EUR} - CR \cdot \Delta \cdot S^{EUR}$ EUR/USD
II USD/EUR	Sell forward $CR \cdot \Delta \cdot S^{EUR}$ EUR/USD	Do nothing
III EUR/USD	Sell forward $B^{EUR} \cdot \left(1 - e^{-r^{EUR}t} \cdot N\!\left(d_1 - \sigma_{XS}\sqrt{t}\right)\right)$ EUR/USD	Sell forward $B^{EUR} \cdot \left(1 - e^{-r^{EUR}t} \cdot N\!\left(d_1 - \sigma_{XS}\sqrt{t}\right)\right)$ EUR/USD
IV EUR/YEN	Sell forward $CR \cdot \Delta \cdot S^{YEN}$ YEN/EUR and Sell forward $\Pi^{EUR} = B^{EUR} + CR \cdot S^{YEN} \cdot Y \cdot e^{-qt} \cdot N(d_1)$ $- CR \cdot K^{EUR} \cdot e^{-r^{EUR}t} \cdot N\!\left(d_1 - \sigma_{YS^{YEN}}\sqrt{t}\right)$ $- CR \cdot \Delta \cdot Y \cdot S^{YEN}$ EUR/USD	Sell forward $\Pi^{EUR} = B^{EUR} + CR \cdot S^{YEN} \cdot Y \cdot e^{-qt} \cdot N(d_1)$ $- CR \cdot K^{EUR} \cdot e^{-r^{EUR}t} \cdot N\!\left(d_1 - \sigma_{YS^{YEN}}\sqrt{t}\right)$ $- CR \cdot \Delta \cdot Y \cdot S^{YEN}$ EUR/USD After having converted the $CR \cdot \Delta \cdot S^{YEN}$ YEN proceeds into EUR.

The Outright Investor

Referring to case II, the outright investor is not hedged versus yen. Therefore, he or she must sell yen forward versus euro in an amount equal to the hedge neutral position. (See Table 15.8.)

Table 15.9 summarizes the actions to be taken to neutralize the currency risk for both the outright investor and the delta neutral hedger in each of the four possible currency cases.

Part Four

SPECIAL TOPICS

16

MANDATORY CONVERTIBLE SECURITIES

INTRODUCTION

Mandatory Convertible Securities (MCS) are known by a variety of acronyms (see Appendix 1). Since General Motors launched the first issue in 1990, MCS have grown to constitute about 14% of the total U.S. convertible market. Because these securities are the most equity-like of all convertible securities, they performed very well as a group during the late 1990s due to the strong bull market in the United States. Corporate issuers find these securities compelling, since they combine the tax benefits attributable to debt securities with the equity credit of preferred stock. Consequently, it is expected that these securities will continue to grow in popularity both in the United States and abroad.

Mandatory Convertible Securities should be thought of as yield-enhanced equity. Unlike normal convertible securities, they provide little downside support. This is because, unlike a traditional convertible bond, they have no terminal value. With a convertible bond, the investor expects to receive a minimum of par back at maturity. With an MCS, the final redemption value is uncertain because the security will mandatorily convert into stock at maturity. Consequently, if the stock price declines, so too will the final payout to the MCS holder.

VALUING THE MCS: GIVING UP DOWNSIDE PROTECTION FOR YIELD

One way to think about an MCS is like a traditional convertible bond, where we define the convertible as stock plus a put option (see Figure 16.1). However, instead of retaining the full benefit of the put, the investor elects to sell back a portion of it to the issuer in exchange for more current income (see Figure 16.2).

In keeping with this analogy, we can think of the construction of an MCS as a short maturity convertible note (lines 1 and 2, Figure 16.2) plus the premium received by selling an at-the-money put option (line 3, Figure 16.2).

MSC = Short-maturity note   (1)

$\quad$ + (Out-of-the-money call option on the underlying common
$\quad\quad$ stock struck at the conversion price) · conversion ratio   (2)

$\quad$ − At-the-money put option struck at the issue price on the
$\quad\quad$ underlying common stock   (3)

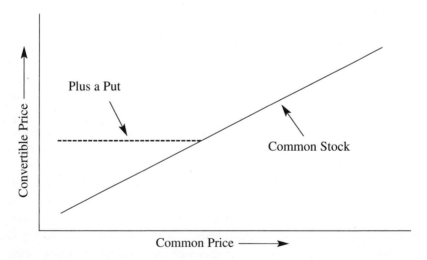

Figure 16.1 Convertible: Stock Plus a Put Option

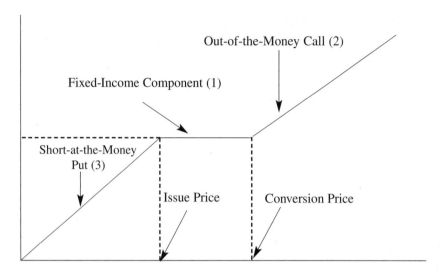

Figure 16.2   MSC: Note Plus OTM Call Option Minus ATM Put Option

Conceptually, this approach is appealing but in practice it is flawed. If the issuer goes bankrupt, the investor can lose only on the investment once and will not be obliged to make good on the short-put position.

VALUING THE MCS: FROM BUY WRITE TO CALL SPREAD

Although the consistency of thinking about the MCS in terms of a traditional convertible bond is satisfying, there is another more intuitive approach. The more commonly accepted approach is to think of the MCS as being long the stock and short a call spread. This concept evolved out of what was traditionally known as a buy write. Investors who own a stock have occasionally sought to increase the yield on their holdings by selling an out-of-the-money call option. This is known as writing a covered call, or a buy write. The premium received from writing the call increases the income to the investor. Of course, writing an out-of-the-money call against a long stock position caps the investor's total return should the stock price rise above the call price. In fact, this became a problem for the first generation of MCS, which were nothing more than covered call structures with maturities of generally three years. (See Figure 16.3.)

Investors were initially attracted by the higher current yield offered by these structures. However, when the ensuing U.S. bull market of the late 1980s caused stocks to advance strongly, the cap disenchanted investors. To calm disgruntled investors, clever investment bankers took the next logical step. They thought of a way to give the investor enhanced current yield but without completely capping the up side should the stock rally strongly. This was achieved by embedding a call spread into the MCS rather than simply shorting one out-of-the-money call option. A call spread involves simultaneously buying and selling call options on a stock with identical maturity dates. Being long a call spread means buying one call and then selling another call with a higher strike price. The investor will have to pay a premium because the call purchased is closer to the money (and thus more expensive) than the proceeds received from selling the out-of-the-money call. The investor's loss will be limited to the net premium paid for buying the call spread. The gain will be capped by the spread between the two strike prices less the premium initially paid to buy the spread.

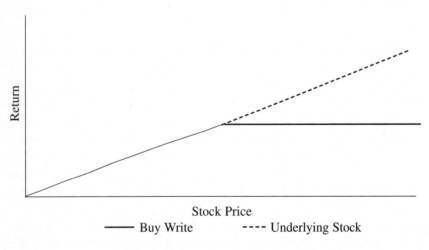

Figure 16.3 Buy Write: Buy the Underlying Stock and Write a Call Option

To be short a call spread is exactly the opposite. The investor buys an out-of-the-money call and then sells a call struck closer to the money. In this case, the investor receives a net premium since the call sold is closer to the money and has a higher premium than the call purchased. The most the investor can gain is the net premium collected should the stock fall. The most that can be lost is the spread between the two strikes less the premium collected.

An MCS is nothing more than a yield-enhanced equity. The yield, or income, is the net premium received from selling the call spread (lines 2 and 3, Figure 16.4). An MCS consists of the following pieces:

MCS = Underlying common stock (stock price · Lower
     conversion ratio)   (1)

    + (Out-of-the-money call option on the underlying common
       stock struck at the upper strike price) · Upper conversion
       ratio   (2)

    − At-the-money call option on the underlying common
       stock struck at the lower conversion ratio   (3)

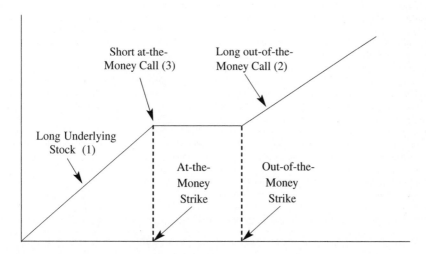

Figure 16.4 The Anatomy of an MCS

+ Present value of the incremental income over the
common dividend   (4)

The first thing we are doing when we buy the MCS is to buy the stock as in line 1. The second step is to short one at-the-money call struck at the issue price as in line 3. By selling this call, two things happen. First, we receive a premium. However, we do not receive the premium up front but rather in the form of a quarterly dividend or coupon payment over the life of the security. Second, we have capped any further upside participation in the stock. The third step is to take some of the proceeds from the sale of the at-the-money call in line 3, and buy a portion of an out-of-the-money call as in line 2. Buying this long call then reinstates our upside participation in the stock, but only after the stock price rises above the out-of-the-money strike price. This gap is known as the flat or dead zone. The net premium received from writing the at-the-money call and purchasing a partial out-of-the-money call is effectively the present value of the income differential between the MCS' yield and the common stock yield. Figure 16.5 shows the payoff of the MCS at maturity with its component parts labeled.

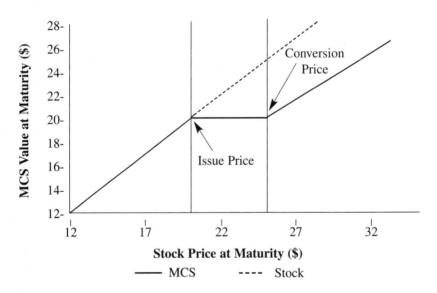

Figure 16.5 Payoff of an MCS at Maturity

THE MYSTERIOUS CHANGING CONVERSION RATIO

A unique characteristic of the MCS is that the conversion ratio at maturity changes depending on the price of the stock. Typically, the issue price of a mandatory convertible security is equal to the price of the stock at the time of pricing. This is also the strike price at which the short-call option in the call spread is struck (the lower strike). At issue, the mandatory is priced with a so-called conversion premium, which determines the level of the strike price for the long call option in the call spread (the upper strike). At maturity, if the stock price has fallen below the issue price, investors usually receive the lower ratio number of shares (which is typically 1). If the stock price is between the issue price and the upper strike price, then investors receive stock worth the issue price (which is generally a ratio between 1 and the upper ratio). This ratio is determined by dividing the issue price by the stock price at expiration. If the stock is above the upper strike, the investor receives the upper ratio number of shares (which is normally less than 1). The upper ratio is calculated by dividing the issue price by the conversion price. The conversion ratio is variable only between the issue price and the conversion price. If the stock rises above the conversion price or falls below the issue price, the conversion ratio will be fixed. Figure 16.6 shows

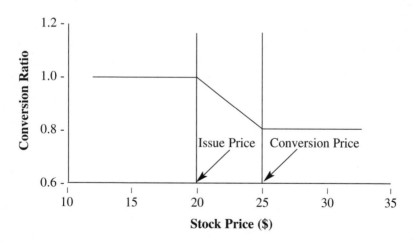

Figure 16.6 MCS: The Mysterious Changing Conversion Ratio

how the conversion ratio changes at maturity depending upon the price
of the stock.

PERFORMANCE BASED CONVERSION PREMIUM

The conversion ratio at the lower strike point is always bigger than at
the upper strike point. This means that if the stock goes up from the issue price, the participation is at first delayed until the point of the upper strike is reached (the flat zone), and then rises at a reduced rate
equal to the upper conversion ratio. On the downside, participation is
one-for-one with the stock. An interesting way to think about this slid-
ing conversion ratio is that the investor does not actually pay the conversion premium up front as in a traditional convertible security. This
is because the MCS is usually issued at the same price as the stock into
which it is mandatorily converted. From the investor's point of view, as
the stock price rises from its issue price to the conversion price, the conversion ratio will decline from 1 to .83 (assuming a 20% initial conversion premium). The declining ratio, and subsequent decline in
conversion value, represents the conversion premium paid by the investor. From the issuer's point of view, the premium can be viewed as
performance based. If the stock performs well and rises above the upper strike by maturity, the issuer will have only to deliver .83 shares in
our example (see Figure 16.7). The .17 shares difference represents the
premium the issuer earns. In this fashion, both the issuer and the investor benefit if the stock performs, thus aligning their interests.

AN MCS EXAMPLE

To fully understand how the MCS works in practice, consider the following example (Table 16.1).

DEFINITIONS OF TERMS

Break Even in Years

This represents the time, in years, required to recover the premium
paid for the MCS. The premium paid represents the difference be-

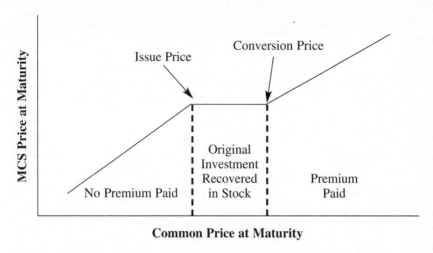

Figure 16.7 MCS: Performance Based Conversion Premium
Source: Morgan Stanley

tween the price of the MCS and parity. Since the conversion ratio is continually changing in the MCS, we use a conservative assumption and use the upper (or smaller) conversion ratio to establish parity. This parity figure (in points) is then divided by the present value of the net cash flows between the MCS and the common stock to derive a payback in years. The attractive yield advantage often permits the premium to be recovered before the call or expiration date.

Conversion (Issue) Premium

The premium of the MCS is really relevant only at the time of issue. At that moment, it is defined as the percentage difference between the issue price (e.g., $25.00) and the conversion price or upper strike price (e.g., $30.75). In this case, the initial conversion premium is 23% (i.e., ($30.75/$25.00) − 1). After issue, the conversion ratio is constantly changing, rendering the concept of a conversion premium largely irrelevant.

Credit Spread

Unlike with traditional convertible securities, the credit spread of the MCS is used only to discount the net cash flows between the dividend

Table 16.1 Mandatory Convertible Security Example: 6.5% Due 25–Dec–02

Stock Data		MCS Data	Issue Information	
Issuer	XYZ Corp.	XYZ Corp.	Issue Price	$25.00
Price	$27.875	$27.000	Issue Date	25-Dec-99
Dividend	$0.000	$1.625		
Premium	23.000%			
Current yield	0.000%	6.019%	Yield	6.500%
Next dividend	NA	25-Mar-00	Maturity	25-Dec-02
Frequency	NA	Quarterly	Call Date	25-Dec-02
Credit rating	A	Parity	$22.662	
Risk-free rate	6.000	Points	$4.337	
Credit spread	0.750%	Break-even years	0.988	
Upper ratio	0.8130	Years to maturity	3.003	
Lower ratio	1.0000	Stand-still YTM	3.723%	
Upper strike	$30.750			
Lower strike	$25.000			
Upper vol.	30.000%			
Lower vol.	30.000%			

Valuation	
Long stock value	+$27.875
Long 0.8130 calls struck at $30.750	+$5.411
Short 1.0000 calls struck at $25.000	–$9.228
Present value net cash flow	+$4.391
Fair value	$28.450
Over/(under) value	–$1.450
Percent rich/(cheap)	–5.369%

paid on the MCS and the dividend paid on the common stock. The terminal value of the MCS at maturity is not known with certainty in advance but depends on the stock price. Moreover, there is little risk of default because the company can always issue more stock to satisfy the mandatory conversion at maturity. The credit spread reflects the riskiness of the issuer's ability to pay its dividends and is expressed as a basis point spread over the equivalent maturity risk-free Treasury yield, in this case 0.75% for an A-rated issuer.

Call Date

Most MCS are noncallable for life. In some cases they may be called before maturity at a small premium to the issue price. Usually, this premium amortizes to the issue price at maturity. The higher the stock price goes, the more likely the event of a call, as the issuer will seek to force conversion into the fewest shares possible (the upper ratio).

Conversion Price (Upper Strike Price)

This is the price at which the MCS are convertible into common stock at a premium to the issue price.

Fair Value

The fair value of the MCS is the price at which it could be theoretically replicated in the open market. In the secondary market, the fair value is the sum of the stock underlying the MCS (the current stock price times the lower ratio), plus the long call, minus the short call, plus the present value of the income advantage. A fair value above the current trading price of the MCS indicates a superior risk/reward profile relative to the common stock.

Issue Price (Lower Strike Price)

The issue price of the MCS is usually the same as the common stock price at the time of issue. The issue price is also the par value of the security and is used to establish the lower strike price of the call spread.

Long Stock Value

This is calculated by multiplying the stock price by the lower ratio. In determining the fair value of the MCS in the secondary market, this component does not change. We are always long an amount of stock equal to the lower ratio. Against this position, we are short a commensurate amount of calls and long a smaller amount of calls. Upon conversion, we will receive an amount of stock somewhere between the lower and upper ratios depending on the price of the stock.

Present Value of the Income Advantage

This is the present value of the amount by which the income from the MCS exceeds the dividend yield on the common stock. The discount rate used is the risk-free rate plus the credit spread.

Stand-Still Yield to Maturity

This represents the yield to maturity of the MCS assuming that the stock price remains unchanged. This yield includes income earned on the security plus any capital gain or loss incurred. This capital gain or loss is often overlooked by investors, who instead focus on current yield. Because the MCS is converted into stock at maturity, any premium or discount in the price of the MCS prior to maturity must be fully amortized when we are calculating the stand-still rate of return. The higher the return, the more attractive the MCS is relative to the common stock.

Upper/Lower Volatility

These are the volatilities that are used to price the two embedded call options in the MCS. To be conservative, we use the same volatility assumption for both the upper and lower strike prices. In reality, the upper strike usually carries a higher volatility than the lower strike because investors are willing to pay more for an out-of-the-money call, which they can acquire for a lower cash outlay. Incorporating a volatility spread into our example would increase the fair value of the MCS by increasing the value of the long-call position.

SENSITIVITY ANALYSIS

In order to appreciate how MCS trade in practice, the following section will demonstrate the sensitivity of the previous example to a change in the stock price, interest rates, credit spread, and volatility. The base case of XYZ Corporation uses a common stock price struck exactly in the middle of the upper and lower ratios in order to give symmetry to the analysis.

Stock Price Sensitivity (Delta)

Because the MCS are essentially yield-enhanced common stock, they are very sensitive to a change in the underlying stock price. This is true for movements both up or down in the stock price. This is because the MCS, unlike traditional convertible securities, do not have a predetermined terminal value at maturity. Figure 16.8 demonstrates that for a 10% move up or down in the stock price, the theoretical price of the mandatory will change by plus or minus 7.3%.

Interest Rate Sensitivity (Rho)

Because the MCS are akin to stock rather than debt, they are not very sensitive to changes in interest rates. A change in interest rates will affect the discounting of the income advantage between the MCS and the common stock dividend. It will also affect the pricing of the call options embedded in the security. However, since we are both long and short a call, the two offsetting calls largely neutralize the effect of a change in interest rates. This behavior is markedly different from traditional convertible securities, especially busted convertibles, which are highly sensitive to a change in interest rates (see Chapter 17). Mandatory convertibles, by definition, can never become busted.

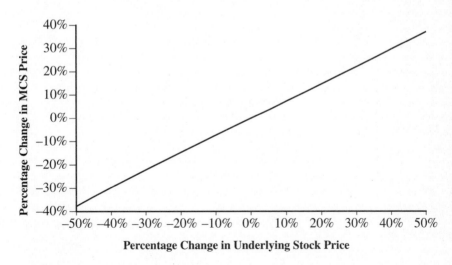

Figure 16.8   Sensitivity of an MCS to a Change in the Underlying Stock Price

Figure 16.9 demonstrates that a 1% parallel shift in interest rates will change the price of the XYZ mandatory by about 0.55%.

Credit Spread Sensitivity

Although a change in credit spread can often have a significant effect on the pricing of a traditional convertible security, its impact is minimal on an MCS. In an MCS, a change in credit spread affects only the present value of the income advantage. As illustrated in Figure 16.10, if the credit rating of XYZ Corporation were downgraded from A to BBB, raising its credit spread by 0.50% from 0.75% to 1.25%, the theoretical price of the MCS would fall by only 0.11%.

Volatility Sensitivity (Vega)

Because of the offsetting nature of the embedded call spread in mandatory convertibles, a change in volatility has a minimal effect on pricing. One curiosity with the MCS is that a change in volatility will affect the price of the MCS differently depending on where the stock price is relative to the upper or lower strike price. When the stock price is below the lower strike price, a reduction in volatility will slightly increase the value of the MCS and vice versa. Traditional con-

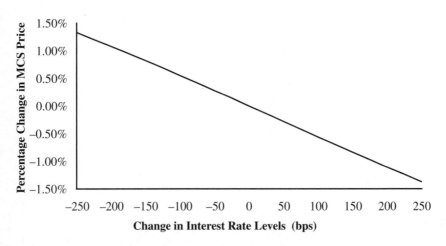

Figure 16.9   Sensitivity of an MCS to a Change in Interest Rates

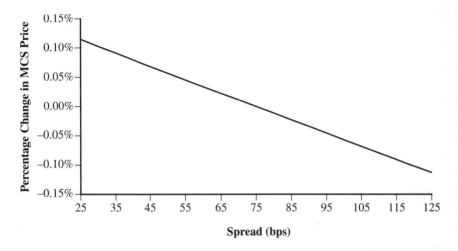

Figure 16.10   Sensitivity of an MCS to a Change in Credit Spreads

vertible securities exhibit the opposite price behavior. An increase in volatility always increases their value. With the stock price of XYZ Corporation at $20, a 10% decline in volatility from 30% to 20% increases the price of the MCS by 1.45%. A 10% increase in volatility from 30% to 40% decreases the value of the MCS by 1.02%. (See Figure 16.11.)

Conversely, when the stock price is above the upper strike price, the price behavior of the MCS is reversed and an increase in volatility will slightly increase the value of the MCS and vice versa. The reason for this unusual price behavior is explained in option pricing theory by the concept of gamma.

Gamma Sensitivity

Gamma is defined as the rate of change in delta. Delta is the rate of change in the price of a derivative security for a one-unit change in the underlying asset, in this case the stock price (see Chapter 9).

Common stock has a delta of 100% and a gamma of zero. A deep in-the-money option also has a delta approaching 100% and a gamma of zero. This is because the option is merely a surrogate for stock. A deep out-of-the-money option has a delta approaching zero and also a gamma of zero. This is because the option has very little equity sensitivity.

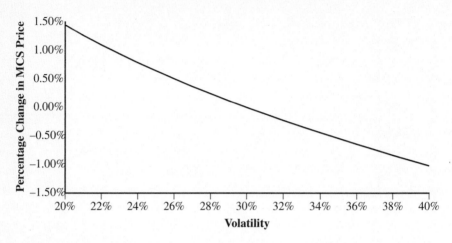

Figure 16.11   Sensitivity of an MCS to a Change in Volatility

In the MCS, we are short a greater number of calls than we are long (short a ratio call spread). The gamma of our embedded call spread will vary depending upon where the stock price is relative to the upper and lower strikes. When the stock price is far below (above) the lower (upper) strike price, the gamma will approach zero. When the stock price is nearest the lower strike price, the gamma will actually be negative, since the weighting of the short call will be greatest at this point. This means that an increase in the stock price at this point will decrease the delta. Again, this is diametrically opposed to what we would expect from a traditional convertible bond in which the delta always rises with an increase in stock price. Figure 16.12 illustrates the gamma of the XYZ mandatory.

The impact that this gamma profile has on the delta of the XYZ mandatory is illustrated in Figure 16.13 for various levels of stock price volatility. As anticipated, the delta approaches 100% as the stock price falls far below the lower strike price. At this point, the delta of the call spread is zero, leaving only the long stock position that has a delta of 100%. As the stock price rises and approaches the midpoint of the call spread, the delta declines rather than rises because the negative gamma of the short-call option dominates the combined gamma of the call spread. As the stock price continues to move up, the delta begins to increase again as gamma turns positive. When

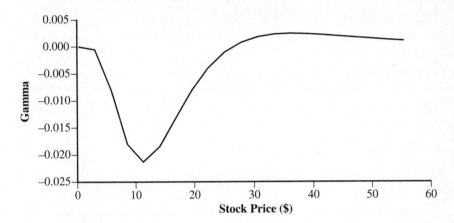

Figure 16.12   Sensitivity of Gamma to a Change in the Underlying Stock Price

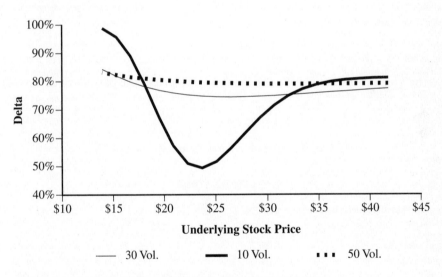

Figure 16.13   Sensitivity of Delta to a Change in Volatility

the mandatory is deep-in-the-money, the stock position is neutralized by the short call leaving only the long call position. The delta of the long call is 100%, but since we own only a partial call, the delta of the mandatory will be capped at the upper conversion ratio.

The change in delta becomes more muted as the time to maturity increases, volatility increases, or the spread of the call spread decreases.

PRICE EFFECTS OF HEDGING THE MCS

As described in Chapter 12, convertible arbitrage consists of buying a convertible security and simultaneously shorting a delta neutral amount of the underlying common stock. With traditional convertible securities, a hedge arbitrageur would be required to sell short increasing amounts of common stock as the share price rose in order to maintain a market neutral position. Because of the negative gamma characteristics of the MCS, a hedger may be required to purchase more shares to remain delta neutral as the stock price rises. This influence will benefit the price of the MCS. Conversely, should the price of the common stock fall, the reverse effect would tend to put downward pressure on the price of the MCS.

FALSE ILLUSIONS IN VALUING THE MCS

Current Yield

A common mistake in valuing the MCS is to rely on their current yield. In the case of a fixed-income security, the current yield is calculated by dividing the coupon by the current price of the security. For example, a straight bond maturing in five years with an 8% coupon trading at 110% has a current yield of 7.27%. The current yield reflects the return the investor makes today for holding the security. This return does not take into consideration the fact that the 10% premium paid for the bond must be amortized to its maturity. The yield to maturity is then a much reduced 5.67%. The same problem exists when evaluating the current yield of an MCS. The current yield may be misleading, since the difference between today's price and the final redemption value at maturity must also be amortized. The discrepancy between current yield and the yield to maturity (or stand-still rate of return) of the MCS is greatest when the price of the stock has fallen dramatically. A classic example of this situation occurred in April 1998 when the price of Cendant stock fell by 47% due to an accounting scandal. With the stock at $19, Cendant's mandatory convertible traded at $32.25. Although the current yield appeared to be a very attractive 11.63% on a BBB-rated credit, the stand-still rate to maturity was actually only 5.82%.

Credit Rating

The credit rating of the MCS relates only to the issuer's ability to make coupon (or dividend) payments. Unlike a bond, the redemption value of an MCS is not fixed but is solely a function of the issuer's stock price at maturity. There is no predefined principal amount to return at maturity. Thus, the existence of a strong credit rating is of little comfort should the stock price fall. The only component of the MCS that is affected by the credit rating is the credit spread used to discount the net present value of the income flows between the MCS and the common stock. As we have seen, the sensitivity of a change in credit spread to the value of the MCS is relatively inconsequential.

Conversion Premium

It is very tempting to describe the MCS in terms of their conversion premium and conversion price but this is a misconception. The only time when it is possible to use these terms is at the time of issue. At that time, an initial conversion premium is used to determine a conversion price. This conversion price is used only to establish the upper ratio in the call spread. Henceforth, the concept of conversion premium is fallacious since the conversion ratio itself is always subject to change depending upon the current stock price. Moreover, many mandatory convertibles are not convertible by the holder before maturity. Thus, the concept of convertibility is moot. In cases where early conversion is allowed, the number of shares into which the issue may be converted is equal to the smaller of the two ratios. Therefore, it is generally inadvisable for the investor to convert before maturity. At maturity, the issuer usually has the option to pay the holder in either cash or stock.

MCS PRODUCT EVOLUTION

Earlier in this chapter we described how the original mandatory convertible structures were nothing more than synthetic buy writes. This then evolved into a long stock position plus a short-call spread, which gave the investor added income but without being fully capped on the upside. A compelling reason for the successful proliferation of mandatories has been their advantages to issuers. Ultimately, the product has evolved to combine the best features of both debt and equity, permitting tax deductibility with equity credit.

From the issuer's perspective, the best way to segment the MSC structure is between the objectives of primary and secondary stock distribution. (See Figure 16.14.)

PRIMARY DISTRIBUTION

Equity MCS

Initially, MCS structures were used to raise equity capital. Such structures were similar to traditional convertible preferred stock in that they paid a dividend and were convertible into the issuer's common stock with voting rights upon conversion. They differed in that they were mandatorily convertible into common stock. Like traditional convertible securities, MCS involved the forward sale of equity at a price higher than the current stock price, but without the traditional downside support or investment value of a normal convertible. In exchange for giving up this downside support, the investor received a higher dividend. The problem for the issuer was that this higher dividend was not tax deductible, making it too expensive. A novel innovation got around this problem: the pairing of the equity MCS with a debt security. This became known as a parallel debt MCS or debt MCS.

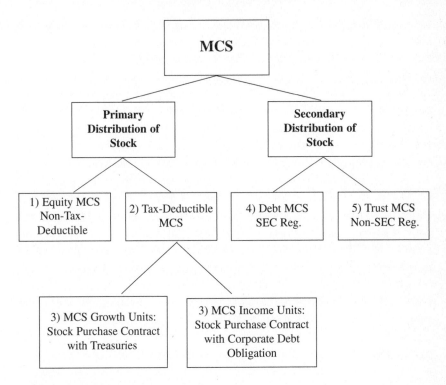

Figure 16.14 MCS: Basic Structures
Source: Morgan Stanley

Parallel Debt MCS: Forward Contract Plus U.S. Treasury Note

The parallel debt MCS was accomplished by describing the embedded call spread in the traditional mandatory structure as a stock purchase contract and concurrently issuing a debt security. The stock purchase contract provides for the three possible conversion outcomes at maturity, which are identical to the call spread payout we have described at length previously. The contract also calls for the investor to pay for the purchase of the stock when the MCS mature. This purchase price is equal to the issue price of the MCS.

All the proceeds from the sale of the MCS are invested in U.S. Treasuries with maturities corresponding to that of the MCS. The yield from the Treasuries is supplemented with an additional fee from the issuer to arrive at the stated yield on the MCS. This supplemental adjustment fee, or contract fee, is nontax-deductible for the issuer.

The issuer then enters the public debt market to issue an interest-bearing note with a maturity and face amount similar to the terms of the MCS. However, the two offerings are completely separate and are not in any way contingent upon each other. This independence is essential because if the debt were issued with the express purpose of supporting the MCS, the tax authorities would likely treat the note as equity and disallow the tax deductibility of interest payments.

At maturity, the investor delivers either cash (the settlement fee) or the maturing Treasury note to satisfy the terms of the purchase contract. The Treasury has been pledged by the investor as collateral to insure that the issuer's stock is purchased at maturity. The collateral agent typically applies the proceeds of the maturing Treasury note to purchase the issuer's shares at maturity. This ensures that the issuer receives the initial proceeds of the forward contract at maturity. The issuer can then use these proceeds to retire the corporate debt obligation that was issued simultaneously with the MCS, or retain the cash.

In this structure it is important to note that the issuer is not dependent upon the decision of the investor. At maturity, the issuer will receive either the maturity value of the Treasuries or the settlement fee, which is equal to the issue price. The other distinction is that the issuer does not purchase the Treasuries and so does not own them. The Treasuries are owned by the investor. This can be important in the event of a bankruptcy, in which case the investors and not the issuer would be entitled to the proceeds from the Treasury securities.

Finally, the investor also enjoys a tax benefit from this structure since that portion of the income received from the Treasury coupon payments is exempt from state and local taxes. (See Figure 16.15.)

MCS Trust Units with Corporate Debt or Treasuries (Income or Growth MCS)

Although the idea of collateralizing the stock purchase contract with Treasuries and then issuing concurrent debt was truly novel, it was not optimal for the issuer. It was not optimal from a tax perspective because only the cash flow from the debt security was tax deductible and not the contract adjustment fee. In the structure described previously, the issuer could deduct the interest paid on the concurrent debt obliga-

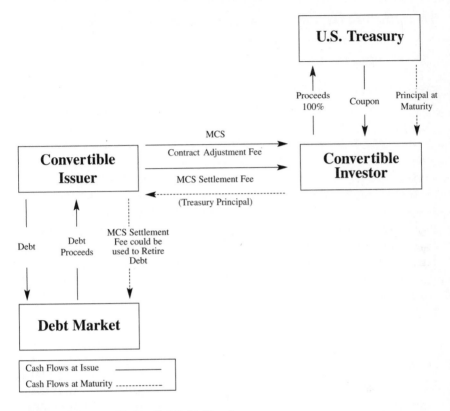

Figure 16.15   MCS: Parallel Debt Structure
Source: Morgan Stanley

tion, but because Treasuries were being used to fund the coupon on the MCS, a large contract adjustment fee was required to make up the difference. The obvious next step was to replace the Treasuries with the issuer's own debt. This would allow the issuer to minimize the contract fee and thus reduce the nontax-deductible portion of the coupon, thereby reducing the overall after-tax cost of the financing. This substitution allowed the issuer to capture the benefit of its own credit spread.

The problem with making this substitution was that it would eliminate the parallel structure used previously. The parallel structure had been required in order to satisfy the tax authorities that the two issues (the MCS and the concurrent debt) were not contingent upon each other. The way to overcome this problem was to create the MCS unit in which the two components (i.e., the conversion feature and the fixed income security) were detachable from each other. The MCS unit can then be split into a growth unit and an income unit. The growth unit consists of a forward contract, a zero-coupon Treasury note, and a contract adjustment fee. The income unit consists of a forward contract, a trust preferred stock or a debenture, and a contract adjustment fee. To facilitate this structure, the issuing company sets up a wholly owned financing trust to issue the MCS. The only asset of the trust is subordinated debt equal to the issue size of the MCS. The trust collects the proceeds from the sale of the MCS and invests them in the debt of the issuer. At maturity, the forward contract is executed and the proceeds are used to retire the issuer's debt. The issuer treats the coupon paid on the debt to the trust as an intercompany loan. The interest expense associated with this is tax deductible. Meanwhile, on the consolidated balance sheet the combined obligation appears as minority interest. As a result, the company enjoys not only a tax deduction, but equity credit from the rating agencies as well.

Separate Maturities and the Remarketing Agent

To further establish that the component parts of the MCS are not contingent upon each other, they have different maturities. The forward contract usually matures in three to five years, while the debt portion matures two years later. To accommodate this complication, the MCS unit contains a remarketing feature. At the maturity of the forward contract, the investor will choose to either use the fixed income component to settle the forward contract or pay the settlement amount in cash. If the investor uses cash, then the fixed-income security remains outstanding. If the investor chooses to use the fixed-income security to satisfy the forward contract, then the fixed-income piece will be remarketed in the public debt market as a two-year obligation. The underwriter of the issue will coordinate this remarketing procedure for a small fee. The yield will be set according to current market conditions.

Put and Call Features

To ensure that the fixed-income component will be separated from the forward contract, these structures may also contain put and call provisions. Investors are given two puts on the trust preferred they own. The first put is at par on the expiration of the forward contract. If interest rates or credit spreads have risen since the time of issue, the value of the trust obligation will have fallen below par. In this case, the investor will surely relinquish the debt to the contract settlement agent to satisfy the terms of the forward contract. This is clear, since the settlement amount is equal to the issue price of the security, which is equal to the par value of the debt. It is rational for the investor to use the debt, now worth less than par, to satisfy the settlement amount. The contract settlement agent will then remarket the trust obligation at the prevailing market rate so as to restore its value to par. At this point, the investor will be mandatorily converted into the shares of the issuer, who will have issued a new straight debt obligation with two years to maturity.

The investor's second put option on the debt is at a price above par 90 days after the expiration of the forward contract. This is relevant only if the investor elects to pay cash to meet the settlement amount rather than relinquish the debt. This could happen if interest rates or credit spreads had fallen during the term of the MCS. In this case, the debt would be worth more than par and it would be advantageous for the investor to pay the settlement amount in cash and then sell the trust obligation for a profit. This second put feature would allow the investor to take a view on interest rates for 90 days after the expiration of the forward contract with limited downside risk.

Finally, in some cases the underwriter is given a call option on the trust obligation 90 days before the expiration of the forward contract. In this case, should the value of the trust obligation significantly exceed par at this point, the underwriter would likely call the trust preferred and remarket it for a profit to itself. This action would result in an early call of the MCS for the investor. The purpose of these puts and calls is to increase the chances that the trust preferred will be separated from the forward contract. As noted earlier, it is essential to establish the independence of the two components in order to preserve the U.S. tax deductibility of the structure.

SWAPPING THE FIXED-INCOME COMPONENT: CORPORATE VERSUS TREASURY MCS

The fact that the MCS unit can be separated into two pieces presents the investor with an opportunity. The investor can swap the debt portion of the security between either the issuer's debt obligation or a zero-coupon Treasury note. If the investor chooses to retain the more risky corporate debt obligation in the structure, the yield will be higher than if it is replaced with a zero-coupon Treasury. This is the first time in history that an investor has the option to change the income and equity sensitivity of a convertible security. When the corporate debt obligation is used, the structure is known as income MCS. When the zero-coupon Treasury is used, the structure is called growth MCS.

Mechanics of the Swap

At any time before the expiration of the forward contract, the investor may convert the original income MCS into a growth MCS. To do so, the investor will sell the corporate debt obligation at the current market price in exchange for cash. The proceeds from this sale will be used to purchase a zero-coupon Treasury note with a maturity corresponding to the maturity date of the forward contract. The terms of the forward contract will remain unchanged. The effects from this swap are as follows.

Income Effect

The income to the growth MCS holder will be reduced. Income to the growth MCS holder will consist of the contract adjustment fee plus the accrual from the zero-coupon Treasury note. The growth MCS holder will give up the income from the corporate debt security previously enjoyed by the income MCS holder.

Cash Proceeds

The investor making this swap will receive net cash proceeds from the trade. This is because the proceeds from the sale of the corporate debt obligation will be larger than that required to buy a zero-coupon Treasury note with a face value equal to the settlement amount of the forward contract. This cash difference represents the income the investor would have received over the life of the MCS. By receiving this cash up front, the investor reduces the cost basis of the security. The cash can be used to make another investment or to buy more of the growth MCS, thereby increasing the investor's exposure to the stock.

Insolvency Risk

Another consequence of substituting the corporate debt security for a Treasury instrument is that in the event of bankruptcy, the MCS holder is relieved of the obligation of the forward contract. In this case, the holder would be left with the Treasury notes with a par value equal to the issue price of the MCS. Of course, if the issuer remains solvent and its stock trades down to $0.50, the investor will receive $0.50 times the lower conversion ratio worth of stock.

Note

To facilitate this swap, MCS units are usually issued with a face amount of $50. Since zero-coupon Treasury notes sell in denominations of $1,000, any swap from the income MCS to the growth MCS must be made in units of 20 (20 times $50 equals $1,000). This differs from nonunit type MCS that have an issue price equal to the current stock price. Determining the upper and lower ratios of the call spread is easily achieved by dividing the $50 issue price by the upper and lower stock prices used to establish the call spread.

OTHER MECHANICS OF THE SWAP

In executing a swap from an income MCS to a growth MCS, investors may be surprised that the value of the income MCS may not equal the value of the growth MCS plus cash received. There are three reasons for this.

Credit Spread

At the issue date, the income stream from the MCS is initially priced at a certain spread over U.S. Treasuries. When the swap is made, this credit spread may have changed. If the issuer's credit quality has declined, the spread will have widened and the present value of the future income stream will be reduced. If the issuer's credit quality has improved, the spread will have narrowed and the swapper will receive a cash pick-up.

Note

An absolute change in the level of interest rates will not substantially alter the cash flows. For example, if interest rates rise after the issue date, the reduced value of the cash flows is compensated for by the lower price required to purchase the zero-coupon Treasury notes. The opposite would be true after a decline in rates.

Par Value of the Trust Obligation

The second element that is affected by the swap is the valuation of the debt security embedded in the structure. At the time of issue, the par amount of this security is held as collateral against the forward contract. It is not discounted for credit risk. However, once it is separated in the swap, it no longer serves as collateral for the forward contract and must be discounted to reflect the issuer's credit quality. This discounting reduces the cash proceeds paid to the investor.

Accrued Interest

If the debt security used in the MCS is preferred stock, there will be no accrual of interest between payment dates. The investor will lose the value of this interest when the investor is making the swap. This problem can be avoided if the debt security used in the MCS is an interest-bearing note. In this case, accrued interest would be paid to the investor at the time of the swap.

SECONDARY DISTRIBUTION

Trust MCS

Using trust-type mandatory securities to monetize a company's stake in a nonstrategic asset has become increasingly popular. Examples of this structure include Houston Industries into Time Warner, Tribune into Mattel, and Media One (ATT) into Vodafone. The advantage of this structure is that it allows the issuer to immediately raise money from the sale of its stake but defer the realization of capital gains taxes until the security matures. Usually, this is after a period of three to five years. However, the latest innovation of this structure has allowed for extended maturities of up to 60 years. In Europe, exchangeable convertibles are often used to accomplish this purpose.

The issuer of this type of MCS enjoys several other advantages. First, a floor on the value of the stake is determined at the time of issue. However, if the value of the stake rises during the term of the MCS, the issuer will retain some of the upside benefit, since the number of shares delivered at maturity will be reduced. Second, the mandatory structure assures that the stake will be monetized, unlike a traditional exchangeable convertible where the issuer might have to deliver cash at maturity should the stock fail to perform. A case in point is Tenet Healthcare, which used a traditional exchangeable convertible bond to monetize its holdings in Vencor. Vencor subsequently filed for bankruptcy, but Tenet is still obliged to repay the principal of the bond at maturity. Third, the MCS is structured as debt because the consideration at maturity can be paid in either cash or stock. This means that the coupon paid by the issuer can be deducted for tax purposes. Finally, the issuer retains its voting rights on the monetized stake until maturity. (See Figure 16.16.)

Trust MCS: Non-SEC Registrants

As we have seen, the use of a trust structure has enabled issuers to deduct the coupon paid to the trust as interest expense as it flows

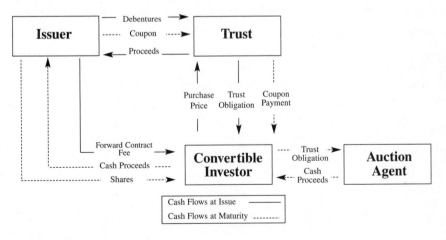

Figure 16.16 MCS: Basic Trust Structure
Source: Morgan Stanley

through to the investor in the form of a dividend on the MCS. The use of a trust structure is also beneficial to insiders or investors who are non-SEC registrants and wish to monetize their holdings in a company. In this case, the trust is used as a conduit. The trust issues an MCS and distributes the majority of the proceeds to the selling shareholders (e.g., 80%). The remaining 20% of the proceeds are used to buy zero-coupon Treasury strips with maturities corresponding to the quarterly payment dates of the MCS. As before, if the stock performs well during the term of the security the selling shareholders will benefit, because a lesser number of shares will be needed to satisfy conversion. Any capital gain due on the sale of the original stake will be deferred until maturity. (See Figure 16.17.)

ACCOUNTING TREATMENT

EPS Dilution: Equity MCS (As-If-Converted Method)

When we are calculating the dilutive effect of convertible securities on earnings per share, two methods may apply. As with traditional convertible securities, the equity MCS use the as-if-converted method while tax-deductible MCS or debt MCS, use the Treasury method.

In the case of equity MCS, the as-if-converted method is used only if it will have a dilutive effect on earnings per share. To test this, two calculations must be performed. Equation 16.1 assumes that the MCS is fully converted. The number of shares into which the MCS may be converted is calculated at the beginning of each reporting period using the average stock price over the preceding period. These shares are then added to the weighted average number of shares outstanding in the equation's denominator. Since the MCS are assumed to have been converted at the beginning of the period, the numerator must be adjusted to include any preferred dividends that were previously deducted from net income.

$$\frac{\text{Net income ascribed to shareholders + Preferred dividends}}{\underset{\text{outstanding}}{\text{Total shares}} + \underset{\substack{\text{would convert given the current} \\ \text{market price of the common stock}}}{\text{Common shares into which the MCS}}} \qquad (16.1)$$

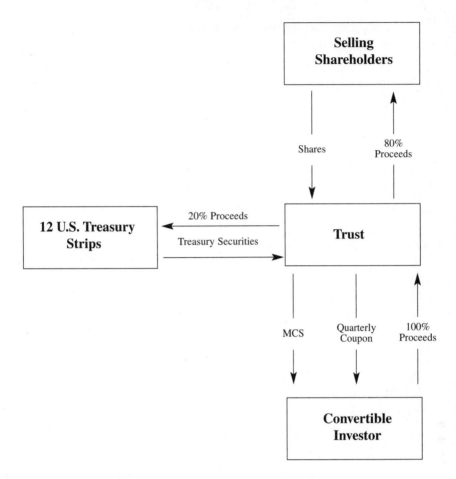

Figure 16.17 MCS: Trust Structures for Non-SEC Registrants
Source: Morgan Stanley

The resultant earnings-per-share figure must then be compared to the calculation given in Equation 16.2, in which no conversion is assumed. In this case, the preferred dividend remains in the numerator (i.e., it is subtracted from net income) and there is no adjustment to the number of shares outstanding.

$$\frac{\text{Net income ascribed to shareholders} - \text{Preferred dividends}}{\text{Total shares outstanding}} \quad (16.2)$$

If the earnings-per-share figure derived from assuming full conversion is greater than if no conversion is assumed, the as-if-converted method is not used because it would be antidilutive. This situation may arise if the preferred dividend paid is particularly high. If so, then Equation 16.1 will be less dilutive than Equation 16.2, and no assumed conversion is made to calculate earnings per share.

SEALED AIR CORPORATION

An example can be seen in the case of Sealed Air Corporation's third quarter 1999 results. In March 1998, Sealed Air issued 36 million shares of convertible preferred stock (not an MCS) with a face amount of $50. Each share was convertible into 0.89 shares of Sealed Air's common stock at a price of $56.52 per share. If fully converted, the preferred would create an additional 31.7 million shares of Sealed Air's common stock. The relevant facts are summarized below.

Third Quarter 1999 Results

Net income	$53.7 M
Preferred dividend	−$17.9 M
Net income ascribed to common stockholders	$35.8 M
Weighted average common shares outstanding	83.6 M
Shares underlying the convertible preferred	31.7 M

On an as-if-converted method, the company's third quarter earnings per share would be $0.47 per share calculated as follows:

$$\frac{\$35.8M + \$17.9M}{83.6M + 31.7M} = \frac{\$53.7M}{115.3M} = \$0.47 \text{ per share}$$

Without taking the dilutive effect of the convertible into consideration, earnings per share were $0.43.

$$\frac{\$53.7M - \$17.9M}{83.6M} = \frac{\$35.8M}{83.6M} = \$0.43 \text{ per share}$$

Due to the high preferred dividend, the as-if-converted method is antidilutive and is not used for purposes of calculating earnings per share.

In the case of Sealed Air, this proved to be an important distinction. Most analysts had incorrectly based their consensus earnings estimates for the company on an as-if-converted basis, which was expected to be $0.45. When the company correctly reported its basic earnings of $0.43, the stock fell 8%, as many market participants believed the company had missed its numbers. Later, it became clear that the company had actually beaten its expected results by reporting $0.47 on an as-if-converted basis and the stock recovered the next day.

EPS DILUTION: TAX-DEDUCTIBLE MCS (TREASURY STOCK METHOD)

Debt MCS, or tax-deductible MCS, are structured as a combination of debt and a forward stock purchase contract. These structures use the Treasury stock method for computing basic and diluted earnings per share. Under this method, the common stock price is the most important factor in determining whether the MCS will be dilutive.

Under the Treasury method, the number of shares to be created from the MCS is calculated using the following formula.

$$\begin{array}{l}\text{No. of MCS} \\ \text{issued} \cdot \text{Conversion} \\ \text{ratio}\end{array} - \left(\frac{\text{No. of MCS issued} \cdot \text{Issue price}}{\text{Current market price}}\right) = \begin{array}{l}\text{Shares added to total} \\ \text{shares outstanding}\end{array}$$

In the formula above, the conversion ratio equals the number of shares into which the MCS would be converted at the time of the calculation. The time of the calculation may be at any time during the term of the MCS, but is usually determined at the beginning of the reporting period. As we have seen, the conversion ratio for the MCS typically varies between 1 and 0.80 shares depending upon the price of the common stock and initial premium at issue.

The Treasury stock method differs from the as-if-converted method in two important ways. First, during the life of the MCS, it assumes that the forward contract will be exercised only if the stock price exceeds the uppermost conversion price. This differs from the as-if-converted method, in which dilution may occur even if the stock price is below the conversion price. Of course, at maturity the mandatory convertible will be converted into common stock regardless of the stock price, and the full dilutive effect will be realized. The second important distinction is that the Treasury method assumes that the cash proceeds from the original sale of the MCS will be used to purchase the shares upon conversion. This has the effect of limiting the dilutive effect of the conversion. As we will see in the examples following, if the stock price is below the upper strike price in the MCS, then no dilution will occur until final maturity. If the stock price rises above the upper strike price during the term of the MCS, then additional shares will be added to the total number of shares outstanding, and dilution will occur. However, since it is assumed that the cash proceeds from the sale of the MCS are used to pay for the stock when it is eventually issued, the stock price must rise substantially for any significant dilution to occur.

XYZ Corporation (Treasury Method)

To illustrate how this method works in practice, we recall the MCS example of XYZ Corporation from earlier in this chapter.

Issue price	$25
Conversion (issue) premium	23%
Conversion price (upper ratio)	$30.75 ($25 · 1.23)
Number of MCS issued	10 M
Shares outstanding	50 M
Conversion ratio	
If stock is below $25	= 1.000
If stock is above $30.75	= 0.813
If stock is > $25 and <$30.75	= 1.00 to 0.813

Example 1

If Stock Price Is below Issue Price

If we assume that the share price drops to $20, we know that the conversion ratio applied under the Treasury method formula would be 1.000. We then apply the formula as follows:

$$10M \cdot 1.000 - \frac{10M \cdot \$25}{\$20} = -2.5M \text{ shares}$$

Since the result is negative 2.5 million shares, we make no adjustment to the total shares outstanding because the result would be antidilutive.

Example 2

If the Stock Is Trading between Issue Price and Conversion Price

If the stock is trading between the upper and lower strike prices at $27.875, we know that the appropriate conversion ratio would be 0.8968 ($25/$27.875). Using these inputs yields the following result:

$$10M \cdot 0.8968 - \frac{10M \cdot \$25}{-\$27.875} = 0 \text{ shares}$$

For all stock prices between the upper and lower strike prices, the result of the formula will be zero and there will be no dilution.

Example 3

If the Stock Price Is Higher than the Upper Strike Price

If the stock price rises above the upper strike price to $35, we know that the conversion ratio will be capped at the upper conversion ratio of 0.813. Using these values, the number of shares to be added to the total outstanding would be:

$$10M \cdot 0.813 - \frac{10M \cdot \$25}{\$35} = 0.987M \text{ shares}$$

Using the 50 million total shares outstanding, the MCS would be 1.94% dilutive (0.987 M/50.987 M). Considering that XYZ Corporation's MCS represented 20% of its equity market capitalization at the time of issue (10 M/50 M), a 40% rise in the stock price from $25 to $35 results in a relatively small amount of dilution.

TREASURY STOCK METHOD: INCOME STATEMENT AND BALANCE SHEET IMPLICATIONS

In the income statement, trust preferred payments from the tax-deductible MCS are treated as a minority interest expense and not as a preferred dividend. That portion of the payment that is a contract adjustment fee is nondeductible and does not run through the income statement. Instead, a liability for the present value of all future contract adjustment fees is created on the balance sheet with a corresponding debt to shareholders' equity. The MCS are carried on the balance sheet as minority interest.

In calculating basic earnings per share, minority interest expense is deducted from net income (just like preferred dividends) and no shares from the forward contract are added to the total number of shares outstanding. In calculating diluted earnings per share, minority interest continues to be deducted from net income (unlike traditional convertibles, where preferred dividends are added back to net income) and the number of shares to be added to the total outstanding is calculated according to the Treasury method.

MCS: U.S. TAX TREATMENT

Equity MCS are treated like preferred stock. Dividends received by investors are taxed as ordinary income. Corporate investors are eligible for the Dividend Received Deduction (DRD), which allows them to deduct 70% of the dividend, provided the security has been held at risk for 46 days during each dividend period. Gains or losses are recognized upon the sale of the security. If the MCS are exchanged into the stock of the issuer, then no gain or loss is recognized until the stock is sold. The holder's cost basis will be the cost reflected in the MCS. This cost basis is reduced by any fractional cash distribution at the time of the exchange. A gain or loss will be recognized immediately if the holder receives all cash in lieu of stock upon conversion.

Debt MSC are treated like debentures. Interest received is treated as ordinary income. Since no dividend is paid, the DRD is not applicable. Upon exchange, the holder will be subject to a taxable event if cash is received instead of stock. If the exchange is into stock, then no gain or loss is recognized until the stock is sold. If the MCS are sold before maturity, a gain or loss is recognized. The holder's tax basis will be reduced by the amount of accrued interest assumed to accrue during the holding period. This interest will be taxed as ordinary income.

Tax-deductible MCS funded with Treasuries, corporate debt, or corporate trust preferred stock are not eligible for the DRD. Coupons or dividends received from corporate obligations are taxed as ordinary income. Coupons funded by U.S. Treasuries represent a tax-free return of capital and are free of state and local taxes. Upon exchange or sale, the tax consequences are the same as described previously.

Trust MCS are treated as forward contracts. Coupons are taxed as ordinary income unless funded by U.S. Treasuries as discussed previously. If sold before maturity, a gain or loss will be recognized based on the holder's cost basis. Purchase of stock pursuant to the forward contract is not a taxable event. However, any cash received in lieu of fractional shares is taxable. The cost basis of purchased shares is equal to the cost basis of the trust MCS.

CONCLUSION

Mandatory convertible securities have become an important part of the U.S. convertible market. The tax advantages afforded by the structure have made them appealing to a host of issuers, including those who traditionally would not utilize the convertible market. Consequently, the product has helped to grow and broaden the scope of the convertible market. We expect this trend to continue in the United States and gradually develop abroad as well. Although it is important

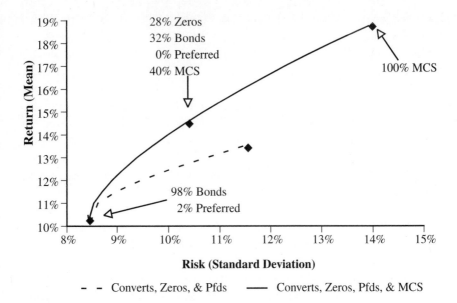

Figure 16.18 Comparison of the U.S. Convertible Market Efficient Frontier with and without MCS (January 1995 through December 1999)
Source: Gabelli

to recognize the risks associated with the MCS, there is no doubt that they play a legitimate role in the composition of a diversified convertible portfolio. The efficient frontier figure (Figure 16.18) suggests that during the five-year bull market period from early 1995 through 1999, investing 100% of portfolio assets in the MCS would have been the optimal choice. Reducing the volatility of the portfolio to a more modest 10% indicates a weighting of up to 40% in the MCS when complemented by a healthy dose of zero-coupon convertible bonds. Surprisingly, the MCS fully replace the convertible preferred category.

17

BUSTED CONVERTIBLES
Market Overview

WHAT IS A BUSTED CONVERTIBLE?

A convertible is busted when the underlying stock is far out-of-the-money (i.e., the stock price is far below the convertible's conversion price). At this point, the convertible trades on its fixed-income characteristics. Since the equity component of the security is of minimal value, busted convertibles have low sensitivity to movements in the stock price and a high conversion premium. The area constituting busted convertibles is illustrated in Figure 17.1.

WHEN IS A CONVERTIBLE BUSTED?

There are various methods for determining when a convertible is busted. Busted convertibles are characterized by low equity price sensitivity (i.e., low deltas), large conversion premiums, and high yields to maturity. But what should the cutoff points be?

It is generally accepted that a theoretical delta below 40% constitutes a busted convertible. Unfortunately, calculating the delta is

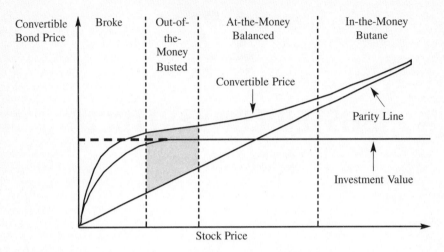

Figure 17.1   Secondary Market Behavior: Busted Convertibles

cumbersome. It requires inputting data into the Black–Scholes model (see Chapter 7). Designating a specific conversion premium is easier to calculate but subjective (see Chapter 1). A conversion premium greater than 75% is often used as a benchmark. Since busted convertible investors are motivated by income, yield to maturity would seem a likely determinant. Perhaps all convertibles yielding more than 10% to maturity should be deemed busted. Unfortunately, this level is a moving target dependent on the current level of interest rates. A relative value indicator would be more meaningful. For example, busted convertibles could be defined as those with a yield to maturity of at least 500 basis points over comparable Treasuries. Again, this is a laborious calculation to formulate and monitor.

The simplest way to identify a busted convertible is to examine the ratio between the current stock price (i.e., S) and the conversion price (i.e., CP). The minimum point at which an investor will exchange the convertible for stock is when this ratio is equal to one. At this point the convertible is at-the-money. When the ratio is greater than one, the convertible is in-the-money. It is out-of-the-money when the ratio is less than one. This analysis originated in the Japanese equity warrants market where the conversion price was the warrant's exercise price (i.e., E). In our case, for simplicity, we retain the stated conversion price rather than the adjusted exercise price (see Chapter 8) to make the calculation. A busted convertible is defined as any convertible with a S/CP ratio below 0.5. This method is easy to use for all convertibles except for those issued under an original issue discount (OID) or premium redemption structure. These structures accrete in value to maturity. Although the conversion ratio remains constant, the conversion price is constantly moving away from the investor at the accretion rate. The conversion price is calculated by dividing the conversion ratio into the accreted notional value of the security (see Chapter 2).

MARKET OVERVIEW

Traditionally, convertibles have been viewed as a safer alternative to equities because of their fixed-income component. Convertibles provide an opportunity to participate in the stock's upside potential without suffering all the downside risk. In 1999, growth in the U.S. convertible market was tied to the growth in technology, media, and telecommunications (TMT) companies. At the peak, TMT companies made up about 70% of the U.S. convertible universe on a market-weighted basis. As of March 2001, this figure fell to about 45% of the total market following the collapse of the TMT bubble in March 2000. Many of the New Economy companies had limited track records, minimal revenues, and negative operating earnings. These companies have highly volatile share prices. However, it is precisely this high volatility that gave them a comparative advantage as issuers in the convertible market. Here they are able to monetize this volatility by issuing a call warrant on their stock in exchange for low coupon financing. In the straight high-yield market, they would be made to pay a high coupon. Unlike their Old Economy counterparts, who enjoy long operating histories and stable cash flows, the New Economy issuers offer a markedly different risk/reward profile. Many New Economy convertibles were priced during the euphoria of the Internet bubble when share prices were trading on extremely high valuations. When prices fell, the size of the busted convertible market relative to the market as a whole increased commensurately (see Figure 17.2).

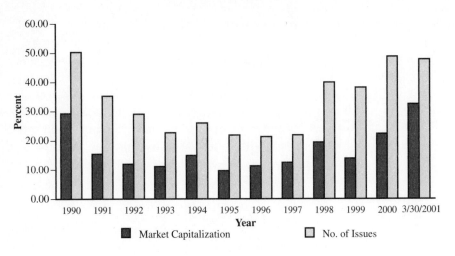

Figure 17.2 U.S. Busted Convertibles: Market Capitalization as a Percentage of Total Market Capitalization
Source: Lehman Brothers, March 2001

BUSTED CONVERTIBLES BY SECTOR

Reflecting the composition of the overall market, the majority of busted convertibles are to be found in the technology (34% of market) and telecommunications (30%) sectors. Convertibles in the health care (9%) and consumer cyclical (6%) sectors also comprise a significant portion of the busted universe. Other important sectors include capital goods (6%), consumer noncyclicals (6%), and basic industry (4%). (See Figure 17.3.)

BUSTED CONVERTIBLES BY PRODUCT TYPE

The majority of busted convertibles are convertible bonds, which represent 63% of the universe. Convertible preferreds make up 15% and zero-coupon convertibles 22%. Relative to the market as a whole, there are fewer zero-coupon convertibles in the busted universe. This is reasonable because zeros are generally issued by better quality companies and are less likely to become busted. Surprisingly, convertible preferreds are proportionally underrepresented. One might ex-

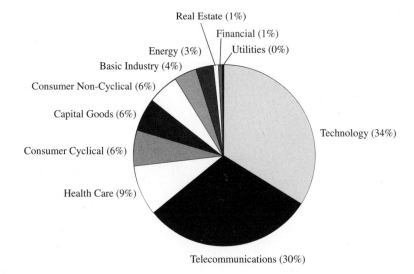

Figure 17.3   U.S. Busted Convertibles: Market Sector
Source: Lehman Brothers, March 2001

pect them to represent a larger percentage of the busted universe because of their weaker investment values and their ability to defer dividend payments. (See Figure 17.4.)

BUSTED CONVERTIBLES BY CREDIT QUALITY RATING

The average credit quality of the busted convertible market is BB–, versus BB+ for the entire domestic universe. Only 38% of busted convertibles are rated investment grade, versus 46% for the broader market (excluding mandatories). The relatively poor credit quality of both markets is due to the large portion of speculative TMT issuers. (See Figure 17.5.)

Both micro- and macroevents can precipitate a deterioration in the value of a firm. On the micro side, poor management and bad execution can reduce profitability and cause the share price to decline. On the macro side, increased competition from new technologies or a changing regulatory environment can reduce the value of the firm. If

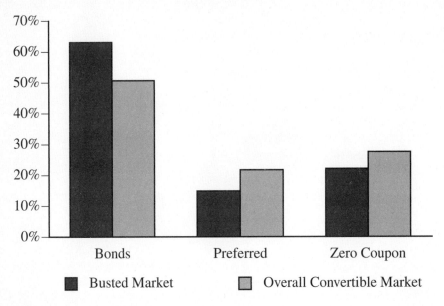

Figure 17.4   U.S. Busted Convertibles: Product Type
Source: Lehman Brothers, March 2001

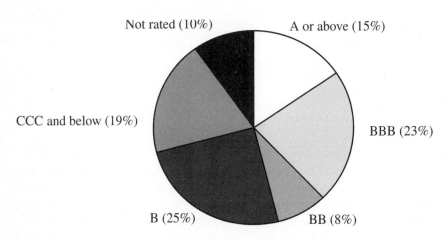

Figure 17.5   U.S. Busted Convertibles: Credit Quality
Source: Lehman Brothers, March 2001

the firm does not adapt, the share price will decline and the convertible will become busted.

DEFAULT RATES: CONVERTIBLES VERSUS JUNK BONDS

In the late 1990s, the high-yield or junk bond market (i.e., bonds with sub-investment grade credit ratings) grew rapidly to more than $600 billion. Junk bonds have played an important role in funding emerging growth companies and in financing industry consolidation. Although junk bonds and convertibles, combined, account for only about 2% of the $40 trillion domestic equity market, they have become increasingly popular with investors as a means of gaining equity-like returns with less risk. Understanding the causes of default, as well as the history of default rates, is helpful in evaluating busted convertibles.

There are three main factors that affect default rates: credit quality, macroeconomic conditions, and time. In 1999, the heavy issuance of nonrated, TMT companies changed the overall composition of the domestic convertible market. As of March 2001, the amount of nonrated issues constitutes about 10% of the overall market. Among rated issues, the number rated CCC+ or below has tripled over the past four years and they now make up 19% of the market. Consequently, nonrated and lower-rated issues represent about one-third of the overall market. Moreover, from mid-1998 through the end of 2000, there have been five times as many credit downgrades as upgrades for existing corporate issuers. These trends help to explain the recent rise in default rates.

Macroeconomic conditions also influence default rates. Economic downturns reduce profitability and cash flow, which inhibit a company's ability to service debt. After the rapid economic growth in the late 1990s, the Federal Reserve Board began raising short-term interest rates to cool the expansion. The rise in the interest rates and the slowing economy precipitated a rise in default rates.

The passage of time is an important element in determining the probability of default. This aging effect illustrates that first-time issuers are most likely to default three to four years after issuance. There is no conclusive evidence to explain this phenomenon. One hypothesis is that

Figure 17.6   Speculative Grade Default Rates (January 1990 through March 2001)

Source: Lehman Brothers, March 2001

companies that issue junk bonds are likely to have sufficient cash flow to make only the first few payments. Others profess that the aging effect is tied to the business cycle. Weak companies who issue debt during an economic upturn default when the economy slows three years later. Unfortunately, this theory does not explain why domestic default rates have been continually increasing despite the record U.S. economic expansion. Ultimately, predicting default rates is more of an art than a science.

Figure 17.6 displays the varying levels of default rates over the past decade for all speculative-grade issues, both convertible and high-yield. The sharp rise in default rates illustrated at the far right of the figure is explained by the large amount of issuance in the 1996–1997 period.

18

INVESTING IN BUSTED CONVERTIBLES

ADVANTAGES OF BUSTED CONVERTIBLES

Despite the negative connotation, busted convertibles present investors with unique opportunities. In contrast to junk bonds, the upside potential is not capped. Returns from high-yield debt consist of coupon payments and limited capital gains as the bond accretes to par at maturity. Convertibles, with their embedded equity warrant, enjoy unlimited upside potential if the stock price recovers. With busted convertibles, the equity warrant, being deep out-of-the-money, is often mispriced. Investors are effectively buying high-yield debt with a free equity kicker. Consequently, busted convertibles are a more attractive investment than high-yield debt in a modern economy that has shifted from slow-growth, cyclical companies to more volatile growth companies. As with junk bonds, busted convertibles offer investors high current income and/or attractive yields to maturity or put. Similarly, these securities help diversify unsystematic risk in a portfolio.

DISADVANTAGES OF BUSTED CONVERTIBLES

Busted convertibles are often illiquid. This results from the small size and research-intensive nature of busted convertibles. When convertibles make the transition from being balanced to busted, there is a shift in the investor base. Traditional convertible investors become sellers as equity sensitivity diminishes, while junk bond investors become buyers as yield increases. Frequently, this transition is separated by a price gap. This gap creates a period of inactivity that reduces liquidity.

Convertible securities are generally subordinate to other creditors in the event of a liquidation or bankruptcy. Although they rank before equity holders, the risk of loss is greater than for senior or secured creditors.

Although traditional convertible investors abhor dilution, busted convertible investors dislike recapitalization programs. A stock buyback reduces both the cash balances available for debt servicing and the equity cushion.

Finally, the biggest investment risk is continued credit deterioration. Analyzing busted convertibles is a research-intensive process involving both equity and credit analysis. It requires an assessment of the company's current stability as well as its future potential. For example, is the company's poor performance due to a temporary problem, or to a fundamental flaw in its business model?

To illustrate, we examine two case studies. The first is Mark IV Industries (Mark IV), an Old Economy industrial company. In this case, the busted-convertible bonds offer an attractive yield, the share price is undervalued, and the credit risk can be assessed using traditional ratio analysis. The second case is Global TeleSystems (GTS), a New Economy broadband telecommunications company engaged in the process of building out its business plan. In this case, it is clear that the convertible preferred offers an attractive yield, but an evaluation of the share price and credit risk is less certain. A comparison of these two cases will provide insight into how to evaluate the merits of busted-convertible investing.

OLD ECONOMY CASE STUDY: MARK IV INDUSTRIES

The Company

Mark IV Industries Inc. is a leading manufacturer of power and fluid transfer products used primarily in automotive and industrial businesses. Headquartered in Buffalo, N.Y., the company had worldwide sales of $1.9 billion in 1999 (the fiscal year ended February 2000). With 47.5 million basic shares outstanding and the stock price at $16.5625 in December 1999, Mark IV had an equity market capitalization of $787 million. Adding $853 million of net debt gave a total enterprise value (EV) of $1.64 billion. With EBITDA (earnings before interest, taxes, depreciation, and amortization) of $279 million, the company traded on an EV/EBITDA multiple of just 5.9 times. Although the stock price had been as high as $27.50 in October 1997, it came under pressure as the Asia debt crisis and a strike at General Motors hurt operating results. Despite these setbacks, management was taking corrective actions. These included the disposition of underperforming assets, employee reductions, strategic acquisitions, and a share-buyback program. In fact, so adamantly did Sal Alfiero, the company's chairman and chief executive officer, believe in the value of the company that he made the following statement in the firm's 1999 annual report: "Our attitude towards stock repurchases will continue to be the same as long as these ridiculously low price levels prevail; simply put ... if you don't want it, we'll take all you've got."

Assuming Mark IV could earn $320 million in EBITDA next year, and applying a more reasonable EV/EBITDA multiple of seven times, the stock was worth $29 per share (see Chapter 19).

THE INVESTMENT OPPORTUNITY

Table 18.1 outlines the details of Mark IV's convertible bond in December 1999. With the stock at $16.5625, the bonds traded at 79.75% on a 5.95% current yield and 58% conversion premium. The S/CP ratio (the current stock price divided by the conversion price) was 0.50, defining the bonds as busted (see Chapter 17). Assuming a credit

Table 18.1   Mark IV Industries: Convertible Terms

Issuer	Mark IV Industries	Size	$275 million
Coupon	4¾% fixed, paid semiannually	Registration status	Seasoned 144A
Credit rating	Ba2/ BB–	Maturity date	1-Nov-04
Security type	Convertible bond	Conversion premium	58%
Convertible price	79.75%	Stock price	$16.5625
Current yield	5.59%	Yield to maturity	10.00%
Conversion price	$32.8125	Conversion ratio	30.476

spread for a BB–rated industrial credit of 400 basis points over comparable treasuries, the bond sat on its investment value of 80% with a yield to maturity of 10%.

Since both the equity story and the pricing of the bond appeared attractive, the only remaining phase of the investment process was to assure that the credit risk was satisfactory.

CREDIT ANALYSIS 101

What Is Credit Analysis?

Credit analysis determines the ability of a firm to meet its obligations to debt holders. A company's financial well-being can be analyzed by examining a number of financial ratios. These ratios are generally grouped into five categories: leverage, liquidity, coverage, profitability, and efficiency. By studying the trends in these ratios, and by comparing them to an industry average, the credit risk can be assessed. Of course, the usefulness of financial ratios is limited—they are by definition based on static, historic data. Experienced judgment is also required in making an informed credit decision. Nevertheless, the framework is useful in terms of leading the analyst to ask the right questions. In the analysis next, we apply this process to Mark IV. Finally, in an effort to use ratio analysis as a predictive tool, we introduce the Altman Z-Score methodology, developed by Professor Edward I. Altman of New York University.

As a basis for analysis, we present in Table 18.2 a common-sized balance sheet and income statement for Mark IV Industries for the

Table 18.2 Mark IV Industries: Common-Sized Balance Sheet and Income Statement

(USD Millions)	1998	%	(Fiscal year ended February) 1999	%	2000	%

Mark IV Industries—Balance Sheet

	1998	%	1999	%	2000	%
ASSETS						
Current assets:						
Cash & cash equivalents	121	5	126	6	2	0
Accounts, notes receivable	466	19	406	20	414	20
Inventories	393	16	298	14	347	17
Other current assets	106	4	133	6	139	7
Total current assets	1,086	44	963	46	901	44
Noncurrent assets:						
Net fixed assets	668	28	562	27	605	30
Other noncurrent assets	666	28	555	27	537	26
TOTAL ASSETS	2,421	100	2,080	100	2,043	100
LIABILITIES & EQUITY						
Current liabilities:						
Accounts payable	222	9	220	11	266	12
Short-term debt	207	9	58	3	59	3
Other current liabilities	199	8	194	9	183	9
Total current liabilities	628	26	472	23	508	25
Noncurrent liabilities:						
Long-term debt	794	33	798	38	796	38
Other	247	10	286	10	335	13
Total liabilities	1,669	69	1483	71	1,566	77
Shareholder equity	752	31	597	29	477	23
TOTAL LIABILITIES AND EQUITY	2,421	100	2,080	100	2,043	100

Mark IV Industries—Income Statement

	1998	%	1999	%	2000	%
Net sales	1,703	100	1,798	100	1,994	100
Cost of goods sold	1,131	66	1,227	68	1,363	68
Selling and administration	271	16	278	15	293	15
Research & development	46	3	51	3	59	3
Depreciation & amortization	63	4	76	.4	91	.5
Operating income (loss)	193	11	116	6	188	9
Interest expense	46	3	49	3	54	3
Income tax expense	56	3	22	1	48	2
Income before XO items	91	5	45	3	86	4
XO gain (loss)	6	0	3	0	3	0
NET INCOME (loss)	97	6	48	3	89	4
Avg. # shares (basic)	64.1		56.9		47.5	
Avg. # shares (diluted)	67.4		65.5		56.2	
Effective tax rate %	28.8		18.9		25.5	
Cash dividends paid	10.8		11.4		10.7	

fiscal years ended February 1998, 1999, and 2000. For industry comparisons, we equate this to the calendar years ended 1997, 1998, and 1999. Our industry comparison consists of six companies engaged primarily in auto parts (i.e., Borg Warner, Dana), industrial products (i.e., Donaldson, IDEX), or a combination of such services (i.e., TRW, Barnes).

LEVERAGE RATIOS

Financial leverage measures the relative amount of risk borne by the shareholders versus the creditors. It measures how much of a protective cushion the assets of the firm provide the creditors. The larger the amount of debt relative to equity, the greater the creditors' risk. Two ratios commonly used to measure this relationship are the debt-to-equity ratio and the debt-to-total capitalization ratio.

Debt-to-Equity Ratio

The debt-to-equity ratio describes a company's capital structure. It provides a measure of how much the owners have at risk versus the creditors. Although a high debt-to-equity ratio may increase shareholder returns, it creates greater risk for the creditors. The ratio is calculated as follows:

$$\text{Debt-to-equity ratio} = \frac{\text{Total liabilities}}{\text{Net worth}}$$

Total liabilities are defined as the sum of the current liabilities plus all other types of long-term debt, including deferred income taxes. Occasionally, deferred taxes are omitted from total liabilities under the assumption that they may be deferred indefinitely. We use the more conservative assumption. In the case of Mark IV, the company's reserves for deferred taxes are not included in total liabilities, so no adjustment is necessary. Net worth is defined as shareholders' equity including minority interest. Mark IV has no minority interest. Table 18.3 shows the trend in Mark IV's debt-to-equity ratio versus the industry average.

Table 18.3 Mark IV: Total Liabilities-to-
Equity Ratio (Times)

	Mark IV	Industry Average
1997	2.22	1.70
1998	2.49	1.65
1999	3.28	2.32

Measured by the book value of the assets, a debt-to-equity ratio of 3.28 indicates that the creditors have 3.28 times more at risk to the company than do the shareholders. In reality, this proportion might be different if the market value of the assets differs significantly from their book value. This is particularly true for older companies that have productive assets (i.e., factories) that have largely been depreciated, or that have significant real estate holdings. This is not likely to be relevant for Mark IV.

The deteriorating trend in Mark IV's debt-to-equity ratio is cause for concern. Closer examination reveals that the deterioration is due to write-offs associated with management's restructuring and share-buyback program. Investors should scrutinize whether or not the company's level of retained earnings is sufficient to fund its future sales growth. Given the existing capital structure and profitability, we can calculate the company's sustainable growth rate as follows:

$$G = \frac{NPM \cdot (1-D) \cdot (1+L)}{A - NPM \cdot (1-D) \cdot (1+L)}$$

where G = Sustainable sales growth rate
     NPM = Net profit margin (Net profit ÷ Sales)
       D = Dividend payout ratio (Dividends ÷ Net profit)
       L = Debt-to net worth ratio (Total liabilities ÷ Net worth)
       A = Total assets ÷ Sales

The equation assumes that an increase in sales requires an increase in total assets, that assets are financed with retained earnings and debt, and that the profit margin and dividend policy remain constant.

For Mark IV, this indicates a sustainable growth rate of 19.6%. In other words, the company could increase its sales at this rate without changing its capital structure.

$$19.6\% = \frac{0.044656 \cdot (1-0.12) \cdot (1+3.28)}{1.02508 - 0.044656 \cdot (1-0.12) \cdot (1.328)}$$

$$= \frac{0.16818}{0.85688}$$

Last year, the company grew its sales by only 10%. In the future, a growth rate of between 5% and 10% is most likely. Consequently, the company is overleveraged for its expected growth rate. If we assume a 10% growth rate, we can rewrite the preceding equation to solve for the required amount of leverage. This indicates an appropriate capital structure of just over one times debt (total liabilities) to net worth.

$$\text{Leverage} = \frac{G \cdot A}{NPM \cdot (1+G)} - 1$$

$$= \frac{0.10 \cdot 1.02508}{0.044656 \cdot (1+0.10)} - 1$$

$$= 1.08$$

The debt-to-net worth ratio should be used as a comparative tool. Different industries have unique capital structures. Higher debt-to-equity ratios are acceptable in industries with stable earnings. Leverage ratios of regulated utilities are justifiably higher than those of biotechnology companies. Mark IV has consistently higher leverage ratios than the industry average. Again, this is cause for concern. Although the company's corporate strategy may be an explanation, we would expect to see a commensurately higher return on equity. If not, this would be a red flag. Fortunately, since its restructuring, Mark IV has increased its net income and return on equity. Moreover, the company has a low dividend payout ratio. All this indicates that the company has sufficient retained earnings to increase its assets, and thus its sales, in the future.

Long-Term Debt-to-Total Capitalization Ratio

This is a more refined version of the previous ratio. It seeks to identify that portion of a company's net assets that are financed with debt rather than equity. A company's net assets are its total assets less its current liabilities. This is also known as the company's permanent capital, or its long-term debt plus net worth. Short-term debt, which is funded from working capital, is excluded because of its seasonality. The analyst needs to consider the degree to which the company's operating cash flow is able to support this leverage. The ratio is calculated as follows:

$$\text{Debt-to-capitalization} = \frac{\text{Long-term debt}}{\text{Long-term debt} + \text{Net worth}}$$

(*Note:* Capitalized lease obligation should be included in the definition of long-term debt.)

As would be expected from Mark IV's leverage position, its debt-to-capitalization ratio is higher than the industry average and has been trending up. A ratio of 0.63 indicates that long-term creditors supply 63% of the company's permanent capital, 40% higher than the industry average. (See Table 18.4.)

LIQUIDITY RATIOS

Liquidity measures the company's ability to meet its short-term debt obligations. Liquid assets are current assets that can be easily converted into cash without suffering a significant discount. In addition to

Table 18.4 Mark IV: Debt-to-Capitalization Ratio (Times)

	Mark IV	Industry Average
1997	0.51	0.31
1998	0.57	0.32
1999	0.63	0.45

cash-on-hand, these include marketable securities, receivables, and inventory. Liquidity also includes the availability of credit lines, bank financing, and access to the capital markets. The desired level of liquidity depends on the nature of the business. If cash flows are highly predictable, then liquidity need not be high. If the business is cyclical, a greater degree of liquidity is required to meet fluctuating demand. Companies may experience a liquidity squeeze if they are growing rapidly, are insufficiently funded (too much debt), or are heavily invested in illiquid assets like plant, property, and equipment. The consequences of insufficient liquidity range from the inability to capitalize on creditor discounts for prompt payment, to bankruptcy. Two commonly used liquidity ratios are the current ratio and the quick ratio. These ratios give creditors a sense of the degree by which asset values can slip before a company has trouble meeting its current liabilities.

Current Ratio

The current ratio compares the company's current assets to its current liabilities and is calculated as follows:

$$\text{Current ratio} = \frac{\text{Current assets}}{\text{Current liabilities}}$$

For industrial companies, a current ratio of 2:1 has traditionally been considered adequate. Generally, the higher the current ratio, the better the credit since there is more security against reduced inventory values or bad receivables. Nevertheless, the ratio requires interpretation. It must be examined in the context of each industry. A large current ratio may indicate a poor management team, which holds idle cash, carries excessive inventory, or extends overly generous payment terms to its customers. The current ratio assesses only the availability of assets, not the quality or composition of those assets. Finally, the ratio provides only a partial indication of a company's debt-paying capacity since an ongoing concern would never completely liquidate all of its current assets to meet its current liabilities.

Table 18.5 shows Mark IV's current ratio compared to the industry average. A current ratio of 1.77:1 means that the company has $1.77 of current assets for every dollar of current liabilities. Thus, the value of its

Table 18.5 Mark IV: Current Ratio (Times)

	Mark IV	Industry Average
1997	1.73	1.52
1998	2.04	1.51
1999	1.77	1.52

current assets could fall by 43.5% (.77/1.77) without impairing its ability to meet its current liabilities through the liquidation of those assets.

The fact that Mark IV has a higher current ratio than the industry would appear to be favorable. However, the company has had problems with obsolete inventory. The fluctuation in this ratio reflects inventory write-downs and improved cash management efforts, which can be seen in the efficiency ratios.

Quick Ratio

A more stringent measure of liquidity is the quick, or acid test, ratio. This ratio includes only the most liquid current assets that can be converted to cash at close to their book value. It excludes inventory and other less liquid current assets, leaving only cash, marketable securities, and accounts receivable. The quick ratio is calculated as follows:

$$\text{Quick ratio} = \frac{\text{Cash} + \text{marketable securities} + \text{accounts receivable}}{\text{Current liabilities}}$$

Traditionally, a quick ratio of 1:1 has been considered good for industrial companies. Table 18.6 shows comparative figures for Mark IV.

The recent drop in Mark IV's quick ratio is not in line with the industry average. An examination of the common-sized balance sheet

Table 18.6 Mark IV: Quick Ratio (Times)

	Mark IV	Industry Average
1997	0.94	0.87
1998	1.13	0.84
1999	0.82	0.84

reveals a sharp decline in cash from 6% of total assets to practically zero. This was explained by a European cash acquisition. However, with a demonstrated ability to access the capital markets, and $450 million in undrawn credit facilities, the decline in the quick ratio would not appear to signal a cash flow problem.

COVERAGE RATIOS

Leverage and liquidity ratios are static. They are derived from the company's balance sheet, which is a historic snapshot. They measure the comfort of creditors in the event of liquidation. Coverage ratios treat the company as an ongoing concern. They give an indication of how well the firm can meet its debt service obligations from its flow of funds. Interest coverage, debt-burden coverage, and the dividend-payout ratio are three commonly used coverage ratios.

Interest-Coverage Ratio

This ratio measures the extent to which interest expense is covered by earnings before interest and taxes (EBIT). It is defined as follows:

$$\text{Interest-coverage ratio} = \frac{\text{EBIT}}{\text{Interest expense}}$$

The numerator of this equation sometimes includes depreciation, a noncash expense. We use the more conservative definition assuming that depreciation is fully reinvested in capital expenditures. Taxes should always be excluded from the numerator because if EBIT is insufficient to meet interest expense, the firm will not pay taxes. The ratio provides a good picture of the extent to which earnings are penalized to finance the company. Unless the company has a high degree of liquidity, a coverage ratio of at least one is usually required to avoid default. The greater the ratio, the more comfort creditors have that the company will be able to service its debt. Table 18.7 lays out Mark IV's interest-coverage ratio relative to the industry.

Mark IV's interest coverage is below the industry average, which is to be expected, given its higher degree of leverage. Nevertheless,

Table 18.7 Mark IV: Interest-Coverage Ratio (Times)

	Mark IV	Industry Average
1997	4.18	11.40
1998	2.35	9.14
1999	3.47	6.48

the trend has been improving, reflecting that the company's restructuring program is beginning to improve operating efficiency. A ratio of 3.47 times means that interest expense could more than triple before the company would have trouble meeting this expense given its current level of profitability.

Burden-Coverage Ratio

The burden-coverage ratio goes one step further by including the current portion of long-term debt in the calculation. It is calculated as follows:

$$\text{Burden-coverage ratio} = \frac{\text{EBIT}}{\text{Interest expense} + \dfrac{\text{Current portion of long-term debt}}{1 - \text{tax rate}}}$$

Interest is a pre-tax expense, while principal is paid after tax. In order to compare like with like, the principal repayment must be grossed up to an equivalent pretax amount. This is accomplished by dividing it by the factor one minus the effective tax rate. Because a company's debt amortization schedule varies from year to year, trend analysis or industry comparisons may be difficult. However, being cognizant of a company's debt amortization schedule is useful information. The busted convertible investor would like to see this spread out evenly over a number of years and not bunched up in any one period. Moreover, it would be comforting to see the company's subordinated convertible debt maturing before its other senior debt obligations. Mark IV's debt amortization schedule and burden coverage ratio are indicated in Table 18.8.

Table 18.8   Mark IV: Burden Coverage (Times) and Debt
Amortization Schedule

						(USD Millions)		
(FYE February)	1998	1999	2000	2001	2002	2003	2004	2005
Burden Coverage	0.83	0.96	1.40					
Amortization Schedule				8.2	58.0	26.2	23.3	300.1

The company faces no significant debt repayments until 1 November 2004 (fiscal year 2005) when the $275 million convertible comes due. The bulk of the company's other senior and subordinated debt matures after the convertible.

Dividend-Payout Ratio

This ratio measures the amount of after-tax profit paid to shareholders in the form of dividends. These are funds that otherwise could be used to grow the business or repay debt. The ratio can be helpful in explaining changes in net worth and leverage. The equation is as follows:

$$\text{Dividend-payout ratio} = \frac{\text{Cash dividends paid}}{\text{Profit after tax}} \cdot 100$$

Table 18.9 illustrates Mark IV's dividend-payout ratio relative to the industry average.

Mark IV has kept its dividend payments steady over the past

Table 18.9   Mark IV: Dividend-Payout Ratio
(Percent)

	Mark IV	Industry Average
1997	11.0	28.5
1998	23.3	28.5
1999	12.0	30.7

three years at about $11 million. The increase in 1998 (fiscal year 1999) is explained by the company's restructuring program, which reduced income from continuing operations. The fact that the company's payout ratio is less than the industry average is positive for creditors. It indicates that the company, which is more highly leveraged than its peers, is not allowing its dividend policy to impede its need to build equity.

EFFICIENCY RATIOS

These ratios determine how effectively management is utilizing the resources entrusted to it. They measure the relative amount of assets needed to support the company's sales. They determine how long it takes for accounts receivable to be collected, inventory to be sold, and accounts payable to be collected. Although investing in companies with low leverage and high liquidity involves less credit risk, efficiency ratios are more difficult to interpret. For example, a high return on assets can be indicative of the type of business (jeweler versus grocery store) rather than its safety. Consequently, these ratios often help the analyst to ask the right questions rather than provide a definitive answer.

Asset-Turnover Ratio

This ratio measures how efficiently a company is using its assets to generate sales. It is calculated as follows:

$$\text{Asset-turnover ratio} = \frac{\text{Net sales}}{\text{Average total assets}}$$

When a flow figure (i.e., sales) is compared with a static figure (i.e., total assets), it is more accurate to average the static figure. This is because the amount of assets is likely to change during the year. Table 18.10 illustrates Mark IV's asset-turnover ratios.

An asset turnover ratio of 0.97 means that Mark IV generated $0.97 of revenues for every $1.00 of assets employed. Although it is lower than the industry average, it has been improving. This may

Table 18.10   Mark IV: Asset-Turnover Ratio (Times)

	Mark IV	Industry Average
1997	0.84	1.47
1998	0.80	1.43
1999	0.97	1.28

indicate that the company's restructuring efforts are beginning to pay off. The analyst should note that the ratio is calculated using the book value of assets. This means that companies with older equipment will tend to show higher turnover ratios than companies with newer equipment. A high turnover ratio may indicate that increased capital expenditures will soon be required. One way to put this in perspective is to calculate the amount of accumulated depreciation relative to plants, property, and equipment.

WORKING CAPITAL MANAGEMENT

Inventory-Turnover Ratio (Days)

This ratio shows how frequently the company's inventory is turned or sold to generate the current level of sales. The equation uses cost of goods sold in the denominator rather than sales to reflect the cost of inventory sold during the year. Sales would distort the relationship because it includes a profit margin. Generally, the faster inventory is turned over, the more efficiently the company is operating. A slowing trend may indicate product obsolescence. However, the ratio requires interpretation. A fast turnover ratio may indicate insufficient inventories, supply shortages, and lost customers. Finally, the ratio may not be comparable among companies, depending on accounting methods and the diversity of business segments. The formula for days inventory is illustrated next together with Mark IV's statistics. (See Table 18.11.)

$$\text{Days' inventory} = \frac{\text{Average inventory}}{\text{Cost of goods sold}} \cdot 365$$

Table 18.11 Mark IV: Inventory-Turnover Ratio (Days)

	Mark IV	Industry Average
1997	115	49
1998	98	50
1999	86	51

An inventory-turnover rate of 86 days means that Mark IV could liquidate its inventory in 86 days assuming the current level of sales. This is higher than the industry average, which is cause for concern. Holding higher levels of inventory may be justified if that inventory commands a higher profit margin when sold. As we shall see, this is not the case for Mark IV, which has a lower return on sales than the industry as a whole.

Accounts Receivable-Turnover Ratio (Days)

This ratio indicates how quickly a company is converting its credit sales into cash. The ratio is calculated as follows:

$$\text{Average collection period} = \frac{\text{Average accounts receivable}}{\text{Credit sales}} \cdot 365$$

Frequently, credit sales are not distinguished from cash sales. Consequently, net sales will surface. The ratio is useful when compared to the collection terms offered by the company. If 30 days are offered, but the turnover figure is 40 or 50 days, this could be an indication of bad debts. As noted in Table 18.12, Mark IV's average

Table 18.12 Mark IV: Accounts Receivable-Turnover Ratio (Days)

	Mark IV	Industry Average
1997	85	48
1998	89	48
1999	75	49

collection period is longer than the industry average. However, at just over 2% of receivables, bad debt allowances appear to be normal.

Accounts Payable-Turnover Ratio (Days)

This ratio measures how quickly the company pays its trade accounts. Terms vary widely by industry. The analyst should be sensitive to changing trends in the ratio. A faster turnover could mean that the company is taking advantage of discounts offered for prompt payment or that suppliers are restricting credit. A longer turnover could indicate more favorable supplier terms, or cash flow difficulties.

$$\text{Days-payable ratio} = \frac{\text{Average accounts payable}}{\text{Cost of goods sold}} \cdot 365$$

Table 18.13 reveals that Mark IV also has a longer days-payable ratio than the rest of the industry. The fact that days payable and receivable are of similar duration indicates that Mark IV's payment terms are unique by industry standards, but does not signal a problem in working capital management.

PROFITABILITY RATIOS

Profitability is another important indicator of financial health. A profitable company is more likely to grow, remain solvent, and repay its debts. Profitability ratios also help to put other ratios into context. For example, a higher leverage ratio without a commensurately higher return on equity could be cause for concern.

Table 18.13 Mark IV: Accounts Payable-Turnover Ratio (Days)

	Mark IV	Industry Average
1997	66	42
1998	63	40
1999	71	37

Return on Equity Ratio

The return on equity (ROE) ratio measures the efficiency with which the company uses its shareholder capital. It says nothing about the amount of leverage employed. The ratio is calculated as follows:

$$\text{Return on equity ratio} = \frac{\text{Net profit}}{\text{Average net worth}} \cdot 100$$

The analyst should be cognizant of the fact that nonrecurring events will distort the net income figure. Mark IV's repositioning expenses explain the decline in ROE in 1998 (fiscal year 1999). Nevertheless, using average net worth, the company's ROE is inferior to the industry average despite its higher leverage. If we calculate ROE based on the net worth figures at year end, the effect of the share-buyback program is revealed as Mark IV's ROE rises to 18.65% versus an industry average of 18.25%. (See Table 18.14.)

Return on Sales Ratio

The return on sales (ROS) ratio measures how much profit the company makes on each dollar of sales. This is also known as the net profit margin and is calculated as follows:

$$\text{Return on sales ratio} = \frac{\text{Net profit}}{\text{Sales}} \cdot 100$$

The ratio gives an indication of how much expenses can change with no adverse impact on profits. Here, the analyst should be prompted to ask other questions like: How volatile are the company's sales? Does the company have the ability to pass on higher expenses to its customers? How much operating leverage is in the business? Companies with volatile sales, weak pricing power, and large fixed

Table 18.14 Mark IV: Return on Equity Ratio (Percent)

	Mark IV	Industry Average
1997	13.06	16.88
1998	7.06	20.77
1999	16.58	18.25

costs should exhibit higher returns on sales. Table 18.15 shows that Mark IV's return on sales has improved since its restructuring, but remains below the industry average.

Return on Assets Ratio

The return on assets (ROA) ratio measures the profitability of a company in terms of how efficiently it uses its assets. In its simplest form it measures net income to total assets. In the equation that follows, we make the common adjustment of eliminating how the business is financed from the net income. This is accomplished by adding interest expense back to net income and then subtracting the tax benefit of the interest expense. The tax benefit is equal to the interest expense times the tax rate. The tax rate is found by dividing income taxes by the profit before tax.

$$\text{Return on assets ratio} = \frac{\text{Net Income} + \text{Interest expense} - \text{Tax benefit}}{\text{Average total assets}} \cdot 100$$

The ratio may be misleading if the company carries significantly undervalued assets on its balance sheet (e.g., land). Table 18.16 shows

Table 18.15 Mark IV: Return on Sales Ratio (Percent)

	Mark IV	Industry Average
1997	5.31	6.25
1998	2.61	5.73
1999	4.46	5.22

Table 18.16 Mark IV: Return on Assets Ratio (Percent)

	Mark IV	Industry Average
1997	5.97	6.75
1998	3.89	7.74
1999	6.27	6.64

the relevant figures for Mark IV. Again, the company's returns are below average but improving.

THE ALTMAN Z-SCORE MODEL: PREDICTING BANKRUPTCY

In 1968, Professor Edward I. Altman of New York University formulated a model to predict financial distress. The model, subsequently revised, remains relevant today. Dr. Altman's Z-score model is a linear function that uses five financial ratios. The model goes beyond traditional credit analysis by selecting the most important ratios and by determining how they are correlated using multiple discriminant analysis. Evidence supports the fact that the model can predict bankruptcy up to two years in advance relatively accurately. Beyond two years, the accuracy of the model decreases and long-term predictions are difficult. The formula is defined as follows:

Z-score $= (1.2 \cdot X1) + (1.4 \cdot X2) + (3.3 \cdot X3) + (0.6 \cdot X4) + (1.0 \cdot X5)$

where $X1$ = Net working capital to total assets ratio

This ratio measures the firm's net liquid assets compared to its size. This ratio is a better predictor of bankruptcy than a deteriorating current or quick ratio because companies with consistent operating losses usually experience shrinking current assets relative to total assets.

$X2$ = Retained earnings to total assets ratio

This ratio measures a firm's cumulative profits relative to its size. Although the ratio is inherently biased against younger companies that have not had time to accumulate retained earnings, these are precisely the companies more prone to failure.

$X3$ = EBIT to total assets ratio

This ratio measures the earnings power of the firm's assets without any influence from taxes or leverage. This is an important measure because ultimately the survival of a firm is based on the earnings power of its assets.

$X4$ = Market value of equity to book value of total
liabilities ratio

This ratio determines the extent to which a firm's assets can decline in value before the book value becomes negative and the firm becomes insolvent. The ratio is an adaptation of the familiar debt-to-net-worth ratio (book values), with the following modification: Equity is defined as the market value of common and preferred stock. Using market values introduces a new dimension into the calculation. For privately held firms, $X4$ can be modified to use the book value of net worth.

$X5$ = Sales to total assets ratio

The asset-turnover ratio measures how efficiently the firm is using its assets to generate sales. (See Table 18.17.)

INTERPRETATION OF THE ALTMAN Z-SCORE

Generally, scores range from –5.0 to 20.0. Scores above 3.0 indicate that bankruptcy is unlikely. Scores below 1.8 indicate an increased risk of failure with scores below 1.2 indicating a strong probability of failure. Scores between 1.8 and 3.0 are generally inconclusive. Since the model is dynamic, while the scores are static, the Z-scores must be evaluated over time. A pattern of low scores can indicate fundamental problems with the firm.

Altman's numeric score is then translated into an overall health rating for the firm. This process takes into consideration the firm's

Table 18.17   Mark IV: Altman Z-Score Calculations

Ratio	Weight	1998	1999	2000
$X1$	1.20	.19	.24	.19
$X2$	1.40	.06	.08	.10
$X3$	3.30	.09	.06	.09
$X4$	0.60	1.42	1.61	1.38
$X5$	1.00	.76	.87	.98
Z-Score		2.22	2.43	2.47

credit rating. If the credit rating is at the high end of the investment grade spectrum, it will bolster the score. Altman's grades range from A+ to F. According to Altman's model, with a Z-score of 2.47 and a current senior debt rating of BB–, the health grade of Mark IV was actually only single B. This is an interesting result because it fore-shadows the possibility of a potential credit downgrade. Altman's model has effectively interpreted the negative credit effects of Mark IV's weaker operating results, higher leverage, and faltering stock price. The score indicates that the company's credit spread should re-flect the lower rating. In other words, in calculating the convertible's investment value, a single B credit spread of 400 basis points should be used rather than the 350 basis points implied for BB– credits. This distinction is worth 3.25 points in the investment value of the bond.

Despite Mark IV's speculative credit rating, the Altman analy-sis indicated that the company was not in imminent danger of bankruptcy. Figure 18.1 illustrates that the market correctly valued this situation because Mark IV's investment value held up at 80%, or a yield-to-maturity of Treasuries plus 400 basis points (i.e., 10.00%).

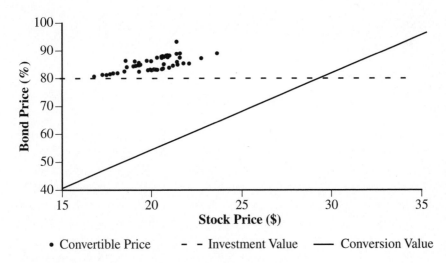

Figure 18.1 Mark IV: Investment Value History
Source: Bloomberg

CONCLUSION (MARK IV)

Our analysis revealed that Mark IV was more leveraged and less efficient than its peers, but that its stock price was clearly undervalued.
Management was aware of the situation and was taking actions to
correct it. Consequently, the company's busted convertible bonds offered investors a classic opportunity to be paid to wait for the company's value to be surfaced. With the bonds still trading in the low
eighties, a catalyst to unlock this value occurred when an investment
banking firm was hired by the company to explore strategic opportunities. Several months later, Mark IV agreed to be sold to a United
Kingdom-based leveraged buyout firm for $23 per share in cash. The
transaction triggered a change of control put at par in the bonds, resulting in a 30% annualized return for investors.

NEW ECONOMY CREDIT ANALYSIS: GLOBAL TELESYSTEMS

Company Description

Global TeleSystems Inc. (GTS) was originally founded in 1983 to provide telecommunications services in Russia and Eastern Europe. The
firm went public in February 1998 at $20 a share and has since ex-
panded through acquisition to become one of Western Europe's largest
broadband network operators.

INVESTMENT OPPORTUNITY

GTS's stock price fell from a high of $100 in November 1999 to $10 in
June 2000. The company had expected to become EBITDA-positive by
the end of 1999. Investors sold the stock when the company extended
this date by one year. Prior to the fall, the stock price appeared to be
inexpensive relative to its peers, based on such measures as enterprise value to sales, and sales to plant, property, and equipment. Equity analysts, using a discount cash-flow model (see Chapter 19),
estimated the stock to be worth more than $40 per share. The terms
of the convertible preferred are given in Table 18.18.

The convertible offered an attractive alternative to both the company's common stock and its debt. The preferred yields only about 2% less than the high-yield debt, but enjoys the possibility of substantial capital appreciation should the stock price recover. Versus the common stock, the preferred pays a 14.36% current yield on a modest 28.5% conversion premium. As can be seen in Figure 18.2, the conversion premium is small because the preferred has not held its investment value.

Table 18.18 Global TeleSystems: Convertible Preferred Terms

Issuer	Global TeleSystems Inc.	Size	$500 million
Dividend	$3.625 paid quarterly	Registration status	Registered
Credit rating	Caa (Moody's)	Maturity date	1-Jan-30
Security type	Cash-pay convertible preferred	Conversion premium	28.5%
Convertible price	$25.25	Stock price	$10.06
Current yield	14.36%	Yield to maturity	NA
Conversion price	$34.50	Conversion ratio	1.45

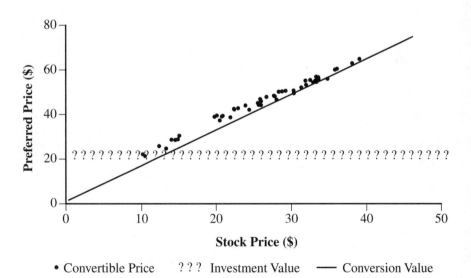

Figure 18.2 Global TeleSystems: Investment Value History
Source: Bloomberg

Table 18.19 Global TeleSystems: Common-Size Balance Sheet and
Income Statement

(USD Millions)	1997	%	1998	%	1999	%
			(Fiscal year ended December 31)			

Global TeleSystems Inc.—Balance Sheet						
ASSETS						
Current assets:						
Cash & cash equivalents	358	41	999	38	1,083	27
Accounts, notes receivable	42	5	175	7	286	7
Inventories	0	0	0	0	0	0
Other current assets	54	6	120	5	318	8
Total current assets	454	52	1,294	50	1,687	42
Noncurrent assets:						
Net fixed assets	260	30	643	24	1,005	25
Other noncurrent assets	163	18	678	26	1,310	33
TOTAL ASSETS	877	100	2,615	100	4,002	100
LIABILITIES AND EQUITY						
Current liabilities:						
Accounts payable	57	7	173	7	199	5
Short-term borrowing	35	4	67	3	122	3
Other current liabilities	51	6	171	6	382	10
Total current liabilities	143	17	411	16	703	18
Noncurrent liabilities:						
Long-term borrowing	610	70	1,725	66	2,430	61
Long-term debt	15	2	75	3	124	3
Total liabilities	768	88	2,211	85	3,256	81
Shareholder equity	109	88	404	15	745	18
TOTAL LIABILITIES AND EQUITY	877	100	2,615	100	4,002	100

Global TeleSystems Inc.—Income Statement						
Net sales	121	100	372	100	852	100
Cost of goods sold	97	80	238	64	524	62
Selling and administration	97	80	279	75	620	73
Depreciation & amortization	19	16	79	21	213	25
Other	0	0	0	0	142	17
Operating income (loss)	(92)	76	(144)	39	(434)	51
Interest expense	27	22	124	33	209	25
Interest income	0	0	53	14	52	6
Income tax expense	2	2	8	2	18	2
Other gain (loss)	(13)	11	(20)	5	(30)	4
Income before XO items	(135)	112	(243)	65	(617)	72
XO gain (loss)	0	0	(13)	3	0	0
NET INCOME (loss)	(135)	112	(256)	69	(617)	72
Avg. # shares (basic and diluted)	98		143		171	
Effective tax rate %	NA		NA		NA	
Cash dividends paid	0		0		0	

Table 18.20 Global TeleSystems: Ratio Analysis

	1997	1998	1999
Leverage ratios			
Total liabilities-to-equity	7.10	5.60	4.40
LT debt-to-capitalization	0.85	0.81	0.77
Liquidity ratios			
Current ratio	3.19	3.15	2.40
Quick ratio	2.81	2.85	1.95
Coverage ratios			
Interest coverage	−3.4	−1.2	−2.3
Burden coverage	−1.48	−0.75	−1.40
Dividend payout	NA	NA	NA
Efficiency ratios			
Asset turnover	0.22	0.21	0.26
Inventory turnover	NA	NA	NA
A/R turnover (days)	77	106	98
A/P turnover (days)	119	175	129
Profitability ratios			
Return on equity	−120.5	−99.6	−53.6
Return on sales	−111.5	−68.8	−72.4

Altman Z-score

$X1$ = Net working capital/total assets
$X2$ = Retained earnings/total assets
$X3$ = EBIT/total assets
$X4$ = Market value of equity/total debt
$X5$ = Sales/total assets

Calculations	1997 (1)	1998	1999
$X1$	.36	.34	.25
$X2$	−.33	−.21	−.29
$X3$	−.12	−.06	−.07
$X4$	.14	2.03	1.97
$X5$	.14	.14	.21
Z-score	−0.19	1.27	1.06

(1) Since the company was not public in 1997, the book value of equity was used to calculate $X4$, and the Z-score coefficients were adjusted as prescribed by Altman as follows: $Z = .72(.36) + .85(−.33) + 3.1(−.12) + .42(.14) + .99(.14) = −.19$

CREDIT ANALYSIS

In Table 18.19 we give a common-sized balance sheet and income statement for GTS together with its relevant credit statistics. As expected,
many of the traditional credit ratios are not applicable. The 1997 Altman Z-score has been adjusted to accommodate the company before it
became public by substituting the book value of equity for the market
value. The scores predict a high likelihood of insolvency, but the model
may be less relevant for a developmental-stage company. Liquidity is ob-
viously a key issue, and here the firm scores well. (See Table 18.20)

CONCLUSION (GLOBAL TELESYSTEMS)

By definition, New Economy credits are young companies in the
process of developing a business plan. Traditional methods of credit
analysis are likely to rank these companies as highly speculative,
which no doubt they are. The example of Global TeleSystems illustrates that the market has a hard time evaluating this credit because
the convertible preferred has no apparent investment value. Herein
lies both a risk and an opportunity. Unfortunately, determining GTS's
creditworthiness is more of a qualitative than a quantitative process.
The analyst needs to answer a number of important questions. Is the
company's business model valid? Will the market for European broadband services be as large as expected? Can the management execute
on this opportunity? What experience have they had? Who is the competition? Is the business plan well funded? Does the company have
sufficient liquidity? Can it access the capital markets if necessary?
And finally, if all else fails, is there a likely buyer for the business at a
price that will protect the creditor's investment? Unfortunately, an examination of these questions is beyond the scope of this text. However, assuming these questions can be satisfactorily answered, the
company's convertible preferred stock may be of interest to speculative investors.

19

THE INVESTMENT DECISION

WHY CONVERTIBLES?

Including convertibles in a portfolio of stocks and/or bonds increases value by enhancing the return per unit of risk. Thus, by definition, convertibles are a unique asset class. This can be seen in Figure 19.1 in which the risk/return profile of convertible securities, as managed by The Gabelli Asset Management Company, is graphed together with other asset classes. That convertibles lie above the capital–markets line illustrates their superior risk–reward characteristics. It is no wonder that convertibles appeal to a wide variety of investors in addition to convertible investors including fixed-income investors, equity investors, and arbitrageurs.

CONVERTIBLES: BETTER THAN A BALANCED PORTFOLIO?

Because convertibles combine the attributes of both equities and bonds, their price performance is nonlinear. This convexity gives convertibles a unique characteristic that cannot be replicated sim-

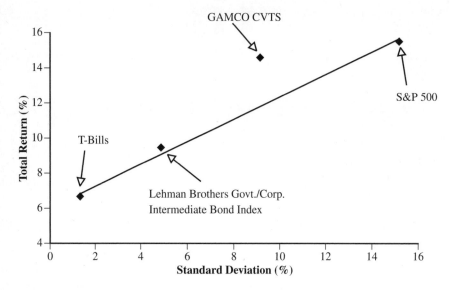

Figure 19.1   Capital–Markets Line (1980–2000)
Source: Gabelli

ply by combining equities and bonds. This quality is demonstrated in Table 19.1, in which our generic XYZ convertible is compared to a balanced portfolio of 50% bonds and 50% stock. As expected, the convertible outperforms the balanced portfolio on both the up side and the down side. If the stock price falls, the convertible will find its investment value and transform itself into the equivalent of a straight bond. If the stock price rises, the convertible will metamorphose into equity. The convertible portfolio is self-adjusting. The balanced portfolio will suffer as the equity component drags down performance in a bear market, and the fixed income component hurts performance in a bull market. Table 19.1 illustrates how the convertible outperforms the balanced portfolio by 16% on the down side and by nearly 9% on the up side, for a 50% move in the stock price over one year. Thus, on average, the convertible is expected to outperform the balanced portfolio by more than 12%. Had we substituted Treasury notes for high-yield debt in the balanced portfolio, the average outperformance would have increased to more than 18%.

Table 19.1   Convertible versus Balanced Portfolio

Stock price change	−50.00%	0.00%	50.00%
Stock price	$50.00	$100.00	$150.00
Estimated convertible price	93.10%	118.60%	151.60%
Balanced approach return			
Stock price (gain or loss)	50.00%	0.00%	50.00%
Straight bond return	8.75%	8.75%	8.75%
50% stock/50% bonds	−20.63%	4.38%	29.38%
Convertible bond return			
Convertible (gain or loss)	−21.50%	0.00%	27.82%
Interest earned	4.22%	4.22%	4.22%
Total return	−17.28%	4.22%	32.04%
Convertible versus balanced	3.34%	−0.16%	2.67%
Percent outperformance	16.19%	−3.64%	9.07%
Average outperformance (high to low)	12.63%		
Convertible participation versus stock	34.57%	NA	64.08%
Convexity	1.85		

THE CONVEXITY RATIO

Table 19.1 also indicates the convertible's performance relative to the stock. The convertible provides 64% of the upside participation with only 34% of the downside movement. This is the classic "two-thirds upside, one-third downside" payoff, which balanced convertible investors seek. This payoff, or convexity, can be expressed as a risk/reward ratio by dividing the upside by the downside participation. The larger the ratio, the more favorable the payoff. In this case, the convexity ratio is 1.85, indicating that the convertible provides 85% more upside participation than downside risk.

CONVERTIBLES: THE INVESTMENT DECISION

Fundamentals First

The first step in selecting a convertible investment is to do your homework on the underlying equity. If there is no compelling reason to own the stock, an outright investor should avoid the investment. This is true even for busted convertibles because the company's ability to meet its obligations is ultimately a function of its success as a business. Conversely, a hedge arbitrageur has more flexibility. The arbitrageur may actively seek out inferior companies with the intention of establishing a bear hedge position (see Chapter 12). In this chapter, we consider the goals of the outright long investor.

Diversification

Equity investors are generally divided into two styles: growth and value. Within these two styles, investment decisions can be further segregated by market capitalization and geography. The success of these investment approaches tends to vary over market cycles. Consequently, investors with a long-term view are well advised to hold a diversified portfolio. (See Table 19.2 and Figures 19.2–19.4.)

EQUITY ANALYSIS 101: GROWTH STOCKS

Growth-stock investors favor companies with successful business models selling at a reasonable price. Characteristics of these compa-

Table 19.2 Investment Returns by Investment Category
A Century of Investing: Compound Annual Rates of Return

Years	Stocks	Bonds	Bills	Inflation
00s	−9.1%	20.3%	5.1%	3.4%
90s	18.2%	8.8%	4.9%	2.9%
80s	17.5%	12.6%	8.9%	5.1%
70s	5.9%	5.5%	6.3%	7.4%
60s	7.8%	1.4%	3.9%	2.5%
50s	19.4%	−0.1%	1.9%	2.2%
40s	9.2%	3.2%	0.4%	5.4%
30s	0.0%	4.9%	0.6%	− 2.0%
1926–2000	11.1%	5.3%	3.8%	3.1%

Note: Stocks: S&P 500 Index; Bonds: U.S. 20-Year Government Bonds; Bills: 30-Day Treasury Bill; and Inflation: CPI Index.
Source: Gabelli

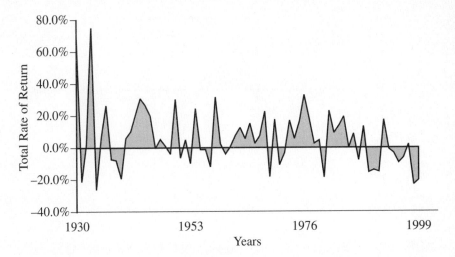

Figure 19.2 Investment Returns by Style: Value Minus Growth (All Capitalizations)
Source: Gabelli

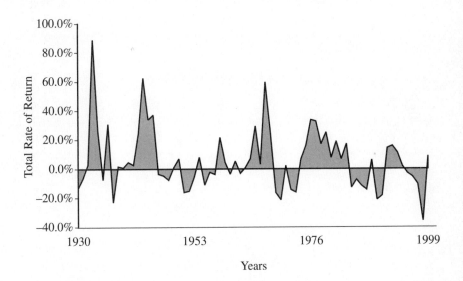

Figure 19.3 Investment Returns by Market Capitalization: Small Minus Large (All Styles)
Source: Gabelli

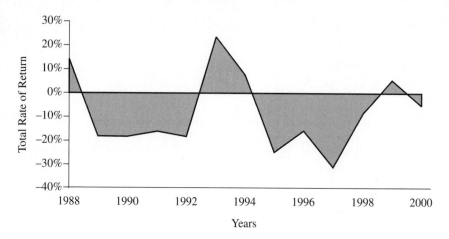

Figure 19.4 Investment Returns by Region: MSCI EAFE Minus S&P 500
Note: MSCI EAFE is the Morgan Stanley Capital International Europe Australasia Far East Index.
Source: Gabelli

nies include a unique product, a dominant market share, or a well-established brand name. These companies enjoy consistent earnings growth and are found in the most vibrant sectors of the economy.

Fair Value Calculation

Howard Ward, portfolio manager of the Gabelli Growth Fund, devised a simple discounting technique for valuing growth stocks. To determine a growth stock's fair value, compound the company's estimated earnings per share at its expected growth rate, discount the result, and apply a terminal multiple. Consider the following example and Table 19.3.

$$\text{Fair value} = \frac{EPS \cdot (1+GR)^{FP}}{(1+r+ERP)^{FP}} \cdot TM$$
$$= \$129.50$$

As with any other model, the results are only as good as the inputs. Of the six variables required, only two are readily observable: the risk-free interest rate and the term of the forecast period. The longer the forecast period, the greater the fair value but the more un-

Table 19.3 XYZ Corporation: Earnings
Valuation Model

Company	XYZ Corporation
(FP) Forecast period	5 years
(EPS) EPS estimate	$4.50
(GR) Estimated EPS growth rate	20%
(TM) Terminal p/e multiple	18X
(RFR) Risk-free interest rate	5.75%
(ERP) Equity risk premium	3.50%
Current share price	$100.00
Fair value	$129.50
Percent undervalued	29.50%

certain the result. For stocks with consistent earnings growth, a five-year period seems acceptable (or at least convenient) because analysts often predict five-year earnings growth rates. By way of contrast, this term falls about midway between the two other commonly used valuation techniques: cash flow multiples (0 to 1 year) and discounted cash flow analysis (7 to 20 years).

The fair value price is calculated by compounding the estimated *EPS* figure by the expected growth rate over the forecast period. This results in an earnings estimate for the last year of the forecast period. This figure is then discounted back to a present value. The discount rate is the sum of the risk-free rate of interest over the corresponding forecast period, plus an equity risk premium. Finally, this sum is multiplied by the terminal P/E multiple to arrive at the stock's fair value.

THE EQUITY RISK PREMIUM

Historic Measures

The equity risk premium compensates investors for the additional risk associated with holding equities over risk-free Treasury bonds. This premium can be estimated by observing the historic data in Table 19.2. In reviewing the data, several questions arise. First, what is the correct time period? Is the recent data more predictive than the long-term average? For argument's sake, we use the long-term average. Second, which return should we use: the arithmetic or the geometric mean? The arithmetic mean measures the average return, while the geometric mean measures the compounded annual return. Which is used can make a big difference. If the stock price rises from \$100 to \$200 in year one (+100%), and then falls back to \$100 in year two (−50%), the arithmetic mean is +25% ((+100% − 50%)/2 = +25%). This seems strange because nothing has been gained over the original investment. The investor's actual return experience is better reflected in the geometric mean, which is zero (($100/$100)^{1/2} − 1.0) = 0%). The geometric mean will always be lower than the arithmetic mean when the series contains at least one negative number. Consequently, geometric means are the preferred measure of historic returns. Finally, what is the appropriate measure of the risk-free rate of return: Treasury bills or long-term Treasury bonds? The latter is the better choice since it matches the long-term duration of equities and is less susceptible to short-term economic influences. Table 19.2 indicates that the equity risk premium of large capitalization stocks over long-term Treasury bonds is 5.8%.

Future Expectations

Although calculating the historic equity risk premium is easy, it may not be useful. What we really want to know is what this premium will be in the future. Recently, analysts have argued that the historic risk premium is too high. Global competition has forced companies to become better managed and more efficient. Consequently, earnings are steadier and more predictable. Meanwhile, the volatility of Treasury bonds has increased. Therefore, the required equity risk premium has declined. Evidence supporting this thesis points out that price to earnings (P/E) multiples have been trending up despite the fact that the economy has continued to grow. Normally, P/E multiples rise in recessions and fall gradually during periods of economic expansion. In other words, a lower equity risk premium has justified higher stock market valuations, which are reflected in higher P/E multiples.

The Gordon Growth Model

One way to estimate the expected or future equity risk premium is to use a single-stage discounted cash flow model known as the Gordon Growth Model. The model defines the present value of an asset as follows:

$$PV = \frac{NCF_0 \cdot (1+g)}{k-g}$$

where PV = present value
   NCF_0 = net cash flow in period 0
   k = discount rate
   g = the expected sustainable long-term growth rate

The formula can be rearranged to solve for the discount rate.

$$k = \frac{NCF_0 \cdot (1+g)}{PV} + g$$

To calculate the equity risk premium for the U.S. market, we use the S&P 500 as a proxy (the underlying asset). The net cash flow of this asset in period 0 is its trailing 12-month dividend payment. The expected long-term growth rate is the estimated growth in nominal gross domestic product (GDP). This assumes that over the long run the growth rate in corporate cash flows will converge with that of national income. If not, the stock market will be worth more than the entire economy, which is illogical. The present value of the asset is represented by its current market price. Plugging these figures into the formula solves for the discount rate (k), which is the cost of capital. The equity risk premium is defined as the cost of capital minus the risk-free interest rate.

Price of the S&P 500	1,430
Trailing 12-month dividend payments	$15.73
Nominal GDP growth rate	5.30%
Risk-free interest rate	5.75%

$$k = \frac{\$15.73 \cdot (1+5.3\%)}{1,430} + 5.3\%$$

$$= 6.45\%$$

$$\text{Equity risk premium} = k - r$$
$$= 6.45\% - 5.75\%$$
$$= 0.7\%$$

The Gordon Growth Model is useful because it allows us to easily calculate the equity risk premium for markets where historic return data is not easily available. Unfortunately, its accuracy is only as good as our estimate of the economy's sustainable long-term growth rate. In practice, the consensus is that the equity risk premium has been declining but that the business cycle is not dead. Most analysts assume that the appropriate equity risk premium is between 2% and 4%.

THE TERMINAL MULTIPLE

Finally, to complete the fair value analysis, a terminal multiple is applied to the discounted EPS estimate. This is a subjective judgment. Depending upon the quality of earnings, a premium or a discount to the company's growth rate is determined. In deference to the vagaries of forecasting, the terminal multiple is usually capped at 30 times the projected EPS figure, regardless of the growth rate.

EQUITIES 101: VALUE STOCKS

Many investors believe that a company's ability to generate cash is the most important factor in determining value. Cash flow is often a precursor to earnings. If a company is investing heavily, interest expense may eliminate its earnings but its cash flow may be positive. Cash flow is defined as earnings before interest, taxes, depreciation, and amortization (EBITDA). Essentially, EBITDA captures the company's operating income and then adds back noncash expenses like depreciation and amortization. It is the simplest definition of cash flow. It does not take into consideration how to grow the business or finance it. Nevertheless, EBITDA is a useful measure for comparing companies across borders. Unlike EPS, extraordinary items and taxation discrepancies do not distort it.

INTRINSIC VALUE

In 1934, Benjamin Graham and David Dodd, in their seminal work, *Security Analysis*, developed the concept of intrinsic value. A stock's intrinsic value is defined as the economic value of the firm as a going concern. It takes into consideration a number of factors including cash flow, earnings power, management, and the investment environment. Due to market inefficiencies (i.e., fads, herd instinct, etc.), a company's intrinsic value may differ from its public market price.

PRIVATE MARKET VALUE (PMV)

In order to highlight the discrepancy between intrinsic value and market price, Mario Gabelli, chairman and chief investment officer of The Gabelli Asset Management Company, coined the term Private Market Value (PMV). PMV defines the intrinsic value of the firm as the price an informed industrialist would pay to own the business. Effectively, it is the intrinsic value plus a control premium. The value investor seeks to identify investments whose public market value is temporarily below its private market value. Unfortunately, cheap stocks may be cheap for good reason. Consequently, Gabelli developed an important corollary to the concept of PMV: a catalyst. A good investment must be both undervalued and exhibit an identifiable catalyst to unlock that value. Catalysts included regulatory changes, reorganizations, spin-offs, share buybacks, and a change in management.

To determine the PMV of a stock, a multiple is assigned to the company's historic or projected EBITDA. To this sum, cash is added and other senior claims (debt) are subtracted to arrive at a PMV available to common shareholders. A fair multiple is determined by calculating the multiples of similar companies in the same industry. Multiples are verified by observing where recent merger and acquisition activity have occurred. Relative value is determined by comparing multiples globally.

In the case of Mark IV Industries (see Chapter 18), a PMV of $29.20 per share was calculated as shown in Table 19.4.

Table 19.4 Mark IV: Private Market Value Model

Company	Mark IV Industries
Estimated EBITDA	$320M
PMV EBITDA multiple	7 times
PMV calculation	
EBITDA times multiple	$2,240M
+ Cash	$2M
− Debt	($855M)
− Minority interest	0
PMV	$1,387M
No. shares outstanding (basic)	47.5M
PMV per share	$29.20
Current share price	$16.5625
Percent undervalued	76.30%

EQUITY ANALYSIS 101:
DISCOUNTED CASH FLOW ANALYSIS (DCF)

In the previous two methods of equity analysis, the company had either consistent earnings or positive cash flow. What if neither exists? In this case, the investor must build a model to forecast the future cash flows of the company. Here a more exhaustive definition of cash flow is used, known as Free Cash Flow (FCF). Free cash flow is defined as net operating profit after tax (NOPAT), less net investments. Net investments include capital expenditures (net of depreciation) and changes in working capital. Forecasting FCF requires assumptions about revenue growth, operating margins, tax rates, and capital spending. The forecasting period is usually 10 years but may vary depending upon how long the company is expected to earn an excess return over its cost of capital (the excess return period). Once the business has matured, it is assumed that it will earn a return on capital equal to its cost of capital in perpetuity. This is known as the firm's terminal value. The terminal value is calculated by dividing the final year's NOPAT by the weighted average cost of capital (WACC). The value of the firm is the sum of its discounted free cash flows, plus its discounted terminal value, plus any cash and marketable securities. Cash flows are discounted at the company's weighted average cost of capital (WACC). Typically, three-quarters of the firm's value (or more) is derived from its terminal value. Once the firm value is calculated, the value to common equity holders is determined by subtracting any senior claims. Dividing this sum by the number of shares outstanding gives the estimated fair value per share. The fair value of Global TeleSystems (see Chapter 18) is estimated in Table 19.5.

Calculating the Weighted Average Cost of Capital (WACC)

A firm's cost of capital is the minimum rate of return that debt and equity holders expect to earn for investing in the company. The before-tax cost of debt is equal to the risk-free rate of interest plus a credit spread. The credit spread is the risk premium demanded by debt holders to compensate them for default risk. Since we are looking for a rate with which to discount the firm's after-tax free cash flows, we need to calculate an after-tax cost of debt. Because interest expense is tax deductible, we calculate the after-tax cost of debt by multiplying the pre-tax cost by 1 minus the tax rate. The after-tax cost of debt is 10.35%, calculated as follows.

After-Tax Cost of Debt

Risk-free interest rate	6.00%
Credit spread	5.50%
Before-tax cost of debt	11.50%
Tax rate	10.00%
After-tax cost of debt	$11.50\% \cdot (1\text{--}10\%) = 10.35\%$

Cost of Equity

The cost of equity is derived from the capital asset pricing model (CAPM) developed in the mid-1960s by three economists: William Sharpe, John Lintner, and Jack Treynor. According to the CAPM, the cost of a company's equity is equal to the risk-free rate of interest plus a company-specific risk premium. As discussed previously, there are various methods for calculating an equity risk premium for the general stock market. To solve for the company-specific risk premium, we multiply the equity market premium by the company's beta. Beta measures the volatility of the stock price relative to the market. It is calculated by performing a linear regression of the

Table 19.5 Global TeleSystems: DCF Model

Period	1999	2000	2001	2002	2003	2004	2005	2006	2007	2008	2009
Period number	0	1	2	3	4	5	6	7	8	9	10
Revenues	852	1,065	1,438	1,941	2,620	3,406	4,258	5,110	6,132	7,051	8,109
% change		25%	35%	35%	35%	30%	25%	20%	20%	15%	15%
Operating margin		−35%	−23%	−17%	−7%	8%	13%	16%	21%	22%	23%
NOPBT		−373	−331	−330	−183	273	554	818	1,288	1,551	1,865
EBITDA		−53	86	194	445	715	1,064	1,431	1,839	2,115	2,514
Effective tax rate		−6%	−6%	−6%	−10%	10%	10%	10%	10%	10%	10%
Taxes		22	20	20	18	27	55	82	129	155	187
NOPAT		−395	−351	−350	−202	245	498	736	1,159	1,396	1,679
Capital expenditures		895	546	563	550	545	554	511	491	494	568
% revenues		84%	38%	29%	21%	16%	13%	10%	8%	7%	7%
Depreciation		320	417	524	629	443	511	613	552	564	649
% revenues		30%	29%	27%	24%	13%	12%	12%	9%	8%	8%
Change in WC		21	22	25	27	24	26	26	31	28	32
% of change in rev.		10%	6%	5%	4%	3%	3%	3%	3%	3%	3%
Free cash flow		−992	−502	−414	−150	119	430	812	1,190	1,439	1,728
PV FCF		−890	−405	−300	−98	70	225	382	503	546	589
Cum. PV FCF		−890	−1,295	−1,595	−1,692	−1,623	−1,397	−1,015	−513	33	622

GTS DCF valuation

PV FCF	622
PV terminal value	5,027
Marketable securities	1,083
Total firm value	6,732

Total firm value	6,732
Less debt	2,552
Less preferred stock	502
Total value of common stock	3,678
Intrinsic value per share	$21.511

stock's excess monthly returns (i.e., the return minus the risk-free interest rate) on the excess returns of the market. The beta of the market is equal to 1.00. If a company has a beta of 2.00, it is twice as volatile as the market. If the market rises or falls by 10%, the stock with a 2.00 beta will rise or fall by 20%. The cost of equity for GTS is calculated as follows.

$$R_e = R_f + \beta \cdot (R_m - R_f)$$

where R_e = Cost of equity
  R_f = Risk-free rate of interest
  R_m = Average equity market return
  β = Beta

Cost of Preferred Stock

Preferred stock is a specialized type of financing that falls between debt and common stock on the balance sheet. It ranks senior to common stock in the event of a bankruptcy but junior to all creditors. The cost of preferred stock is equal to its current yield. This yield requires no adjustment because preferred dividends are generally not tax deductible (see Chapter 16 for exceptions). The current yield of GTS's convertible preferred stock is 14.36%.

Book Value versus Market Value

Now that we know the cost of the various components of GTS's capital structure, we need to weight them accordingly. The book value of debt, preferred stock, and equity is found on the company's balance sheet (see Chapter 18). Book value is an accounting measure that indicates how much money the firm raised when the securities were initially issued. Book values may vary substantially from current market values. Consequently, to compute the current capitalization, we mark each component to market. To calculate the WACC, we multiply the cost of each component by its current market capitalization. Global TeleSystem's WACC of 11.37% is derived in Tables 19.6 and 19.7.

Table 19.6 Global TeleSystems Capitalization:
Book versus Market Value

	Book Value		Market Value	
	Total	%	Total	%
Debt	$2,552	77%	$2,296	54%
Preferred stock	$ 502	15%	$ 254	6%
Common equity	$ 243	7%	$1,710	40%
Total capitalization	$3,297	100%	$4,260	100%

Table 19.7 Global TeleSystems: WACC Calculation

	Cost	•	Weight	=	WACC
Cost of equity	12.30%		40%		4.94%
After-tax cost of debt	10.35%		54%		5.58%
Cost of preferred stock	14.36%		6%		0.86%
Total			100%		11.37%
Cost of capital inputs					
Current stock price			$10.000		
Shares outstanding (Mln)			171		
10-year Treasury bond yield			6.00%		
Credit spread			5.50%		
Preferred stock yield			14.36%		
Equity risk premium			3.50%		
Beta			1.8		
Effective tax rate			10.00%		

Sensitivity Analysis

The predictive power of the DCF model is only as good as its inputs.
For example, if we were to reduce GTS's revenue growth projections
by 5% per annum and increase its WACC to 14% by doubling its credit
spread, the estimated fair value of the stock would drop to $0.21. In
fact, this is exactly what happened to GTS's share price as increased
competition and an inability to access capital markets thwarted the
company's business plan. The DCF model is useful for putting a
framework around a company's value. It helps analysts to ask the

right questions. The analyst must then use qualitative judgment to decide if management's guidance, or parameters implied by the current share price, are reasonable.

CONVERTIBLES: THE TECHNICAL INVESTMENT DECISION

Once the appropriate equity and credit analysis has been completed, a technical review of the convertible is required before making an investment.

Valuation Score

Generally speaking, the theoretical value of the convertible should be higher than its market price. If the convertible is theoretically cheap according to the pricing model, then the investor is adding value to the portfolio by making the investment. If not, the investor would be better off replicating the convertible by purchasing the company's debt and equity separately. The cheapness of the convertible may come from either the bond or warrant component of the convertible. If the credit spread is correct, the convertible is cheap because the implied volatility of the warrant is less than the stock's historic volatility. In this case, the convertible offers the investor a cheaper vehicle into the stock. Conversely, if the volatility assumption is correct, then the investor is buying the issuer's debt at a discount.

For the arbitrageur, technical cheapness is paramount. For the outright investor, a degree of richness may be tolerated. This is because the outright investor may not be able to replicate the component parts of the convertible or may be willing to pay for scarcity value.

Technical Score

In addition to theoretical valuation, a number of other technical factors should be considerations before investing. In Table 19.8, we identify the 10 most important elements of a convertible. To judge the relative merit of a convertible, we divide the convertible universe into three sections: out-of-the-money, at-the-money, and in-the-money. For any given section, we establish an average value for each of the 10 elements. Average values can be taken from various convertible sub-indices or may reflect the individual investors' own criteria.

Scores range from 0 to 100, with 100 being the highest score. The average score is 50. If the convertible scores twice as high as the average (or higher) in any given category, the maximum score is 100. If the convertible ranks 100% below the average (or lower), the minimum score is 0. We have weighted each element equally, but the model allows for bias. For example, an investor in an at-the-money convertible may be more concerned with convexity and downside risk than yield to maturity or yield advantage.

Finally, we combine both the valuation and technical scores to arrive at an overall score. We allow for flexibility in weighting the two scores to accommodate the requirements of each investor. The system

Table 19.8 XYZ Corporation Convertible Bond: Technical Rating System

Characteristics	XYZ Corp.	Category Average	Weight (0 to 10)	Score
Type (OTM= 1, ATM = 2, ITM = 3)	2			
Yield advantage	4.40%	2.50%	10	88.0
Historic-implied volatility	7.00%	5.00%	10	70.0
Yield to maturity-Treasury yield	−3.85%	−3.00%	10	35.8
Downside risk to investment value	−35.00%	−25.00%	10	30.0
Credit rating (1 to 10, 5 = B+)	6	5	10	60.0
Call protection (years)	5.00	3.00	10	83.3
Liquidity (1 to 10, 5 = 150 mln)	9	5	10	90.0
Convexity	2.18	2.00	10	54.5
Delta	75.00%	65.00%	10	57.7
Rho	1.89%	1.75%	10	46.0
Technical score			100	61.5
Valuation score (theoretical-market price)	−3.50%	−2.00%		87.5
Technical score (1)			4	61.5
Valuation score (2)			6	87.5
Final score (1+2)			10	77.1
Buy = 65 to 100				
Hold = 35 to 65				
Sell = 0 to 35				

Note: OTC: out-of-the-money, ATM: at-the-money, and ITM: in-the-money.

helps investors to focus on the key elements of the convertible and to rank them. To illustrate, we return to our generic convertible example, XYZ Corporation (see Chapter 1). We assume that we can purchase the bonds at a 3.5% discount to theoretical value (i.e., 114.625%), and fill in the remaining metrics. A score of 77 ranks 54% above the average at-the-money convertible, indicating that the XYZ convertible is technically attractive.

BUILDING A DIVERSIFIED CONVERTIBLE PORTFOLIO

Earlier in this chapter we demonstrated how diversification is an important characteristic of any successful investment program. The same principle holds true when we are building an individual convertible portfolio. To successfully diversify away individual company risk (i.e., unsystematic risk), 20 to 30 positions are recommended. The portfolio should also be diversified by industry group, credit quality, and product type. These are the basic requirements for any unrestricted convertible portfolio regardless of the investor's style or risk objectives.

Today, the global convertible market is sufficiently broad to satisfy the objectives of almost any investor. Convertible portfolios can be constructed to meet a wide array of objectives ranging from yield-enhanced equity to high-yield bond surrogates. Investors seeking a balanced convertible portfolio need not exclude busted or equity-sensitive convertibles from their portfolios. Investors can cherry-pick from across the convertible spectrum to produce a blended portfolio that satisfies their credit, yield, and conversion premium objectives.

SELL DISCIPLINE

The convertible investor must maintain a strict sell discipline. There are both fundamental and technical reasons to sell. Fundamentally, if the stock price rises above its target price, it should be reviewed. If the anticipated catalyst has occurred and the target price is justified, a sell decision should be considered. In some cases, investors may wish to gradually reduce the position rather than exit it altogether, since momentum may carry the stock price to a premium above its fair value. If the stock price falls, the investor needs to review the original reasons for owning the stock. If the expected catalyst no longer seems likely, or if other factors have changed the original valuation parameters, the convertible should be sold.

The main technical reasons for selling a convertible include a negative yield advantage, loss of call protection, or expensive pricing. If the stock yields more than the convertible, the stock may be the superior investment vehicle. However, this is not a foregone conclusion. The convertible's downside protection or theoretical cheapness may more than compensate for the loss of yield advantage. The loss of call protection puts the investor at risk for both the conversion premium and accrued interest. The investor needs to weigh this loss against the likelihood of a forced conversion (see Chapter 9). Last, a technically expensive convertible may not add value to the portfolio. A decision for inclusion should be made based on the fundamental and technical criteria developed in this book.

EPILOGUE

Convertible securities are the most dynamic and innovative product in the capital markets. Because of their flexibility and diverse investor base, convertible offerings are able to respond quickly to changing market conditions. For example, during the period of Internet hysteria, so-called TMT (Technology, Media, and Telecom) issuers constituted more than 70% of the new issue market. During this period, convertibles became a surrogate for venture capital. Later, after the bubble burst, the convertible market metamorphosed once again by bringing a number of investment-grade issuers to market. As the credit crunch ensued, the high-yield market remained closed while the convertible market was first to reopen to subinvestment-grade issuers.

Even more impressive has been the convertible market's ability to offer unique structures to both investors and issuers alike. Paramount has been the mandatory convertibles that with Houdiniesque skill succeeded in conquering one of the age-old problems in finance: How to get equity credit and tax deductibility at the same time. Aside from mandatories, which we covered in depth, this book has examined only the basic convertible structures. Perhaps, in a later edition, we will explore other fascinating structures like pre-IPO (initial public offering) convertibles, convertibles with downside resets, coupon adjustments, remarketability, and contingency features.

As for the future, one thing is clear. The global convertible market is set to grow. This will be assured not only from the supply side as issuers continue to take advantage of the novel tax and accounting benefits provided by convertibles, but from the demand side as well, particularly in the European market. In Europe, convertibles provide the ideal stepping-stone as investors, prompted by pension reform, finally gravitate toward an equity culture. Convertibles have come a long way since the early days of the U.S. railroads, but the journey is far from complete.

APPENDIX 1:
MCS NAME VARIATIONS

Equity Participating Mandatory Convertibles

PEPS	Participating Equity Preferred Stock
NUPEPs	Note Unit with Prospective Equity Participations
ACES	Automatically Convertible Equities Securities
PRIDES	Preferred Redemption Increased Dividend Equity Securities
DECS	Dividend Enhanced Common Stock
SAILS	Stock Appreciation Income Linked Securities
MARCS	Mandatory Adjustable Redeemable Convertible Securities
TAPS	Threshold Appreciation Price Securities

Tax Deductible Mandatory Convertibles

FSUs	Forward Stock Units
ACES	Automatically Convertible Equity Securities
PRIDES	Preferred Redeemable Increased Dividend Equity Securities
FELINE PRIDES	Flexible Equity-Linked Exchangeable Preferred Redeemable Increased Dividend Equity Securities

Mandatory Exchangeables

PEPS	Premium Exchangeable Participating Securities
PERCS	Premium Exchangeable Redemption Cumulative Securities

PICS	Premium Income Convertible Stock
PRIDES	Provisionally Redeemable Income Debt Exchangeable for Stock
DECS	Debt Exchangeable for Common Stock
ACES	Automatic Common Exchangeable Securities
MEDS	Mandatory Exchangeable Debt Securities

APPENDIX 2:
USEFUL INTERNET SITES

www.aantix.com calculates put and call values using the Black–Scholes model. The calculator can be downloaded free.

www.axone.ch/javacalculators.htm offers free calculators for options, multiple options, bonds, and forward rate agreements.

www.bloomberg.com has free and pay components. For free, you can access a stock's 90-day volatility and dividend yield. The currency calculator calculates exchange rates for more than 200 currencies.

www.cboe.com is the Chicago Board Option Exchange's website. It provides historic volatility data for optionable stocks and other contracts. In addition, it offers extensive literature about options and a free toolbox.

www.convertbond.com is a pay site with a two-week free trial. It gives detailed analysis of more than 800 U.S. convertible bonds. The site provides in-depth research on the U.S. convertible market including earnings estimates, call dates, and a handy portfolio analysis module. Convertbond.com is a division of Morgan Stanley.

www.financialengines.com provides a 30-day free trial to view the risk associated with a stock or mutual fund. It also tests to see if you will currently meet your retirement goals.

www.gabelli.com provides information about the Gabelli Family of Funds, including both the domestic and global convertible products.

www.morningstar.com has a free guide to stocks and mutual funds ranked by category.

www.multexinvestor.com offers free and pay research from many of the top investment firms.

www.numa.com has a free convertible bond calculator that provides you with key valuation data. You need to input the convertible's maturity date, conversion ratio, coupon rate, par value, price, share price, and dividend yield. You can also adjust the share price volatility, the dividend growth rate, the credit spread, and the risk-free interest rate.

www.prophetdataservice.com sells historic price data and daily updates on stocks, futures, and indices. This site has free charts of equities and indices. You must pay for futures and options charts on hundreds of contracts dating back to 1959.

www.riskmetrics.com provides stock price volatility charts. It also includes an interesting tutorial on risk.

www.ubswarburg.com offers an introduction to convertible basics plus the performance of various convertible indices. Access to research requires approval.

GLOSSARY OF NOTATION

A = total assets/sales.

B = investment value.

c = price of European call option or warrant.

C = price of American call option or warrant.

CB = convertible bond.

CF_t = nominal cash flows received in year t.

CP = conversion price.

CR = conversion ratio.

D = dividend payout ratio (dividends/net profit).

d_1, d_2 = parameters in option pricing formula.

$$d_1 = \frac{\ln \frac{S}{K} + \left(r - q + \frac{\sigma^2}{2} \right) \cdot T}{\sigma \sqrt{T}}$$
$$d_2 = d_1 - \sigma \sqrt{T}$$

d = proportional down movement in binomial model.

e = exponential (2.71828).

F = forward or futures price. The symbol F_t is the forward or future price at time t.

G = sustainable sales growth rate.

K = exercise price of option.

k = discount rate.

L = debt-to-net worth ratio (total liabilities/net worth).

NCF_0 = net cash flow in period 0.

NPM = net profit margin (net profit/sales)

$N(x)$ = cumulative normal probability density function.

p = (1) value of European put option. (2) probability under the risk neutral valuation in a binomial model.

P = value of American put option.

P_o = the desired probability of the event occurring.

P_{no} = the probability of the event not occurring.

PV = present value.

q = annualized continuous dividend yield.

$\overline{R}$ = mean return.

R_e = cost of equity.

R_f = risk-free rate of interest.

R_m = average equity market return.

R_i = the return of each ith occurrence.

r = risk-free interest rate.

r^* = instantaneous risk-free interest rate in the foreign country.

S = price of asset underlying the derivative security.

t = current time or time remaining until the receipts of cash flow CF_t.

T = time to the exercise date in years.

TPV = the total present value of all of the bond's future cash flow.

u = proportional up movement in binomial model.

β = beta.

Γ = gamma of derivative security or portfolio of derivative securities.

Δ = delta of derivative security or portfolio of derivative securities.

Π = value of portfolio.

ρ = coefficient of correlation.

σ = volatility.

λ = the ratio of outstanding warrants to the number of outstanding shares.

GLOSSARY OF TERMS

accrued interest the amount of interest that has accrued to the bondholder since the last coupon payment.

arbitrage the simultaneous purchase and sale of securities to take advantage of pricing inefficiencies created by the market.

at-the-money when the underlying stock price is close to the conversion price.

beta a measure of a stock's volatility (i.e., systematic risk) relative to the stock market as a whole.

bond floor *See* **investment value**.

bond value *See* **investment value**.

break-even time the time period, in years, over which the convertible recaptures any premium paid over conversion value by virtue of the yield advantage.

busted convertible a convertible in which the equity has substantially declined below the conversion price and is selling essentially as a straight bond. *See* **out-of-the-money**.

call option the right, but not the obligation, to purchase a security at a specified price for a predetermined period of time. Creates no dilution.

call price the price an issuer agrees to pay an investor, in the event the convertible is called.

call protection insures that the issuer cannot call the bonds away from the investor. There are two types, hard and soft.

callable term applying to convertible securities that contain a provision giving the issuer the right to retire the convertible prior to its redemption date.

conversion parity the value of the shares of the underlying common stock into which the convertible can be exchanged.

$$\text{Parity} = \text{Current share price} \cdot \text{Conversion ratio}$$

conversion premium the difference between the convertible's price and parity, expressed as a percentage of parity.

$$\text{Conversion premium} = (\text{Convertible price} - \text{Parity})/\text{Parity}$$

conversion price the share price at which the convertible can be exchanged for shares upon conversion.

conversion ratio the number of shares of stock into which each convertible can be converted.

$$\text{Conversion ratio} = \text{Bond denomination}/\text{Conversion price}$$

conversion value *See* **conversion parity**.

convertible bonds debt securities issued by a company that are convertible at the investor's option into the common stock of that company.

convertible preferred preferred shares issued by a company that are convertible at the investor's option into the common stock of that company.

convertible security a bond or preferred stock that can be exchanged or converted into the common stock of a company.

coupon rate the annual interest payment received from a bond.

current yield the bond's annual coupon expressed as a percentage of the market value of the convertible security.

$$\text{Current yield} = \text{Annual coupon payment}/\text{Convertible price}$$

delta the sensitivity of an option's value to a change in the price of the underlying security.

dilution the increase in the total number of shares outstanding due to the issuance of new shares, or the conversion of existing warrants or convertibles.

exercise price price at which the underlying stock is delivered in the event an option is exercised.

exchangeable a convertible issued by a company that is convertible into shares of another company.

expiration date the last date to exercise an option.

gamma the sensitivity of an option's delta to a change in the price of the underlying security.

hard call protection a period during which the issuer cannot call the bond under any circumstances.

hedge a position whose specific intent is to neutralize the price risk of an existing position.

in-the-money when the price of the underlying stock exceeds the conversion price.

investment premium the difference between the convertible's price and its investment value, usually expressed as a percentage.

$$\text{Investment premium} = (\text{Convertible price} - \text{Investment value})/\text{Investment value}$$

investment value the value of the straight fixed-income element of the convertible, without regard to its embedded equity option.

mandatory convertible a convertible security in which the holder is obliged to convert into the underlying equity at maturity.

option the right to purchase or sell an asset or security at a predetermined price for a set period of time.

out-of-the-money when the stock price is less than the conversion price.

par value the face value of a bond, which the company promises to repay at maturity.

parity *See* **conversion parity**.

provisional call protection *See* **soft call protection.**

put option the right, but not the obligation, to sell a security at a specified price for a predetermined period of time.

put feature the bondholder's privilege to force early redemption.

rho the sensitivity of an option's value to a change in interest rates.

short selling selling borrowed shares of a common stock.

soft call protection the issuer has the right to call the convertible under certain circumstances, for example, if the underlying stock trades at a price that exceeds the conversion price for a set period of time.

theta the sensitivity of an option's value due to a change in the time to expiration.

vega the sensitivity of an option's value to a change in volatility.

volatility the degree to which the price of a security tends to fluctuate over time.

warrant a long-term right to buy or sell a certain number of shares at a predetermined price for a specific period of time. Dilution is created.

warrant premium the difference between the market value of the warrant and its exercise price expressed as a percentage.

yield advantage the difference between a convertible's current yield and the underlying stock's dividend yield.

$$\text{Yield advantage} = \text{Current yield} - \text{Dividend yield}$$

yield to maturity the bond's internal rate of return to maturity.

yield to call the bond's internal rate of return to the call date.

zero-coupon a bond that pays no coupon and is usually issued at a deep discount to par.

BIBLIOGRAPHY

Altman, Edward I. *Corporate Financial Distress and Bankruptcy.* New York: John Wiley & Sons, 1993.

Bear Stearns. *Convertible Default Rates* by Joseph Montemayor, December 1999.

Bear Stearns. *Convertible Default Rates—An Update* by Joseph Montemayor, June 2000.

Black, Fisher, and Myron Scholes. "The Valuation of Option Contracts and a Test of Market Efficiency." *Journal of Finance*, vol. 27, May 1972.

Bookstaber, Richard M. *The Complete Investment Book.* Glenview, Il: Scott Foresman & Company, 1985.

Bookstaber, Richard M. *Option Pricing and Strategies in Investing.* Menlo Park, Ca: Addison-Wesley, 1987.

Brealey, Richard A., and Stewart C. Myers. *Principles of Corporate Finance.* New York: McGraw-Hill, 1996.

Calamos, John P. *Convertible Securities.* New York: McGraw-Hill, 1998.

Connolly, Kevin B. *Pricing Convertible Bonds.* Chichester, Great Britain: John Wiley & Sons Ltd., 1998.

Cox, John C., and Mark Rubenstein. *Options Markets.* Englewood Cliffs, N.J.: Prentice-Hall, 1985.

Credit Suisse First Boston. *EVA Primer* by Al Jackson, Michael J. Mauboussin, and Charles R. Wolf. February 1996.

Credit Suisse First Boston. *Convertible Make-Whole Provisions.* by Jeffrey A. Seidel et al. March 2000.

Deutsche Bank. *Convertible Quarterly Review: Second Quarter 2000* by Jeremy Howard et al. July 2000.

Deutsche Morgan Grenfell. *Japanese Convertibles: 5-3-3-2 Reform Fears Exaggerated* by Jeremy Howard and Glyn Randles. March 1997.

Deutsche Morgan Grenfell. *Enhancing Fixed Income Performance: How Convertibles Can Help* by Jeremy Howard. October 1998.

Ferguson, Niall. *The Cash Nexus: Money and Power in the Modern World,* 1700–2000. New York: Basic Books, 2000.

Goldman Sachs. *Goldman Sachs/Bloomberg Convertible Indices* by John McGeough, April 1999.

Goldman Sachs. *Convertibles as an Asset Class–2000 Update* by Scott Lang et al. March 2001.

Graham, B., D. L. Dodd, Sidney Cottle, et al. *Security Analysis.* New York: McGraw-Hill, 1988.

Helfert, Erich A. *Techniques of Financial Analysis.* New York: Mc-Graw-Hill, 1997.

Hoyt, Edwin P. *The Goulds: A Social History.* New York: Weybright and Talley, 1969.

Hull, John. *Options, Futures, and Other Derivative Securities.* Englewood Cliffs, N.J.: Prentice-Hall, 1989.

Ibbotson Associates. *Stocks, Bonds, Bills, and Inflation—2001 Yearbook.* Chicago: Ibbotson Associates, 2001.

Jefferies. *The Jefferies Global Convertible Bond Indices,* 1995.

Jefferies. *The Jefferies International Convertible Bond Index,* by Adrian Hope. October 1995.

Jefferies. *Risk and Return Characteristics of International Convertible Bonds* by Adrian Hope, Simon Ruddick, and Guy Ingram. September 1996.

Lehman Brothers. *Having Your Pie and Eating It Too . . . How the Tax Deductible Mandatory Structure Can Improve Equity Sensitivity* by Ravi Suria. July 1999.

Lehman Brothers. *Mandatories Demystified: The Mandatory Convertible Security Universe and How to Value It.* by Ravi Suria. January 2000.

Lehman Brothers. *September Busted Convertibles Report* by Ravi Suria. September 2000.

Lehman Brothers. *Broadening the Horizons: How Convertibles Can Benefit an Equity Investor* by Grant Mackie. January 2001.

Lehman Brothers. *Explaining the Basis: Cash versus Default Swaps* by Dominic O'Kane and Robert McAdie. May 2001.

Lehman Brothers. *Make the Most of It: Intraday Volatility and Rehedging Strategies* by Grant Mackie. June 2001.

Lummer, Scott L. and Mark W. Riepe. "Convertible Bonds as an Asset Class: 1957–1992." *The Journal of Fixed Income,* vol. 3, no. 2, September 1993.

Mann, Prem S. *Statistics for Business and Economics.* New York: John Wiley & Sons, 1995.

McKinley, John E. et al. *Analyzing Financial Statements.* Washington, D.C.: American Bankers Association, 1988.

Merrill Lynch. *Convertibles Can Outperform Stocks.* by Lorraine Gringer and James Peattie. July 1996.

Merrill Lynch. *Convertibles' Risk Adjusted Outperformance Explained and Measured* by T. Anne Cox. October 1997.

Merrill Lynch. *Convertible Structures—Evolution Continues 1999 Update* by T. Anne Cox. January 1999.

Merrill Lynch. *A Comprehensive Introduction to International Convertibles* by Lorraine Lodge and James Peattie. March 1999.

Merrill Lynch. *The Merrill Lynch G300 Convertible Indices* by Caspar Cook, Lorraine Lodge, and James Peattie. June 1999.

Merrill Lynch. *Introducing Interactive Convertible Research on the Web* by T. Anne Cox. November 1999.

Merrill Lynch. *Hedging Convertibles* by James Peattie and Lorraine Lodge. December 1999.

Merrill Lynch. *Convertible Structures—The Inner Workings* by T. Anne Cox. August 2000.

Merrill Lynch. *Global Convertibles 1st Quarter 2001 Review* by T. Anne Cox. April 2001.

Merrill Lynch. *Convertible Monthly* by T. Anne Cox. April 2001.

Morgan Stanley Dean Witter. *Guide to PEPS: Premium Exchangeable Participating Securities* by Anand Iyer. December 1998.

Natenberg, Sheldon. *Option Volatility and Pricing Strategies.* Chicago: Probus, 1988.

Nelson, Wayne F. *The Best Kept Secret on Wall Street.* Chicago, Ill.: Dearborn Financial, 1993.

Noddings, Thomas C. *Convertible Bonds.* Chicago, Ill.: Probus, 1991.

Philips, George A. *Convertible Bond Markets.* Great Britain: MacMillan Business, 1997.

Salomon Smith Barney. *Demystifying the Role of Hedge Funds in the Convertible Market* by Venu Krishna. May 2000.

Sharpe, William. *Investments.* Englewood Cliffs, N.J.: Prentice-Hall, 1985.

Stigum, Marcia. *Money Market Calculations: Yields, Break-evens, and Arbitrage.* Homewood, Il.: Dow Jones-Irwin, 1981.

Warburg Dillon Read. *Warburg Dillon Read Global Convertible Index.* by Katalin Tischhauser, 1998.

Warburg Dillon Read. *Convertible as an Asset Class: a Study of Historic Returns* by Katalin Tischhauser. March 1999.

Warshow, Robert I. *Jay Gould: The Story of a Fortune.* New York: Greenberg Publisher, 1928.

William Blair & Company. "William Blair & Company Convertible Rating System," *Convertible Research* by Richard Cunniffe. February 2–7 2000.

William Blair & Company. "Short Selling—a Traditional Convertible Hedge Strategy," *Convertible Research* by Richard Cunniffe. July 2–7 2000.

Zubulake, Laura A. *The Complete Guide to Convertible Securities Worldwide.* New York: John Wiley & Sons, 1991.

INDEX